# Rebbe Nachman Says...

*The Teachings of Rabbi Nachman of Breslov*
*As Taught by Rabbi Shlomo Carlebach z"tl*

Compiled by Zivi Ritchie

ShlomoCarlebach@gmail.com

**Tel: 972-2-9961805**
**02-9961805**

**www.ShlomoC.com**

# *Rebbe Nachman Says...*

The Teachings of Rabbi Nachman of Breslov
As Taught by Rabbi Shlomo Carlebach z"tl

Compiled by Zivi Ritchie

Editing by Tzvia Ehrlich – Klein

ISBN: 978-0977622894

*Leiluy nishmat*, **in memory of Rabbi Michael Dorfman z"tl**

For more information about Rabbi Shlomo Carlebach books, Email:

ShlomoCarlebach@gmail.com

**Tel: 972-2-9961805**
**02-9961805**

**www.ShlomoC.com**

# Table of Contents:

| | |
|---|---|
| **Foreword** | 5 |
| **Acknowledgements** | 6 |
| **Jump in Through the Window!** | 7 |
| **What do you Really Want?** | 8 |
| **Servant of G-D** | 9 |
| **Be What you Have to Be** | 10 |
| **Honor** | 10 |
| **Soul** | 11 |
| **Stories** | 12 |
| **DON'T GIVE UP!** | 13 |
| **The Banker from Odessa** | 15 |
| **Joy and Oneness** | 17 |
| **Three Lessons** | 23 |
| **A Little Anthology of Rebbe Nachman's Teachings About Joy** | 24 |
| **Wholeness of the Soul** | 32 |
| **Holy Arrogance** | 34 |
| | |
| **Yom Tov** | |
|     **One Ounce of Joy** | 44 |
|     **Rosh HaShanah** | 45 |
|     **Learn How to Get Up – Sukkot** | 45 |
|     **Hanukah** | 48 |
|     **"*Ohr Haganuz*" A Hidden Light Hanukah** | 49 |
|     **Purim and Holy Pride** | 52 |
|     **Purim** | 62 |
| | |
|     **Pesach:** | |
|         *Maos Hittim* | 64 |
|         *Noam Elyon* | 64 |
|         **Don't Take any Time** | 65 |
|         **Crossing the Red Sea** | 66 |
|         *Geula Shleima:* **The Fixing of Fear** | 68 |
| | |
|     *Rosh Chodesh* | 70 |
|     **Shabbos** | 73 |
|     **On *Bentshing Gomel* – Shabbos** | 73 |
| | |
| **Sit your Mind Down - Likutei Moharan Tinyono 10** | 76 |
| **Praying in the Field  - Likutei Moharan Tinyono 11** | 78 |
| **Simplicity - Likutei Moharan Tinyono 12** | 79 |

| | |
|---|---|
| Singing | 79 |
| Alone | 87 |
| Joy | 89 |
| Teaching Rebbe Nachman in Prison | 93 |
| A Letter to you from Rebbe Nachman | 95 |
| Holy Words | 97 |
| Maturity of the Mind | 99 |
| Three Things Widen your Mind | 100 |
| Five Levels of Understanding | 101 |
| Light and Vessels | 102 |
| Living Words | 109 |
| Happiness and Prophesy | 109 |
| Imagination | 112 |
| Dreams | 113 |
| Wisdom of your Heart | 116 |
| Still be Holy | 124 |
| Silence | 125 |
| *Haneor Balayla* | 130 |
| The Depths of *Mikva* | 147 |
| The Only Counteraction for Anger is if you're Filled with Joy | 151 |
| Anger | 156 |
| Angry at Myself | 157 |
| *Hisbodedus* | 168 |
| A Free Gift from G-d - Likutei Moharan Tinyono 78 | 172 |
| Only G-d can Help | 179 |
| Wedding | 181 |
| Hearing your Soulmate | 181 |
| What is the Point | 182 |
| Rebbe Yisroel Dov Odesser zt"l | 185 |
| Oral Law | 187 |
| Eating | 191 |
| Tell it Straight | 192 |
| The World is Getting Better | 192 |
| Mixing the Ingredients | 193 |
| A Taste of How Holy your Soul is | 194 |
| Yerushalayim | 196 |
| Days are Coming | 212 |
| Glossary | 224 |

# Foreword

I thank Rebbe Shlomo Carlebach for giving us his holy teachings. He selflessly dedicated his entire life to teaching, counseling, and uplifting us. He gave us a great heritage of teachings. I remember being at a class with him in 1994 in Jerusalem, and before Rebbe Shlomo Carlebach started the class, he asked if anyone had brought a tape recorder. When he saw that no one had brought a tape recorder to record him teaching, he got upset and said that he will not teach the class! I was used to seeing Rebbe Shlomo Carlebach always calm and forgiving in any circumstance, so to see him getting upset, and, even more so, not willing to teach the class, after we had traveled all the way to hear him, showed me how important it was to him that we record his teachings. (In the end several people went to bring tape recorders from their houses, and only after they came back and started recording, did he start teaching.) Another lesson I learned from this is that he wanted us to record the classes. He could have easily brought a tape recorder to all of his classes and do the recording himself, but he purposely did not do that. He wanted us to record his teachings and to spread them to the world.

Rebbe Shlomo Carlebach taught:

> "The Bal Shem Tov had a daughter named Udele. Udele had a daughter named Feigele. Feigele had a son, Rebbe Nachman. He was something very special. Special is not the word. The special thing about him was that, besides that he was such a great holy master, he had a student named Rebbe Nosson, who wrote down everything he said. There were a lot of great people in the world, but very few people had the privilege of having somebody following them around day and night in order to write down everything he is saying."

I thank G-d for the special privilege of bringing to you the teachings of Rebbe Nachman as Rebbe Shlomo Carlebach gave over to us. I thank all those who helped in publishing this book, and to all of you who will help spread it further by learning from it, living it, teaching it, telling your friends about it, lending it to your friends, and buying extra copies to give as gifts.

Zivi Ritchie

### In loving memory of Pesach ben Mordechai and Mendel ben Aharon

A thousand thanks to Zivi Ritchi for bringing to print Reb Shlomo's deepest teachings of Rebbe Nachman's awesome and wonderous wisdom. The world will surely be a happier and holier place now that "Rebbe Nachman Says" has arrived.

Blessings Forever,

Baruch and Rachel Freedman
New Outreach Project

# Acknowledgements

I especially thank my holy wife, Galit, may she be blessed with great *nachas*. She is the one who really deserves all of the credit. Her diligently taking care of the family is what allowed for the tremendous amount of time dedicated to writing this book.

I thank Galit for the endless hours of taking care of the physical needs of children, and I especially thank her for teaching our children *emuna* [faith]. As Rebbe Shlomo Carlebach taught:

> "According to Chassidus, the mother teaches the baby belief and the father teaches the baby truth. How do I know the truth? Unless I believe, I'll never get to the truth. Rebbe Nachman says that the whole world is operating on the basis of belief. A child goes to school and the teacher teaches him the ABC, and the child completely believes the teacher. Imagine if the child would be an intellectual. "How do you know this A is an A and this B is a B?" Thank G-d we teach kids the alphabet while they still believe. The whole world is based on alphabets. The mother teaches the alphabet, which is the utmost of belief and the utmost of truth: this is really an *alef*, this really is a *beit*."

> "Rebbe Nachman says, the woman has more *emuna* [faith] in the world than man does. Can you imagine how deep this is? Do you know how much faith you need in a baby, in order to bring it down to the world? You *mamash* have to believe in him, that he's going to make it, that this baby is going to bring the Mashiach. Because if you don't have faith that this baby will do it, then you have no right to bring it down to the world…. The way you believe in G-d is how much you believe in children….

> Why is Sarah called 'our mother Sarah?' Because from the moment she married Abraham, she was in training to be a mother to Yitzchak.
> You know, to bring down a baby like Yitzchak, you need training. That is why it took her 90 years of training every second, to bring down Yitzchak. *Mamash*, G-d was testing her for ninety years. Sarah believed in G-d so much, and just as much, that's how much she believed in Yitzchak."

The merit of the strong *emuna* that Galit has, and her heartfelt prayers, brings blessing to our house and to the success of this publication. *Eshet chayil*, a woman of valor *mi yimtza*.

Zivi Ritchie

ഇ〇ര

# Jump in Through the Window!

Late one night a young man was waiting in front of Rebbe Nachman's house. Rebbe Nachman looked out of his window and said, "In the middle of the night you have to talk to me? What do you want to talk to me about?"

He was nearly crying and he said, "I don't know what I am born for."

So Rebbe Nachman put his hand on his head and said, "You know something, I'm just walking up and down here in my room and I'm thinking the same thing. I'm troubled about the same thing. You better come in fast, but don't go through the door, jump in through the window! Don't waste even the two half seconds to go through the door. Jump right through the window."

You know friends, this road is not traveled anymore. Are people walking around thinking, "I wish I would know what I'm born for?" You know what kind of world we are, sadly, living in? Not our world, but the outside world? If someone would say to their parents, "Tell me really, what am I born for?" You know what their reaction would be? "You better see a psychiatrist fast! You're talking completely crazy! What do you care what you're born for?"

Do you know why they have this reaction? Because they don't know the answer, they just don't know the answer.

But the truth is that now there is a great revival in the world. People begin to ask each other, "What am I born for, what is this all about?"
And the answer has to be, "Jump in through the window. Jump in through the window, and fast!"

## Mt. Sinai

It says, "If I hadn't been on my way to Mt Sinai, I'd be long lost." Do you know where Mt. Sinai is? Mt. Sinai is there, where people know that the world is still a desert. Mt. Sinai is there, wherever people really would like to hear G-d's voice. Mt. Sinai is wherever people are really troubled, and are asking, "What am I born for? What am I doing here?" and they are really waiting for the answer.

So friends, could you possibly jump through this open window, and could we get much closer, because we all are troubled about the same thing, so let's get close.

## To be free

When we came out of Egypt, G-d did the ten plagues and all the miracles; G-d turned over the earth. We walked through the Red Sea; He turned over the waters. When G-d spoke to us on Mt. Sinai; He turned over the heavens.

To be free is also very hard. To be free you literally have to turn over the earth, and even the waters. You literally have to walk through the waters where there is no way. Everybody thinks you are drowning. If you want to be free, you better be ready to walk through the water.

In fact, this isn't enough. If you want to know why you are free, if you want to know what you are born for, you have to be ready to turn over Heaven! You have to turn over Heaven. And you can turn over Heaven.

The Kotzker Rebbe asked one of his Chassidim, "What do you think man is born for?" So he answered, "To lift up the earth." He says, "That's all? Man is born to lift up Heaven!"

The angels ask each other, "Where is G-d?" And we answer them back, "He is right here," meaning to say, we know G-d better than the angels.

Every human being knows G-d in a different way.

Rebbe Nachman talks about it so often. There is a passage in the Psalms: David *HaMelech* says, "I know G-d is great." So Rebbe Nachman says, what does David *HaMelech* mean to say, "I know that G-d is great.?" Rebbe Nachman says that it is not only that the way I know G-d nobody else knows Him, but that the way I knew G-d yesterday is not the way I know Him now.

And do you know something? The way I knew Him before I began talking to you, is not the same way that I know Him right now.

If you really have to turn over Heaven, do you know what is the prerequisite? Really asking G-d, "What am I born for?"

෫෬

# What do you Really Want?

## Your own preciousness

I really don't know how much I am worth. If G-d would give me a taste of my own *neshama* [soul], my whole life would change.

The question is not only if you know that you are precious. Because if I walk around and say, "I am precious, but you… listen, I know you are not," it means you never tasted your own preciousness. Because your own preciousness is so divine and so holy that if you *mamash* know what is precious about you, then every person you meet, you bring forth their preciousness too.

Who are all the big Rebbes? Why when I stand next to the Lubavicher Rebbe, when I stand next to the Amshinover Rebbe, I am a different person? Because, at that moment, that which is precious about me, is *mamash* shining. So their presence is so special.

**What do I really love?**

Rebbe Nachman says… Do you really think we love what we want to love? Most of us love everything we don't really want to love.

Friends, sometimes you can spend a thousand years, and only in the last minute of your life is it clear to you that everything you did in your life you didn't want to do it. "This is not what I want."

When do you reach the moment that it is clear to you; "What do I really love? What do I really want?" It is at those great moments when you are alone with G-d. When your own preciousness is shining so much. We need this the most.

Why is it that when you stand by the holy Wall something happens to you and you realize, that maybe all those things you want, you don't really want.

Friends, I just want you to open your hearts. What is the holy Wall? How did King Solomon build the holy Temple? King Solomon collected the preciousness of every human being in the world. Unbelievable. And from that he built the House of G-d. Obviously he didn't build it just from stones. That is just the outside. But the inside….

ஐௐ

# Servant of G-d

Rebbe Nachman asks the question: Are we G-d's servant or people's servant? There is no in between. Everybody is somebody's servant. Are you G-d's servant? If you are, then you are the freest person in the world because you know exactly what is right. If you really know what is right, then you don't listen to anybody, just what your soul tells you is right. The Gemara says that the freest person is the one who is G-d's servant. If you are man's servant, then you are a slave. If you are G-d's servant, you are completely free, really, really free.

Rebbe Nachman says, what is it to be in exile? To be in exile means you know everything, but you don't know it clearly. And to be free means it is shining, it's really shining.

છા૭ર્ણ

# Be What you Have to Be

Rebbe Nachman says, there are two kinds of evil. One is when I want to give charity, and my evil inclination comes and says, "Don't give." Then there is a general evil that is not concentrated against any specific action or thing. It is concentrated against my being what I am supposed to be. This evil doesn't mind what I do - "Do anything you want to be holy. Be Holy, who cares? Just don't be what you have to be" - because this is deeper than anything in the world. Evil is trying to stop every person from being what he or she is supposed to be. "Don't be a Jew. Even if you want to be what you are, don't be real about it." Evil is holding out with its last strength, "Just don't be completely what you have to be." We have to cut off this evil.

છા૭ર્ણ

# Honor

**Your own honor, or G-d's honor?**

Rebbe Nachman's Torah teaching, on *chodesh* Ellul begins, *mamash*: The first step in *teshuva* is that you care about G-d's honor. He says, are you concerned with your own honor, or are you concerned with G-d's honor? You see, if all you are thinking about is your own honor...

> Imagine someone says: "Tonight I walked into a big conference, and I was really disturbed. I walked in, and the *gabbi* [beadle] wasn't there to tell them to get up. What's going on here? Then they called up this Rabbi first, that Rabbi second, and they only called me up to speak fourth. What a *chutzpah* [nerve]. And they didn't give me all my correct titles, and they forgot to mention the two PhD's I have. You know, but because I am humble, I didn't say a word."

How does that sound to you? Small creep... Small creep. If you are concerned with your own honor, you are becoming so small, even a garbage pail is too big for you. But if you say, "I don't care about my *kavod* [honor], I want G-d's honor to be big in the world." Ah, suddenly your *neshama* becomes so big....

**You can fool your head**

I can imagine that I am the greatest. Nobody stops me. You know, Rebbe Nachman says, sadly enough, you can fool your head, but you cannot fool your *kishkes* [stomach]. The *kishkes* are *mamash* real; if you didn't eat, you are hungry. ☺ But I can imagine that I am just absolutely the greatest scholar in the world. I look in the mirror, I look at myself, and, "I can't believe that such a person exists." ☺ It is possible to think like that. And how many people really do walk around thinking like that; "How come the world hasn't discovered me? *Gevalt*, what a person I am. If I wouldn't believe that the Messiah is greater than me, I would think I could be the Messiah." ☺

There is a Satmar chossid, who calls me up every few weeks at night, and he says to me, "*Oy*, people persecute me."

I said, "*Oy, gevalt*, I am so sorry. Why do they persecute you?"

He begins laughing, "Ha, ha, ha." He says, "The Messiah shouldn't be persecuted?" ☺ (Ha, ha)

ഇ)രൂ

# Soul

Our holy master Rebbe Nachman says that not only the soul has a soul – but my body also has a soul - the inside of my body. You know, imagine if all I used my hand for was just to take, and I never used my hand to give. Rebbe Nachman says I can get physically sick from this. My hand is crying, "Why didn't you use me for the right purposes?" You know, if my ears only hear terrible things, if my ears never hear something holy, then physically my ears are angry at me: "Why didn't you do something with me which I really want to?" Not only my soul is angry, the inside of my body is too.

Rebbe Nachman says the deepest thing. What are hands for? Hands are for reaching. How do you reach out to another human being? It is beyond giving and taking, reaching... reaching out to G-d in Heaven, *gevalt*. You know, there's a *Zohar* which is most beautiful: Jacob, when he prayed, he was holding out his hands. *Gevalt*! He was reaching up to Heaven. Esau, when he prayed, his hands were always down. He didn't want to reach G-d. He just wanted to get something from G-d. Do you know, friends, the whole wedding ceremony is between the hands. Because, you know, a lot of people love each other, but they don't reach each other. And the deepest thing is to reach each other.

There's another very important thing. Many things are very beautiful, but they don't move. You know what feet are? Not only physical feet - the inside of my foot wants to move! Not to move to a new neighborhood - inside moving! Just moving!

I want to bless all of us that we should reach out to each other and that everything we want to do for the world and for G-d should be moving, moving, moving, moving, moving.

Friends, how far away are we from the day that the whole world should reach out to each other and dance? You know how far we are? Less than one second! It's so easy. And yet the world is not doing it. Not because it's so hard. Because the world refuses to do that which is easy. You know, if the word "peace" would take fifteen years to write down, every nation would say, "Hey, we are the first ones to make peace!" But it's so easy! All it takes is, one handshake and one kiss. So they say, "Who needs it." right? But, friends, you and I, we are not ashamed to be simple. You know what is the most simple thing in the world? That there is one G-d in Heaven. Is there something simpler than that? No "x" - no zeroes – nothing - just one G-d. One G-d.

෨ଠୠ

# Stories

Two people came to Rebbe Yisroel Rizener: one, a storyteller who had written a book of stories, and the other, a great scholar who had written great treatises on *halacha* [Jewish law]. So the *shames* [beadle / secretary] asks the Rizener who he wants to see first. The Rebbe says, "I want to see the storyteller first." The secretary was really astounded that the Rebbe would call in this storyteller in preference to this great scholar, but he didn't say anything. So he ushers in the little storyteller, and the Rebbe looks at his book and says, "Oh, this is such a beautiful story, it's the greatest story I ever read. The story is really holy." Then the Rebbe asks to see the scholar, and his great treatise on *halacha*. He is looking at the book and he says. "Oh, this is so deep, it is really from Mt. Sinai." Then they both leave, and the secretary comes in and asks, "I don't understand it. Here is a great scholar who has studied many years, and he is one of the greatest men, and you ask him to come in second. First you speak with the storyteller?"

"So," the Rebbe says, "I'm just doing it the way *HaShem* did it in the Torah. First *HaShem* was telling stories - He told the story of creation, the story of the flood, the stories of Abraham, Isaac, and Jacob. The story of slavery, the story of redemption, and then He led us to Mt. Sinai. After He told us all these stories, He gave us the Laws."

**Tell G-d your story**

Rebbe Nachman says, G-d created man because He loves stories. The whole world is G-d telling a story. G-d is telling us stories, creating the world, creating people, telling long stories. There is such a thing as prayer, which is very deep, but, Rebbe Nachman says, prayer is not the deepest depths of closeness to G-d. The deepest depths of closeness to G-d is when you can tell G-d your story.

The Tree of Knowledge is theories, and the Tree of Life is stories.

Everything we understand comes from our consciousness. Where do stories originate? Imagination. The truth is, the story comes from beyond my consciousness, but it flows into my consciousness. The story itself is really beyond.

You know, my beautiful friends, the older you get the less stories you tell. Have you ever noticed, people don't tell stories anymore. You know, for me, a young person is somebody who is telling stories. An old man is somebody who stopped telling stories long ago.

Rebbe Nachman says that when you dream, you always dream stories, not theories. When your imagination is completely free, then you dream stories.

When people sit and tell each other stories, they really become friends.

ഇൽ

# DON'T GIVE UP!

Rebbe Nachman tells a story of a poor woodchopper who found a diamond under a tree in the forest. He went home to his little village and asked people, "How much is this treasure worth?"

"We're not equipped to know," the people told him. "It looks like millions of rubles. You have to go to Moscow to find out what it is really worth."

The poor woodchopper didn't actually own a single ruble, nor even a penny, but he did have the diamond, so he started off for Moscow. When he stopped at an inn, he ordered the best food, and ate like crazy. When the innkeeper asked him, "Can you pay?" he said, "I'm sorry to tell you that I can't pay, but I do have this treasure here." Even if the innkeeper didn't know exactly how much it was worth, he knew it was worth millions, so he said, "We trust you. When you come back from Moscow, please allow us the great honor of serving you."

So the woodchopper continued on his way to Moscow. He finally arrived in Moscow, and there they told him, "Even in Moscow we are not equipped to tell you how much your treasure is worth. You have to go to London, and in London they will tell you."

The woodchopper still didn't even have a single penny, but who cares? He has this tremendous treasure. He went to a ship, and they said, "You have to buy a ticket."
"I have no money," he said, "but I have this treasure."

The Captain said, "Oh, what an honor for us to have you on our ship," But he is thinking, "Such a wealthy man, maybe even the wealthiest man in the world." The Captain gives him a cabin, and the woodchopper received special treatment, special waiters, and special butlers. Everybody was waiting on him, even though he was still wearing his dirty shirt (because he didn't have any money with which to buy a new one). He still looked like the poorest beggar in the world.

The waiter who came in to serve him his meal, spread out a very fancy tablecloth. *Nebech*, the poor woodchopper never ate on a tablecloth in his life. He put the diamond on the tablecloth, since just to look at it made him feel good. While eating, he looked at the treasure and thought, "Thank G-d. This is the greatest thing in the world."

One day, when the woodchopper finished eating, he fell asleep at the table. In a ship, when you want to clean crumbs off of the tablecloth, you just shake it out the window. So, that is what the waiter did. Upon awakening, the woodchopper realized what had happened, and thought to himself, "*Oy!* I don't have my treasure anymore! *Oy vey, Oy vey!*"

Rebbe Nachman says, "Don't give up." The woodchopper didn't give up. He knew one thing: "If I tell the Captain that I lost my treasure, he'll throw me right out the window, too. I'm traveling here for free. In the meantime, nobody knows about it. Nobody knows I'm bankrupt, so I won't tell."

Five minutes later the captain came in. "I've got to talk to you," he said to the woodchopper. "I want you to know that I was once a famous bank robber and a pirate. Now I have stopped. But before, when I was in India, I found a great treasure chest of unbelievable jewels. I cannot bring it into England under my name, because if they see my name they will arrest me. I know that you are also rich. Would you mind bringing my treasure into England under your name?"

"Okay," says the woodchopper. So the ship's captain signed the treasure over to his name, and the Captain told him, "Before we leave the ship, I will give it to you. You take it with you, and at night I will come to your hotel and pick it up from you.

Our little woodchopper was a really honest man. When they arrived in England, he took his little suitcase, went to the hotel, and waited for the Captain to come. One day. Two days. The woodchopper started getting nervous. On the third day, the waiter from the ship came to tell him, "The saddest thing happened. The Captain had a heart attack and died. He had no family."

The woodchopper realized that the treasure was his to keep. He also realized that it was only his because he hadn't given up. If he had said to the Captain, "I lost my treasure out the window," the Captain would never have trusted him anymore.

Rebbe Nachman says, "Never give up."

Basically, what was really meant for him was the Captain's treasure, not the treasure he found under the tree. G-d has His ways of giving you your treasure. Hold on. Don't tell [The woodchopper did not tell anyone that he lost the diamond]. Don't give up. Sometimes it is just a matter of minutes. Minutes. Hold out just one more minute. Hold out!"

When Rebbe Nachman was on his deathbed, he summoned all his strength, and he yelled so loud that people blocks away could hear him. "Don't give up! Don't give up!" Even we, here, one hundred and sixty-seven years later, can still hear him yelling, "Don't give up! Don't give up!"

ഇൗരു

# The Banker from Odessa

In Odessa, there was a *Yid* [Jew], a banker. He was a little bit religious, the way assimilated Jews lived in those days. He had a bank, and he was very rich, but he was a little bit connected to *Yiddishkeit*.

One day his accountant brought him all the account books. He looks at the books and he sees one thing: Unless I have two million rubles in four days, I am bankrupt.

Today when people are bankrupt, do you know what they do? First thing, they go to Switzerland, and send a letter to all the people to whom they owe money: "I wish you were here." What is declaring bankruptcy today? It is a joke. You declare bankruptcy, and you never pay the people back. In those days, in Russia, if you became bankrupt, you were on the next train to Siberia. Heavy. Heavy, heavy.

So it was clear to him: "The first thing I am going to do after four days if I cannot get the two million rubbles together, is, I am going to commit suicide. I don't want to go through being in Siberia, and I can't go through this whole thing."

So he went to a pharmacy and bought himself some real heavy drugs, poison. But then he thought, "Where should I commit suicide? At home? I have little children. I don't want to do it there." So he decided, "I will do it in *shul* [synagogue]."

He went to *shul*, and you know, today a *shul* has *siddurim* [prayer books], in those days, the *shul* also had *sforim* [holy books], and there were *mamash Shasim* [books of Talmud]. He put the poison under a *sefer* [holy book] on the highest shelf. He waited four days. He tried everything. *Mamash*, he thought he had good credit, but he didn't get a penny. On the fourth night, it was clear to him, "Tomorrow morning they will find out that I am bankrupt; I am going to commit suicide."

He went to *shul*. In those days, approximately one hundred and fifty years ago, there were no electric lights, just little candles. He put a candle on the table, and reached out his hand to get the poison. He was shaking so much that a lot of books fell down. *Nebech*.

Rebbe Nachman's *sefer*, Likutei Moharan, in the first printing, there is an entire page that says, "Rebbe Nachman says: *Yidden*, don't ever give up."

When the *sefer* fell down, and he went to pick it up. He bent down and he saw; Rebbe Nachman says: Don't ever give up.

So it was *mamash* clear; what a message before you want to commit suicide! So you know what he did? He took that *sefer*, put the candle on the table, and just looked at the page all night long. He said, "Rebono Shel Olam, if you send me this message, I am begging you, Rebono Shel Olam, don't disappoint me. I am not committing suicide tonight, so please let there be a miracle tomorrow."

In short, for five days, every day, when he was in his office, every time there was a knock on the door, he was sure it was the police. But nothing happened. For five nights, every night he was sitting in the *shul* all night long, looking at this page.

On the fifth day he got a letter from a bank in Amsterdam, and they wrote to him, "Please forgive us a thousand times. Ten years ago we took a loan from you for two million rubles. We completely forgot to pay it back, and we just found in our books that we never paid it back. We are sending it to you now." *Gevalt.*

So that night he goes back to the *beis medrash* [synagogue study hall], and takes the book again. Then he thinks, "I don't even know who wrote this book." So he sees; *Heilege* [holy] Rebbe Nachman, grandson of the Bal Shem Tov. And then he opens the book. He knew Hebrew well. He opened the book to the first torah teaching, "*Ashrie Temimei Derech.* You have to put in your *koach* [strength] into *davening* [praying]." He thought, "Ahh, this is so beautiful, so beautiful."

This was the first night that he was a little bit relaxed, and he fell asleep over the *sefer*. In his dream he saw a young man, about thirty five, or thirty six years old, who said to him, "I want you to know, my name is Nachman from Breslev, and I am the one who wrote this book."

Rebbe Nachman, *nebech*, (we should all live long), he passed away when he was thirty nine years old. Rebbe Nachman did not have a long beard; he had a little beard, and *peyos* [side-locks]. The *Heilege* Rishner also did not have a long beard: he had little beard, and long *peyos*.

And you know, before Rebbe Nachman passed away, he was yelling at the top of his lungs, "*Yidden, nisht kin miyaesh*, don't give up."

And Rebbe Nachman said to him in the dream, "I want you to know, before I left the world, when I yelled, '*Yidden*, don't give up,' I was thinking of you." Unbelievable.

The banker, in his dream, says, "So what should I do now?"

Rebbe Nachman answers, "I'll tell you what you have to do now; I want you to sell your bank. You have enough money to live in Eretz Yisrael [Israel]. I want you to go to Eretz Yisrael, and I want you to print my book in Eretz Yisrael."

I just want you to know that I met an old Breslover Chossid in Yerushalayim, who was nearly a hundred years old, and he was a *talmid* [student] of this Jewish Banker. Unbelievable. He was the first one to print Likutei Moharan in Eretz Yisrael. And he was a *talmid* of this *Yid*. I met him in a *beis medrash* in Yerushalayim.

ഇ

# Joy and Oneness

Rebbe Nachman says… the holy master Rebbe Nachman says… The greatest sin in the world is to be sad. The greatest sin in the world is not to be filled with joy.

### Joy brings what we want

You know, my beautiful friends, all of us want so much… we need so much…. Do you know why we don't have it? Because whenever you ask for something from Heaven, whenever you ask for something from another human being… do you know when they deliver the goods? At that moment when you are filled with joy.

Just imagine if I am asking for millions of tons of things from heaven, and here, so to speak, the heavenly mailmen come knocking on my door; they want to give me everything. I open the door, and I am sad, broken. First of all, who wants to have anything to do with a sad person? So they throw me a few crumbs and they take off. And, even deeper than this, G-d wants to give me so much, you need a lot of strength to carry it. And you know, when you are full of joy, you are full of strength, you can carry anything, you can carry the whole world on your head, on your shoulders. You can carry the whole world on one finger. But if you are sad, you can't take the whole thing. You take only a little bit, and the Heavenly mailman takes off.

You know beautiful friends, if you ask somebody for a favor, and you sit there and you cry and cry, they can't get rid of you fast enough.

If you are filled with joy… if you are filled with joy, if your heart is dancing all the time… your eyes are dancing, then people want to be close to you so much.

### Joy brings peace

You know, friends, what the world needs most? Everybody thinks we need peace. Yes, we need peace, but you know why we don't have peace? Because we don't have enough joy in the world.

And this is what the holy Rebbe Nachman says… people only hate when they are sad.

Imagine there is somebody in the world who I hate the most, I can't stand that person. I just hate the person. And every day I hate that person more. And imagine that my daughter is getting married, and at the height of the joy of my daughter's wedding, I take my daughter by the hand and I get on the table and I start dancing. It is the happiest moment of my life. *Gevalt, gevalt,* how could I ever thank the One, the Only One, for that great moment? You think I am in paradise? Ha, much higher than paradise. At that moment the door opens, and my arch enemy walks in. So I am asking you, my dearest brothers and sisters; what do you think will happen? You know what will happen? In the middle of the dancing - and remember I told you, I am beyond paradise - something will happen to me, and I will reach even higher and even deeper. I jump off the table and run to the door, and I will embrace and kiss my arch enemy. And I will say, "My most beautiful, most precious friend, where were you at the wedding?" And I won't be lying, because at that moment it will be clear to me that we never hated each other.

Friends, there is only one anti-hatred; it is joy. And if you and I are dreaming of one day the whole world being one, know it is only with joy.

## Sadness makes you so dirty

You know beautiful friends, we all have certain reflexes, they don't come from our head, they come from the inside of our inside. Do you like to hold hands with a person who has dirty hands? No. And even if you have to because you have good manners, so you shake hands, but you try to get your hand back as fast as possible. Someone with clean hands? You like to shake hands. And if you love somebody, you hold their hands forever.

Our holy Rabbis teach us that sadness makes you so dirty. I don't know what it is… it is a spirit of uncleanliness, a spirit of unholiness, which descends upon you.

And believe me friends; most friendships break up because there is not enough joy in the world.

*And here, I want you to know something. Rav Nachman says; why are you so sad? Because everything goes wrong in your life. But, gevalt, gevalt, do you know why everything goes wrong? Because you are so sad.*

## The gift of joy

But again, my friends, if you will ask me, "I am so sad. How do I get happy?" Believe me, I wish I would know the answer. I can only bless you, that G-d should give you the gift of joy.

Life is in the hands of G-d, joy is in the hands of G-d. And G-d is giving joy to those who He feels fit. And even if you are not fit – misfits like you and me – there is only one way… there is only one way; to pray and to pray…. To pray and to pray.

Friends, you pray for everything. But do you know what Rebbe Nachman says? Every second, every split second, you have to ask G-d, and cry, and beg Him; '"Please G-d, let my heart be filled with joy."

**One ray of light and another ray of light**

My beautiful friends, let me sing with you a prayer. This is what it says:

*Simcha Leartsecha*, let there be joy… let there be joy in Your whole world.

*Vesason Leirecha*, let there be bliss in the holy city.

*Utsmichas keren leDavid avdecha*, let the salvation grow.

You know, beautiful friends, the salvation of the world, the redemption of every individual, doesn't happen suddenly. It comes slowly.

One morning, one early morning, or maybe late at night. It was so late, it was so late… it was so late… the world was so dark… so dark, but it was one minute before dawn. And, you and I know, that whenever the world is darkest, dawn is breaking. So the Zohar HaKodesh, the holy Zohar, the book of splendor, the text book of the deepest, deepest secrets of our holy teachings, this is what it says:

Once, late at night, Rebbe Shimon Bar Yochai and his son, Rebbe Eliezer, were standing on the mountain. It was so dark, it was so dark, *gevalt*, what a dark period to live in, right after the destruction of the Temple. Suddenly, one ray of light, one holy ray of the sun… for one second – a ray of light. And then another ray, just a little bit less dark. And slowly, slowly, G-d's greatest light, the sun, is coming to shine for the whole world.

And imagine, you and I are standing with them on that holy mountain.

And Rebbe Shimon Bar Yochai said to his son, "Eliezer, my son, do you see… do you see? This is the way the redemption of the world, the redemption of Israel, the rebuilding of the holy city will happen: One ray of light, and another ray of light, and another ray of light, until, until, until, until, the whole world will be filled with joy and with light.

*Simcha Leartzecha, vesasson leirecha, utsmichas keren leDavid avdecha, vearichas ner leben yishai meshichecha bimhera biyamenu.* [Let there be joy in Your whole world. Let there be bliss in the holy city. Let the salvation grow. One ray of light, and another ray of light, until the whole world will be filled with joy and with light.]

## Oneness

You know friends, some day there will be peace in the world, there won't be any committees, there definitely won't be a United Nations, there won't be any politicians. I hope they will be around, but they won't dare open their mouth. Just one human being to the other. People will hold each other's hands... and suddenly, suddenly, G-d will give us the gift of the greatest joy in the world... the greatest joy in the world.

What is the greatest joy in the world? Do you know what sad is? Loneliness. The deepest sadness is loneliness. And being one with another human being is the greatest joy. Can you imagine being one with the whole world? What joy! Unbelievable, unbelievable!

## Don't run away. Run to.

You know, my beautiful friends, whenever a person is sad, they want to run away from the world, run away from themselves, run away from their friends, run away from G-d. What happened to Adam and Eve? The first mistake - they ran away. Away from G-d, away from paradise - hiding.

You know, sometimes you talk to your best friend, the person you love the most, but you can't get through to him, he is hiding. He is building walls around himself. What do you do? Listen to this true story:

Rebbe Nosson, Rebbe Nachman's greatest pupil, had a distant cousin who was very wealthy, but suddenly he went bankrupt. He ran away, and he decided to go to Odessa. There he had a rich uncle, and he hoped to get a loan from him. He passed through the city of Breslov. By that time, after walking for a few weeks, he was so downhearted, so broken, Even his shirt had not been washed in months.

He came to Rebbe Nosson, and Rebbe Nosson said to him, "Where are you going?"

He says, "I am going to a rich uncle in Odessa, I will get a loan from him – a million rubles, and I will reestablish my business."

Rebbe Nosson said, "*Oy vey, gevalt,* are you mistaken. You know, the way you look right now, he won't even let you into his house. He will put ten rubbles in your hand and say, 'Listen, this is all I can do for you.'"

He said, "What should I do?"

This is what he told him: Instead of running away... You are running? Good. - Don't run away. Run to. Run to the One... run to the Only One who can help. Instead of running away – just remember friends – instead of running away, run to. Run to the One... the Only One.

You know, when something hurts you, don't run away from your friends. This is the time to run to your friends. This is the time to run to G-d – to your Friend.

You know, when children are little, what do they do? When they are crying, do they run away? No. They run to their parents. Sadly enough, when we get older, we get perverted, we run away from.

So Rebbe Nosson said to him, "Don't run away. Go back to your city, go back to your wife, to your children, but run to G-d. You are bankrupt? You have no business? Go to the *beis medrash*, go to the house of G-d, to the house of prayer, the house of study, and learn day and night. You have no business? Beautiful! It is time to learn, it is time to pray, it is time to fill your heart with the most lofty, with the holiest teachings in the world. And I promise you, G-d will help you."

He listened to Rebbe Nosson, and he went back to his city, and the people didn't believe it; they knew he is bankrupt, that he ran away from all the people to whom he owed so much money. He is back? He doesn't run away? And they asked, "What is he doing?" and they were told, "He is learning day and night." People were so impressed – this is a true story – that within a few days they gathered together so much money, that they gave him a loan, and he reestablished his business.

You see, when you run to G-d… leave it up to the One, to the Only One. When you run to your best friend, He will always help you.

**A true friend**

So friends, if you are very, very sad, is there one person you can run to?

Do you know what a true friend is? A true friend is somebody who, when you tell them why you are sad, you are not sad anymore.

Do you know what the holy Bal Shem Tov brought into the world? That everyone needs a *Rebbe,* a holy master. Every person in the world needs a good friend.

**Parents and children**

Every child needs a father and mother. Do you know what a father and mother are for? Not to tell the children that they are doing wrong. That, they know on their own. Parents are to run to… to run to….

You know, G-d said to Eve, "You will have trouble having children after you ate from the Tree of Knowledge." Eve knew that she is in this world to bring children to the world, so she thought to herself, "What is the greatest thing I can do for my children? I will eat from the Tree of Knowledge, and I will tell them what is right and what is wrong." G-d said, "Look at yourself, you are running away from me. Don't you know, what a mother is… do you know what a mother is for? When children are crying, they run to their mother, to their father." So He says, "*Oy* Chavale [Eve], I am so sorry, it will be hard for you to have children if you don't know the secret of what a mother is really for, what parents are really for."

You hear me, brothers and sisters, fathers and mothers all over the world? I bless you that when your children are crying, they should come running to you.

## Let all of us run to Yerushalayim

And I bless you and me and all of us, the whole world, that instead of running away from each other, let's run together … let's run to the One, to the Only One.

When the Messiah is coming, and the Holy Temple will be rebuilt, the prophet says… and this is what He said, "My house is a house of prayer, for all the nations of the world." You know what will happen someday? Someday the world will realize, "There is no other way. Wars will bring us nowhere. Hatred doesn't lead anywhere. There is only one way; let us all run to Yerushalayim, to the holy city. Let's run to the One to the Only One… let's run to the One, to the Only One." And at that moment, when the whole world will run to G-d and to each other, at that moment the world will be filled with joy.

Do you know how beautiful it is to know that you have one good friend. There is someone who loves you. There is someone who helps you.

## Cry with all your heart

But one more little advice friends; do you know why we are never really happy? Because when we have to cry, we don't really cry. We are living in a world that when you are over a certain age, you don't cry. What is wrong with crying?

We don't know how to cry, we don't know how to laugh. We laugh at dirty jokes, but we don't laugh out of joy anymore.

You know when children are little, when they cry – they cry. And when they laugh - they laugh.

I can only tell you, that whenever you want to cry, cry with all your heart. You know how you will feel after you really cry? But cry before the One. I bless you to have one friend to cry with. Then, suddenly, great joy from heaven will descend into your heart.

଼ଠଐ

# Three Lessons

Rebbe Nachman, the holy master, says, in order to serve G-d you have to learn, you have to know, three lessons.

The first lesson is that you must learn how to walk, and you must learn how to stand. When you do a *mitzvah*, when you do something good, you're walking in G-d's ways. When you're praying, you stand before the Only One. But only those who are walking know how to stand, and only those who are standing know how to walk. This is the first lesson.

The second lesson is a bit harder: learn how to fall and how to get up. If you are falling, don't be sad; you know G-d is teaching you how to get up. If you don't fall, how can the One, the Only One, teach you how to get up? So when you're falling, let your heart be filled with joy, because the Only One, who knows and can teach you, is showing you how to get up.

The third lesson is the hardest: I have a feeling that this lesson is about you and me, about all of us. What do you do when you're falling, and you can't get up? What do you do when your heart is so broken, your spirit is so destroyed, that there's nothing to hope for, nothing to look back to? Rebbe Nachman says, in the meantime, keep on walking, in the meantime, keep on praying, in the meantime, keep on loving, until the day when it's revealed to you that you never fell. How could it be possible to fall when The Only One is holding you so close.

≈◌≈

Rebbe Nachman says, when you want to jump over a rope, you don't stand in front of the rope and jump over. You have to go back a little. Then you jump. This is one of the classic Torah teachings of Rebbe Nachman. If you find yourself far away, *oy, gevalt*, is G-d preparing you to jump! G-d is preparing you for the highest jump ever.

≈◌≈

# A Little Anthology of Rebbe Nachman's Teachings about Joy

**What is joy?**

What is the difference between sadness and joy? Joy really fills you; whatever you have becomes fuller. Sadness empties you out; "I don't have this, I don't have that," So… even what you have, you don't have.

## Don't be sad about the future

People walk around sad because they don't know what to do with their future.
You have this minute, right now! What are you doing with it?

The difference between sadness and joy is very simple: sadness always tells you, *"Oy vey!* What are you going to do in ten minutes? What will you do ten years from now?"

If you are really filled with joy for one minute, then you will also know what to do the next minute.

What is G-d giving you? He is giving you this minute. He hasn't given you tomorrow: He promised He will give tomorrow. So of course I don't know what to do tomorrow, because I didn't receive it yet!

Sadness is being overly concerned with what I don't have - and I really don't have tomorrow yet.

## Completely 'being'

Why are you filled with sadness if somebody dies, G-d forbid? Because that somebody is no longer there, right? The depths of joy is 'being' and the depths of sadness is 'not being.' If you get something, you are happy. The more you get it, the deeper you get it, the deeper your joy is.

Have you ever seen people who are so happy when they have an excuse to be sad? One woman said to me, "I can't talk to my mother unless I am sick." When this woman is sick, then her mother has something to say to her.

There are certain parts of a person that only react to 'not being.' We have to wipe that out.

## There are some people who say, "I am just happy."

There are some people who say, "I am just happy." Have you ever seen a woman coming out of a beauty parlor saying, "It is a beautiful day, and I am happy." What are you happy about? What did you get? You got today, but what are you doing with it? Don't kid yourself. You cannot be happy unless you have something. If you say "I'm just happy," why? Because instead of the beauty parlor charging you $35 they only charged $29 and you gave a tip of $2 so you saved $4?

Rebbe Nachman says: if you are happy for no reason, without doing something good, you are just kidding yourself. On the contrary, the reaction to this kind of joy will be that five minutes later you will be knocked down low.

If you can be happy just because you are alive, then you have something - if you really feel it.

Everyone says that they are happy that they are alive, but the question is, are you really receiving life? That is the highest level there is.

Most people don't realize that life is a gift from G-d, and most people are not happy.

It says, *"schar mitzvah: mitzvah* [the reward for a good deed is another good deed]." The reward of a *mitzvah* is a *mitzvah*, and the reward for joy is joy.

How does G-d pay you for being happy? He gives you another minute of happiness. So if this one minute of happiness is real, the next minute also will be. But if you say, "I'm so happy to be alive," and the next minute you are walking around downcast, then there was something wrong.


**Existing**

The truth is I am always standing before nothingness, because the next minute has not yet been created, so I am non-existent yet for the next minute. I'm not there yet. Time isn't there. The world isn't there. The world is here, right now. One split second, one billionth of a split second in the future has not yet been created. I am always standing between 'being' and 'not being,' between Heaven and Hell. Hell is the utmost of not being.

What is happening in Hell? I am not burning like a hamburger. In Hell I realize that I was non-existent. Do you know how it feels if you are suddenly non-existent? G-d forbid that it ever happens to anybody. Imagine, suddenly you don't have a hand. What a horrible feeling. Imagine if you are there, and then suddenly you see that you are not there. You would see yourself as actually not being. It is unbearable.

There are two kinds of 'not being.' One way of not being is when you are just physically not there - but imagine if you are there and yet you are simultaneously not there. That is what really hurts. If I love somebody very much and they are not here, so they are not here. It is sad. But imagine if they would be sitting next to me and they won't talk to me. That is a deep kind of 'not being' which really hurts. Hell is that I am there, but I am not there.


**Sadness is a sickness**

Sadness is a sickness, not an emotional problem. It is absolutely a sickness and you have to get rid of it.

The Bal Shem Tov says if you want to know whether you are really serving G-d, it is simple: If my heart is filled with joy each time I put on *tefillin*, and each time I do something good my heart is filled with joy, then I am serving G-d. If I am not on that level, then I am just doing mechanical things. Though even that is very holy, and I'll be rewarded in Heaven for doing it, but it is heartbreaking.

## If you are sad, you make G-d uncomfortable

If you look sad, what happens to the person sitting next to you? He feels a bit uncomfortable. In fact even if they love you a lot, they will just overcome those uncomfortable feelings and say, "I have got to stick it out and stay with him. He's my friend, so I have to stick around while he is crying." But this doesn't go, right?

But imagine if you are sitting there and *mamash* laughing like the Ropshitzer Rebbe. Laughing your head off. Then, everyone will feel so comfortable. Why? It's very simple. Imagine if you looked down into the abyss, to the abyss of the abyss; it would be very uncomfortable - frightening. The truth is, when you see someone sad, at that moment you are *mamash* confronted with nothingness. You see that this person is struggling between 'being' and 'non-being.'

Imagine if you saw me standing on the roof with one foot hanging over the edge. You say, "Listen, do me a favor. You make me nervous, even if you are the greatest acrobat in the world. Put your foot back on the roof! I am afraid to see this. Or, if you want to do it, I just don't want to see it."

You have to realize, it is the same way with G-d. When you walk around sad, you make G-d uncomfortable. G-d says, "I love you. I'm your G-d. I signed a contract with you at Mt. Sinai and I will stick to it; I'll be with you. But I really don't feel comfortable with you when you are sad."

When you smile with joy and you look at somebody, they look back at you; but, when you cry, they can't really look back at you. *Mamash*, they try, but they can't look back at you. You can't say, "We cried eye to eye." It just doesn't go. You can smile eye to eye, but you can't cry eye to eye.

We know this world is just a little mirror of Heaven. You have to realize that it's very beautiful when you cry, but it's not really so good. You make G-d feel uncomfortable about it. It is not so good.

## Crying with 'being' or crying with 'nothingness'

We're not talking about crying in general, we're talking about *atzvut*, this dead kind of sadness.
It depends on how you're crying. You can cry with being, or you can cry with nothingness.

On Rosh HaShanah and Yom Kippur, we are crying all the time. It's the holiest tears.

Imagine if someone says to you, "I love you so much, I really want to be the greatest friend to you," and he is crying while he's saying it (crying with being), it would open up your heart in a thousand ways.

But if someone came crying and said, "I was in the beauty parlor, sniff, sniff, and they cheated me, sniff, sniff, and I overpaid five dollars, boo hoo hoo." what would you feel then? Oy vey. And even if this woman was your mother, and you really love your mother, but you just can't stand it. So you'd say, "*Oy vey*," and you'd pat her on the back.

There is a very deep difference between crying before somebody and crying about something. If you're crying before G-d, it is the holiest thing. Maybe He is crying with you. But if you're crying about something and you're telling it to G-d and complaining, it's not so good. You have to cry before G-d.

**The most important thing you have to know is:**

If you are shining here below, then G-d is shining too.

If you smile down here below, then G-d smiles back at you from above.

Something very holy is going on between you and G-d.

**The difference between *marirut* and *atzvut***

The word sadness is not a good translation. The word *atzvut* means you are sitting there moping away.

There are two kinds of sadness. There is *marirut*, which is bitterness, which is living sadness, and there is *atzvut*, which is dead sadness.

Bitterness is: "I wish I could do better. *Gevalt*, why didn't I do better? I didn't do it right. Why didn't I do better?" I'm sad just knowing that I didn't do it good enough. This is a living sadness. And then I go out from there, and I want to do better.

The Bal Shem Tov says that the difference between *marirut* and *atzvut* is very simple: If you see another person after you cry, do you feel love for them or do you hate them? If you cry in the living kind of crying, then every person looks beautiful to you. You think, "I'm not so beautiful, but they are so beautiful. You are so happy for them." But if you have a dead kind of sadness, *atzvut*, then everyone looks ugly to you.

Sometimes you cry and you look out the window and say, "Oh, those disgusting creatures, walking down the street." With this kind of crying, G-d can't look at you either.

If a person wants to know at what level his joy is, it is very simple. If you feel one with the world, it is because you feel the Oneness of G-d.

So if you walk around and say, "I am filled with joy," but you can't stand people. That means it is not G-d joy.

**The higher it is coming from, the deeper it goes.**

If the joy is really coming from a high place, then it doesn't make you stupid. Some people think, "I am in such a good mood today, I have to tell you a dirty joke." Is this how deep the joy touched you? It brought out all the garbage you had piled up for the last few years? Then it is not the joy we are talking about.

The higher place from which the joy is coming, the deeper it goes. If it doesn't reach you that deep, it doesn't come from that high.

How do you know how deep the joy reaches? If it *mamash* makes you get up and dance like mad, then it reached all the way through you, down to your feet. Otherwise it didn't reach you completely yet.

**Living kind of sadness or dead kind of sadness**

How do you know if you are feeling this living kind of sadness or this dead kind of sadness? When you are in the dead kind of sadness, deep down you really think, "There is no G-d. I think the whole thing is a fake," even if it is only for one split second. If you test yourself you'll see that you are really thinking, "Achh, who needs G-d, who is G-d? The whole thing is a fake." That means, at that moment, you really reached the bottom of dead sadness. Therefore, Rebbe Nachman says, keep as far away from this as you can.

**Joy makes you strong**

Joy is the strongest vitamin.

Joy makes you strong in a million ways, physically, mentally, and spiritually.

There are all kinds of strength. Imagine, I could eat dog food and be strong. That is also called strong. But the highest level of strength that a person needs in order to live in this world is joy.

The whole world is filled with joy, the highest level of joy.

**What makes you happy**

What does it mean to be happy with what you are doing? Everyone says "I'm happy with what I'm doing." What does 'happy' mean? Happy means: If you would be willing to be born, and hang around this world for 80 years just for this one thing, without ever doing anything else again after that - that is called being happy with this thing.

If you can be on this level with every *mitzvah* you do, that you feel: "If I were only born to put on *tefillin* this one morning, if I were born just for this one Shabbos, it would have been enough," - that is called joy.

## Real joy is a combination of truth and believing

There is such a thing as *emet* [truth], and there is such a thing as *emuna* [believing]. Real joy is a combination of truth and believing.

If *emet* and *emuna* are both working strongly inside of you, if you believe what you know, and you know what you believe, then you are filled with joy.

If your joy comes from *emet* and *emuna*, from truth and believing, then it's called Jewish joy, holy joy. Otherwise it is just called pagan joy.

## Imagination

Rebbe Nachman always talks about imagination. He says that if you're sad, it's not that you have sad imagination. When you're sad, your imagination isn't real. Because imagination is flying, it soars, right? But if you're sad, you're so unhappy that you can't fly.

You can imagine that you're flying. But even imagining that you're flying is impossible because you're too heavy when you are sad. But if you're filled with joy, then you *mamash* have wings, and you can fly.

## Being in touch with yourself

The greatest joy in the world is when a person is really his own judge. If a person can sit down and really, like, 'spy on himself,' to know what he did, and what he has to do better, that means he is *mamash* in touch with himself.

Most of the time when you do things, you 'live through them,' then you 'read in the newspaper' that you did it. But you never tell yourself about it. It's much better if you hear it from yourself. If something happens to you, and your best friend hears about it from someone else and not from you, then he may get angry; "Why didn't you tell me?" Can you imagine how angry your soul is, that you never told your own soul what you are doing?

**Suddenly unexplainably happy**

Sometimes you walk along and suddenly you are so happy, yet you don't know why. Rebbe Nachman says it is because, at that moment, they declared in Heaven to give you something, even if it might only arrive in a hundred years from now. But your soul heard of the gift and was happy.

If someone asks you something, and you give him real, true advice, it fills you with joy.

Now Rebbe Nachman says something very crazy / amazing. If you are walking along in the street and suddenly you feel very happy, it's because somewhere in the world a very holy soul was born. Way out / a very high concept.
When you tell stories about holy people, and you tell other people that there are holy people in the world, it fills you with joy.

*Kavod*

What's the utmost of a person's own revelation? When do you reveal yourself the most? When is your honor shining from one corner of the world to the other? Rebbe Nachman says, the utmost of *kavod* [honor] is when you're happy, when holy joy fills you.

There is something about a person, about the real holy honor surrounding him… because joy comes from such a high place, and also *kavod* comes from such a high place….

**Understanding**

Rebbe Nachman says, if you don't understand something, I guess you are sad deep, deep down.

**The snake made Eve sad**

What did the snake really do to Eve? How did the snake get through to her and convince her? Rebbe Nachman says, the snake made her sad. The snake said, "Wow, you can't eat this tree." And she started being so sad.

Rebbe Nachman says, at the end, I want you to know that all this talk is really meaningless, because how can I tell you to be happy? It is up to everyone himself. But I am just begging you, be happy.

ഇൟ

This is very deep… How can you understand what's going on if you're sad?

∞☙

Imagination goes wild when you are sad. You know, when I am sad, I imagine that every person hates me, that every person wants to hurt my feelings. That everybody wants something from me.

∞☙

Tears open the gates, but joy breaks down the walls!

∞☙

Rebbe Nachman says, you are angry at HaShem that everything is upside down, and therefore you are sad, but everything is upside down only because you are sad, if only you were happy, everything would be good!

∞☙

# Wholeness of the Soul

How do you know if you haven't yet lost the wholeness of your soul? You have a soul, and then there is the all-ness, the wholeness of you. How do you know if you still have this wholeness of your soul? It's very simple. If you do something and you're completely happy with it, then you know that your soul is whole, because joy comes from that wholeness of yourself.

You see, as much as you're sad when you're missing something outside of yourself, you're also sad if you're missing a little part of your soul. How can you be completely happy if part of you is missing? But if you're completely happy, if you can for even one moment feel this complete joy, this means that your soul is still complete.

**Love other people**

If you love other people, if everybody is ok in your eyes, you're filled with joy.

I want you to know, the Bal Shem Tov says, that when you're filled with joy, you can meet your biggest enemy and love him. Because you don't care at all. You say, "He hates me, but who cares."

If you can still care if "This one hates me," and "That one likes me," then you're obviously not filled with joy, because otherwise you wouldn't care.

## Yom Kippur

Why does G-d forgive us on Yom Kippur for everything we did wrong? Because there's so much joy. We say to G-d, "Listen, I did this." He says, "Ok, you did it, but who cares." Then we say to G-d, "You know, we are planning to probably do wrong again this year," and He says, "Ok."

## Heaven and Hell

Twice a day, or three times a day, you have to say, "Hear O' Israel, the Lord our G-d, the Lord is One." It says; "If someone reads *Kriat Shema* in the morning and evening; if someone says it and he's *mamash* uttering the letters properly, then they cool Hell for him. If he's supposed to be in Hell, they cool it for him." Like, they put an air conditioner in especially for him.

Now, Rebbe Nachman says, those words have to be understood very deeply. Because you have to understand, what is Hell? Hell is the utmost of non-being. The utmost of being is the Torah. G-d's word is the utmost of being. And if you're not connected to the Torah, if you're not connected to G-d's word, you're not being. Less and less and less. But even when you say "G-d is One," even that can be on the level of non-being if you're not really putting your heart into saying it. You know, I can walk on the street and give a *Yiddele* a nickel, but if I'm not doing it completely, with full intention, then my being is also not completely there.

Obviously Heaven and Hell is not just somewhere; they're not just places, specific areas, Heaven and Hell. The more I'm doing something completely, the more I'm out of Hell. If I say *Shema Yisrael*, G-d is One, and I do it in the most complete way I can, at that moment I'm out of Hell, because I'm really there, connected, actually being. I'm completely with it. But if I'm saying it half heartedly, I'm only half out of Hell. If I say it and I'm only uttering the letters, it's also good. At least Hell gets colder. But if I'm saying it with all my heart, then I'm completely out of there. We never know what kind of a favor we do ourselves, at that moment when we do something completely. It's a very strong [powerful] thing.

Another thought to remember. Heaven is completeness and Hell is incompleteness. A lot of people talk to me after they get married: If it's not completely Heaven, then it's a little bit like Hell. If the couple is not completely together, there is a little bit of Hell in it, right? And if there's a little bit of Hell in it, it's bad. You've got to be completely with it.

Then Rebbe Nachman says a very beautiful thing at the end. One is always complete. Two is never complete. Because it's already divided into two. How complete can it be if it's two? One, *mamash* is complete.

**Psalms**

Rebbe Nachman says that all the prayers which have been prayed and will be prayed until the end of all generations, they're all included in the Psalms. This means that when you read the Psalms you are connecting yourself to all the prayers of the world. This is very deep.

When you pray, you *mamash* have to connect yourself to the prayers of others.

ഇ൨൶

# Holy Arrogance

## Using your emotions at the right time

Every emotion that G-d gave us is for a purpose. To love is for a purpose, to hate is for a purpose. We have the emotion to hate. The question is, what do you hate, and what do you love? You have emotions urging to be silent, and you have emotions that you just have to speak up. You have the emotion to be ashamed, and then you have the emotion that you are not afraid of anybody in the world. We have all this stashed away in our mind. The question is, when are you using it, and where are you using it. That is the whole question.

This is the most heart-breaking thing in the world: G-d gives us at birth, let's say, 100 pounds of love, and, let's say, 100 pounds of hatred. So here I am using up 50 pounds of my love, let's say, for food, or for money. Then, when it comes to a holy thing, I have only 50 pounds of love left. Or, let's say, I am using up 50 pounds of hate on hating my neighbor for no real reason. Then, when I see evil in the world, and I really should hate it, I should be all shook up: "*Gevalt!* What is going on here!?" But I already used up most of my hatred for other things. I don't have it anymore.

Then, listen to this. Let's say G-d gave me 100 pounds of shame to be used for a holy purpose. But I used it up on stupid things; I came into a place and I saw they are doing things that are wrong, but I was ashamed to speak up. And so I used up 50 pounds of my shame on the wrong thing. Then, when it comes do doing the most ugly thing in the world which I should be ashamed to do, and I need 100 pounds of shame in order not to do it, but by then I only have 50 pounds of shame left, so I do it, because I already used up the shame that I needed now.

## Hate evil

Rebbe Nachman says, the world uses up their hate against each other, so they are not hating evil any more. They should hate evil, but they just hate each other; they are just using up the entire 100 pounds of hate, and so when it comes to really hating evil, they don't hate it so much anymore, maybe they even like it. David HaMelech says, "The ones who love G-d really hate evil."

If someone would tell you now, "I want you to go and put someone to shame; I will give you a million dollars for doing it," but you just hate to do it, you really just hate the idea of doing it. You hate it to the utmost, because you know and understand what it means to put someone to shame. You say, "No. I am not going to do it, because I hate it."

But if you hate people, if you are using up your hatred in the wrong place, on people, then, if someone says to you to put someone to shame and you know you shouldn't put someone to shame, but if he offers to give you a few rubles to do it, you don't hate it that much anymore.

If you use up all the love in your heart on money, you don't have enough love left for your own children, because you used it up on money. That's what is going on in the world today. Parents are so busy loving their Cadillacs and their new homes and their new golf clubs that there is not enough love left in their heart for loving their own children.

**Your love gets stronger**

Like exercising muscles, the more you feel love, the stronger your ability to love will get.

It is only if you love what you really want to love that your ability to love becomes stronger. But if you love something which, deep down, you don't love, then the deep muscles of love are not worked on.

How much can you love money? Let's put it on that level. Loving your child with all your heart, is different from the way that the most rotten, low creature loves money. These two different kinds of love do not really have the same effect on the heart, so the one who loves money is not really exercising his love muscles, right? You see, each time you love someone who you really want to love, your ability to love gets stronger. If you love something you shouldn't love, and you don't really want to love, you are just wasting your love, and not exercising your love muscles.

Each time you give money to a poor man, your muscles of giving are being exercised and strengthened.

**Holy *chutzpah***

There is something which is very important. There is such a thing as arrogance, believing that you can do it. For instance, I know this very strongly from my musical performances. Who is a good performer? Not just someone who has a good voice. Some people have tremendous voices but they can't perform, because they don't believe that they can do it. When you stand before an audience, you have to believe that you can perform before them. That is really all there is to it. If you are standing there, and if you believe that you can sing a song, that is it. The vibration is tremendous.

Sometimes someone comes on stage and he doesn't believe that he can do it, so no one pays any attention to him. There is something in the air.

But sometimes you have to know that you can't do it, *mamash*. You have to have this holy shame, and know, "I can't do it." Then, at other times, you have to have this holy *chutzpah* to say, "I can do it. I know I can do it." The question is, when are you sure that you can do it, and when do you have this holy shame that you can't do it?

### *Azut d'kedusha* [holy arrogance]

What happens if I want to do something very holy, very strong, and the whole world laughs at me? Everyone thinks I am completely crazy. Then I must have holy *chutzpah, azut d'kdusha*, holy arrogance. If the whole world says that I am crazy, how come I am not crazy? When I was born, G-d gave me the holy arrogance to do what is right.

Say for instance, I believe I should wear a *yarmulke* [skullcap]. I walk into a place, and all the people start laughing, "Are you crazy? A *yarmulke*! You're old fashioned! You're stupid!" So I say, "Oh, I'm sorry. Oh, you are really right. We are living in a modern, civilized world. What do I need a *yarmulke* for?" Rebbe Nachman then asks: What am I doing to myself? It is not that I took off the *yarmulke*. That is beside the point. When I do something because people told me I should or shouldn't do it, or that it doesn't look nice, you know what happens to me? I make a *p'gam*, a blemish; I destroy my holy arrogance. Have you ever seen someone who licks up to the whole world for two pennies? Why are they so low? Because they destroyed their *azut d'kdusha* with their own hands.

G-d says, "Look at yourself. What are you? You were My servant before. I gave you enough *chutzpah* to do right, yet you prefer to listen to people? Okay, be a slave to them. Make up your mind who is your master."

If you are G-d's servant, then you are the highest person in the world because you know exactly what is right. If you know what is right, then you don't listen to anybody - just to what the soul of your soul tells you is right.

If you have *azut d'kedusha*, this holy arrogance, then you can really love people because you are not their slave.

If you lose your holy arrogance, then I am a slave to every *shmendrik* [fool]. I hate this *shmendrik*, because he is my master. I have no dignity, I have no spine anymore. I can't stand people anymore.

It is very strange. We always think that if we don't listen to people who tell us to do wrong, that means we will be pushed off to the side, and we want to be in with the crowd. Just look at the crowd - do you think they love each other? They hate each other. It is 100% true, one billion percent true. Rebbe Nachman's holy words are *mamash* like gold.

Rebbe Nachman says something else. What about the relationship of people to you? If you have holy *chutzpah*, then people really love you. People *mamash* love you. If someone walks in with a *yarmulke*, and everyone laughs at him, and he still wears it - they can keep on laughing. You know what the person who is laughing really thinks? "*Gevalt!* I respect him so much."

But if I wear a *yarmulke* and people say, "Take it off, this is not the place!" and I take it off, people laughingly say, "Really a strong character, this person! Who would want to be his friend?"

You know how people are? When you listen to them, they spit at you. When you don't listen to them, they love you. It's the craziest thing in the world!

When you listen to people, you become their slave, and so you don't love them. Don't tell me you listen to people because you love them. Don't kid yourself. You listen to people because you are not standing on your own two feet. And if you don't stand on your own two feet, then they treat you like a dog who walks on all fours. But if you are strong enough, and you stand on your own two feet, nothing can bend you. Then the world really loves you.

Rebbe Nachman says it is just heartbreaking if you destroy the holy arrogance that you have, because then you become a slave to people. Rebbe Nachman says this very strongly, he says the question is are you G-d's servant, or people's servant? There is no in between.

Everybody is somebody's servant. Are you G-d's servant? Then you are the freest person in the world. Because you know exactly what is right. If you know what is right, then you don't listen to anybody - just to what the soul of your soul tells you is right. The Gemara says the freest person is the one who is G-d's servant. If you are a man's servant, you are a slave. If you are G-d's servant, you are free. Completely free. Really, really free.

### Holy arrogance against my own self

What is *teshuva*? What does it mean to repent? Why basically, did I sin? Because I wasn't strong enough, right? I didn't have holy arrogance against my own self! To repent, to do *teshuva*, to return to G-d, means to correct the holy arrogance within me.

### Mashiach

Who is Mashiach? What will Mashiach do? How will he get us out of exile? How will he get us out of slavery? He will reach the utmost level of not being a slave to people, of not listening to anybody, not even to your own self, not to one's stupid self. He will be *mamash* a servant of G-d completely. He will have the holy *chutzpah* to get the whole world out of exile. Why don't we have the *chutzpah* to get people out of exile, to get the world out of exile? Sadly enough, we are not on the level, we don't have the holy arrogance, we really don't. We listen to ten thousand people. Maybe we listen to ourselves at the wrong moment. We do everything wrong.

## The real humble people

Rebbe Nachman says that the people who have this holy arrogance are the most humble people in the world, the real truly humble people. Their arrogance is not because of "I am," it is because "this is right," – and this gives them strength. If I am doing something because **I** think it is right, or because **you** think it is right, then I am not humble anymore. When I wear a *yarmulke,* is it because **I** want to, because **I** believe in *yarmulke*s? It is because G-d wants me to wear a *yarmulke*! I am a Jew. I want the world to know I am a Jew.

I am not drawing my strength from my stupidity nor my genius. It has nothing to do with me. It is just that I know a Jew has to wear a *yarmulke*, and I am a grandchild of Abraham. This is holy arrogance, to do it just because the thing has to be done.

For instance, I walk on the street and I see someone beating up someone. I walk up, and I knock him off. I am doing it because that is the right thing to do, not because of "I." It has nothing to do with me. The holy arrogant people have no "I," they really have no "I." The non-holy arrogant people also have *chutzpah*, but it is with such a big "I" that it is so disgusting, it smells so bad that nobody can have anything to do with them.

## It's written clearly in the Torah

Rebbe Nachman says that the real *tzadik* is someone who says a teaching, and later, when you look in the Torah, you see that every word he said was *mamash* written openly in the Torah. The question is, why didn't we see it before? Now that the *tzadik* said it, we notice that it was written clearly in the Torah all along.

So Rebbe Nachman says, this is *mamash* a *passuk* [verse] from the Torah, "You are leading the Jewish people with Your holy *chutzpah* back to the holy place." The way King James translates it is "with your strength." Rebbe Nachman says, it means, "with G-d giving us His holy *chutzpah*," which is much deeper.

How will we get back to the Holy Temple? How will we do *teshuva*? What will Mashiach do to us? He will give us back this holy *chutzpah*.

## A person without holy *chutzpah* cannot live

Now Rebbe Nachman says something very, very strong. Why is it considered like murder to put someone to shame? He says it is because when you put someone to shame you are killing his holy *chutzpah*. And a person without holy *chutzpah* cannot live. You are tearing out his heart. He might still be breathing, but the moment you cut off someone's wings, you put someone to shame, you take away this holy *chutzpah* from the person, and you *mamash* kill him.

## Be completely plugged in

Rebbe Nachman says, all *Yiddishkeit*, all service of G-d, depends on how much holy *chutzpah* you have within you. He says you must have holy *chutzpah* against your physical desires, against your spiritual desires, and you must have holy *chutzpah* even against the holiest dreams you have, and just do exactly what you know G-d wants you to do. You must be completely plugged in.

## Friends

Rebbe Nachman asks, what is it to talk to a good friend? It is to take the little friend and instill into him the *chutzpah*, to give him strength to know exactly what is the right thing to do.

What is evil in the world? Imagine a person wants to learn, a person wants to do something holy. Evil doesn't say that it's bad. You know how the devil, so to speak, gets to you? The devil puts on himself the face of a friend, and he talks to you, and he tries to take away your holy *chutzpah*. Evil comes and says, "Listen to me. I've known you so long, I know you very well. You be holy? You be a good Jew? You be learned? Whom are you fooling? You won't be able to do it. I know you." Evil tells you, "Listen, you have to be realistic, and you have to know the world. And this, and that. Be sensible, see a psychiatrist..." and he gives himself the mask of your greatest friend. So Rebbe Nachman says, beware of devils who look like friends.

## *Tzadikim*

Can you imagine? Rebbe Nachman says you must have holy *chutzpah* even against *Tzadikim*, even against holy people. It has to be so strong that if you *mamash* look deep in your soul, and you know what you have to do, there is nothing in the world that can stop you, nobody in the world that can stop you. But you have to be *mamash* plugged in – you have to do it *mamash* on G-d's account.

### *Chutzpah* to get close to G-d

Rebbe Nachman says, not only must you have holy *chutzpah* against the *Tzadikim*, you even have to have holy *chutzpah* against G-d. You have to come to G-d and tell Him, "G-d, I have to be a Jew, I have got to be holy, and I have to be close to You, and You can't push me away." You have to tell G-d, "It is true I tried starting anew fifteen thousand times, and I always fell down again, but G-d, I am telling You the truth. I'll never leave You, so You better let me get close." I want to get close to G-d, and, so to speak, G-d gives me a little kick, He pushes me off. He wants to see how strong I am. By my coming back to Him, I say, "I don't care. You can kick me, I will still come back." It is actually *chutzpah* against G-d. Real *chutzpah*. This is because each time you come back, you come back stronger. And even if you fall again, you come back stronger. Rebbe Nachman says, this is so deep that he can't explain it to you more, but happy is the one who has enough *chutzpah* to get close to G-d.

This is strong stuff. *Oy oy oy oy oy oy oy oy oy oy oy oy.*

Then he says that, the truth is, all the holy *Tzadikim* reached so high, not because they knew more, or because their souls were holier; they got there only because they had this holy *chutzpah*. The people who didn't get there did not have this *azut d'kdusha*.

And, therefore, if someone, sadly enough, comes to you and tells you, "What are you talking about? You want to be a holy Jew? You want to be strong? What do you know? You can't even read Hebrew! You can't do this, you can't do that...." They give you a long account of what you can't do. Rebbe Nachman says, what do you care? The more someone explains to you how bad you are, that means you need more *chutzpah*, right? So get it.

Now listen; Rebbe Nachman says the greatest teaching in the world. What is the greatest evil in the world? The greatest evil comes to me and tells me, "Listen to me, I know the truth. You can't do it. Who are you fooling?" That is the greatest evil in the world. Evil doesn't tell you that this is bad. Evil just tells you, "Listen, I know you so long, I know you very well. You'll be holy? You'll be a good Jew? You'll become a big *lamdan* [scholar]? What are you talking about? I know you all these years. Forget it."

So you have to tell your evil, "Cut it out! I am not listening to you even if it is true." Answer back to your evil, "I am not even listening to G-d if He kicks me. I am not listening to anyone." G-d is only testing you. G-d wants you to become strong.

Rebbe Nachman says, what was the dream Jacob had, the ladder of Jacob? The ladder is this holy *chutzpah*. Jacob saw that there is a ladder, and a person can go up to heaven. How do you go from one rung to the other? Just go.

**You must have a good nose**

But then Rebbe Nachman says, you must be very careful. You must have a good nose [sense] to know what is the arrogance of holiness and what is arrogance of non-holiness. Many people also preach this kind of *chutzpah*, but it is really for the destruction of the world, for your destruction. So you have to know exactly what is holiness and what is not.

Rebbe Nachman says something very strong. The most important thing is, don't be a *shlemazel*. He *mamash* says here "Don't be lazy."

Imagine a person who *mamash* wants to begin to learn, a person who wants to do something good. So the evil inclination comes and says, "Who are you fooling? I know you. You won't be able to do it. You are fooling yourself." What do you do then? You tell your evil, "I have *chutzpah* even against G-d. Even if G-d would tell me not to come close to Him, I wouldn't listen. I'm not listening to anybody. I won't even listen to *Tzadikim* if they would tell me to give up trying to do good." Because G-d is only testing you. G-d wants you to become strong. So when you wrestle, then you become stronger. You have to wrestle with G-d, So to speak. When Yaakov Avinu wrestled with the angel, he was really wrestling with G-d. What does it mean? G-d sends you a little evil in your heart in order to make you stronger.

You see, each time you wrestle, your soul muscles get stronger.

**Don't be a *shlemazel***

How can you know whether your arrogance is holy or not? The only thing I can tell you is that Rebbe Nachman says, "Don't be a *shlemazel*." That means you have to know in your heart whether you are a *shlemazel* or not. Ultimately it is up to your own nose [sensitivities]. You know very well, deep down.

**Shabbos**

The world is bad, not because they don't know enough, it is just because they don't do enough. Have you ever seen a person saying, "Thank G-d I don't keep Shabbos, it brings so much joy to my house"? The lowest, most rotten character knows that that is not true. If someone says, "I don't believe in Shabbos," ok, I have nothing against you. But don't tell me that violating the Shabbos brings joy to you, because even you know that keeping Shabbos brings joy. And don't tell me that not keeping Shabbos brings you close to your children, because you know very well that the only thing that brings you close to your own children is Shabbos.

**Restore this holy arrogance**

Rebbe Nachman says, you need friends to help you restore this holy arrogance, because, in the same way that if a person puts you to shame he kills you - because he takes away your holy arrogance – so, in the same way, you need friends who not only don't put you to shame, but who will give you new life.

**Mashiach *Ben Yosef* and Mashiach *Ben David***

At the end of days, or maybe tomorrow, there will be two Mashiachs, a Mashiach who will be a descendant of Yosef, and Mashiach *Ben* David, who will be a descendant of Yehuda, from the tribe of Yehuda.

Yehuda was the one who did everything wrong. If you remember, Yehuda was the one who told his brothers, "Let's sell Yosef." According to this, in the deepest depths, the whole exile began on account of him. He should have given up then. But he didn't. Then he gets married, and two of his children die. G-d is letting him know, *mamash* you are wrong. Everything goes wrong. Whatever he does is wrong. He makes a guarantee for the safety of Benjamin, and Benjamin gets caught. So what should Yehuda do? He just does not give up. Yehuda is this holy *Yiddele* [Jew] who doesn't give up till the very last second. He doesn't give up. He knows that if Benjamin doesn't come back to Canaan with him he will lose his share in the World to Come. But what does Yehuda do? He says, "I don't care. Even if I don't have a share in the World to Come, you can't knock me out."

The Zohar HaKodesh on the Torah portion of *Vayigash* explains that Yehuda spoke to Yosef, but he really was talking to G-d. He was pouring out his heart. He was saying, "You know, we have an old father," as if he was telling Yosef about Jacob, but actually he was saying to G-d, "You are my Old Father. You are my Father since I was born. I am just a little boy. I am nothing." It is tremendous the way the Zohar HaKodesh translates every word.

So listen to this. Yosef is the one who has the holy *chutzpah* so that he never did wrong. You know how much strength it takes never to do wrong? And Yehuda has this holy strength, that even if he does everything wrong, he still wants to come back.

The world needs both, because we are a combination of billions of little things. Certain parts of us are on the level of Mashiach *Ben* Yosef, certain parts of us never did wrong. We have, thank G-d, the *chutzpah*, the strength needed so that we never did wrong. But other parts of us are completely destroyed, so for that we need Mashiach *Ben* David. Between the two, they correct the whole world.

Before the selling of Yosef, Yosef was holier than Yehuda. When did Yehuda become holy? After he sold his brother Yosef into slavery, after he started doing wrong, then he became so very strong, so holy. In Bereshit it says, "*mi teref bni alisa* - From tearing away my son, you became great and holy." The meaning is, when did Yehuda really become Yehuda? When did he pull out [activate] his holy *chutzpah*, his holy soul, that is the holiness of Yehuda? After he sold Yosef into slavery.

That is why his father favored Yosef. On the level that the children were on initially, Yosef was really the king. There could be only one Mashiach, the son of Yosef. But after Yehuda sold Yosef, and yet Yehuda didn't give up, then suddenly Yaakov realized; Yehuda was even stronger than Yosef. Yehuda doesn't give up praying to the very last second. *Gevalt!*

So you see, we need both. We need someone who gives us the strength not to destroy the holy things we still have, and someone to teach us that even with all the things we have destroyed already, we should not give up, we should come back.

**A time to love, a time to hate**

Deep down we ask the question, when am I supposed to love, and when am I supposed to hate? When am I supposed to be arrogant, and when am I supposed to be bashful? When am I supposed to speak up, and when am I supposed to be silent? Rebbe Nachman says, if I would get to the roots of loving, to the roots of my soul, I would know.

The soul is all one. My body is also one body, but it is not completely one, because my head doesn't look like my foot, right? G-d's Oneness is not really reflected in my body, because there are still differences. Even one finger doesn't look like another finger. My soul is more oneness, because it is one piece. My soul also hears, but for my soul, hearing, seeing, doing, thinking, and feeling are all the same. It is *mamash* one. A human being feels with his heart, thinks with his head, and walks with his feet. Although the body is one, it has different organs.

The soul is *mamash* one. And if I were on the level of my soul, that real oneness… You see, right now, because love is here, and hatred is there, I don't know which one to use. But if I am on the level of complete oneness, then I know exactly when to love and when to hate, because if love and hate are together, then I know when to use them. It is only if love is here and hate is there, if silence is here and speaking up is there, so then I don't know which way to go. If I am not on the level of one, then to love is one department and to hate is another department, because I have different kinds of departments in my heart. But if everything is in the same room, I don't have so much trouble with it, because it is all right there. If I am on the level of one, then I know exactly when to love and when to hate.

If I get to the roots of loving, to the roots of my soul, if I am on the level of my soul, of that real oneness, then I'll know when I am supposed to love, and when I am supposed to hate. When I am supposed to be arrogant, and when I am supposed to be bashful. When I am supposed to speak up, and when I am supposed to be silent.

# ઇ Yom Tov ભ

## One Ounce of Joy

Is there any greater joy in the world than when you see somebody crying, and you give them life, you give them one ounce of joy, you give them one ounce of hope.

Rebbe Nachman says, the greatest crime is to take away somebody's self confidence, to take away somebody's hope.

And the greatest, greatest thing in the world is, if you can give it to somebody. Because the only way of getting into heaven, basically, is by giving it to somebody else. And that kind of joy which comes from heaven, is only given to you at that moment when you give it to somebody else.

You know, it says, *"sisu et Yerushalayim* [give joy to Jerusalem].*"* How do you get joy? By giving joy to Yerushalayim [Jerusalem]. Yerushalayim is that place in our hearts, in the world, which is destroyed. And if you rebuild it a little bit, *gevalt,* is that good.

### A fair exchange

Sweetest friends, believe me... and I am sure you know it anyway; but people who don't believe in G-d don't have joy. They have fun. But joy? No.

I once was sitting with some Communists in Belgium; They were members of Shomer Tsair, Jewish young people, real Communists. I was sitting with them, and I said to them, "OK, you know what? Let's exchange religions. I will be a Communist, and you will be, so to speak, *frum* [religious]. But it has to be a fair exchange. Look what I am giving you. I am giving you Shabbos, Pesach, Shavuos, Sukkot. I am giving you joy. I am giving you heaven to the utmost. What can you give me back for an exchange? Do you have any holiday? Do you have one Shabbos in your life? Do you have one ray of hope, one ray of beauty? You are gloomy people, right? So it is not a fair exchange. So I will stick to mine."

Anyway, it got through to them.

ઇભ

# Rosh HaShanah

One of the most important aspects of Rosh HaShanah is not to say bad things about another person. As you want G-d to give you a chance, also give everyone else a chance to begin again.

So, my dearest brothers and sisters, it's only after Rosh HaShanah when our beginning is so strong, when we get a taste that our inside has never been blemished, and we go to the Holy Cleaner, the Master of the World, who takes out all the stains from our hearts and the dust from our souls. And He is doing it while we are singing and dancing. On Yom Kippur, we tell Him all our mistakes because we now already have so much inner strength.

Please, please, give each other strength. Don't ever stop giving compliments to each other, and, most of all, give compliments to your children, whose self confidence depends on you! On Rosh HaShanah, every second counts like a thousand years.

*Our holy master Rebbe Nachman says: The greatest gift we can give someone is to give him back his self confidence.*

When we make a mistake, not only do we do wrong, but our soul also is shriveling, and we look down at ourselves. A whole year of mistakes - *Gevalt!* How do we look at ourselves? It doesn't take much to give up on somebody else, but to give up on ourselves is always Federal Express.

To have the guts to really begin again takes a lot of inner strength. So on Rosh HaShanah, the holiest day of beginnings, we don't mention our mistakes, in order to have the strength to stand before G-d like newborn babies. Our holy Rabbis teach us that the sound of the *shofar* is the sound of our innermost soul and heart and also the sound of a newborn baby. It is everything. It wakes us up, it gives us strength, it reminds us how holy we are, and how holy we can be, and also how close we are and how easy it is to be the best and most exalted.

Blessings and love,

*Shlomo*

෩෮

# Learn How to Get Up

Rebbe Nachman's holy mother was named Feigele. She was called Feigele *hanevia*, Feigele the prophetess. She had clear vision from one corner of the world to the other. And she was the daughter of Udele, *aish das lamo*, the daughter of the *Heilege* Holy Bal Shem Tov himself.

The Mezritche Maggid said, "Until Mashiach is coming, when one *Yid* [Jew] will give just one *krechts* [crying out to G-d], it is all because of the Bal Shem Tov."

But Rebbe Nachman: *Zeh mesechta bifnei atsmo* [but Rebbe Nachman is a whole tractate himself].

## Two things

Basically this teaching of Rebbe Nachman is two things:

1) How much would you give not to stop breathing? Billions of times more, you have to give everything, not to ever, G-d forbid, not to ever stop being *b'simcha* [filled with joy]. Because if you are not *b'simcha*, if you are not filled with joy, you are dead, a thousand times a second.

2) And then he says, don't ever give up. Don't ever, ever give up.

## Three lessons

The *heilege zeise* [holy sweet] Rebbe Nachman, the *heilege* Rebbe, the Rebbe of all the Rebbes, the *tzadik* of all the *tzadikim*, this is what he said:

If you ever, ever want to be a servant of the One, of the Only One, you have to learn three lessons. You have to know these three things before you begin serving G-d.

The first thing is: You have to learn how to walk. You have to learn how to stand... You have to learn how to walk, and you have to learn how to stand.

When you are praying, when you *daven*, you stand before the One, before the Only One.

When you are doing *mitzvas*, when you do something good, you are walking... you are walking... you are walking in His ways.

But only those who know how to stand, know how to walk.

And those who know how to walk, they also know how to stand.

Learn how to walk… learn how to stand… learn how to walk… learn how to stand….

That is the first torah teaching. The second teaching is:

Learn how to fall… learn how to fall… learn how to fall and to get up.

The second teaching is a little bit harder. Learn how to fall… learn how to fall, and to get up.

So when you are falling, let your heart be filled with great joy, because G-d is teaching you how to get up. Because if you wouldn't fall, you'd never learn how to get up.

When you are falling, let your heart be filled with joy, because the One, the Only One, is teaching you how to get up.

You hear, my friends…. Learn how to walk, learn how to stand. Learn how to fall, and to get up.

Now comes the third teaching: this is hard. Open up your hearts. What do you do when you are falling, and you can't get up? What do you do when you are falling, and you don't stop falling? When you are falling, you are falling, you are falling, and you are still falling. What do you do when you are falling and falling and falling? What do you do when you are falling and nobody holds your hand, nobody is helping you, and you can't get up?

So this is what the *heilege tzadik* Rebbe Nachman says: In the meantime, keep on walking, in the meantime keep on standing… in the meantime keep on standing, in the meantime keep on walking. In the meantime let your heart be filled with joy. In the meantime keep on singing, keep on dancing. Until one day, until one day, one day, one day, it will be revealed to you that you never fell, that you never fell, because how is it possible to fall when the One, the Only One, is holding you so close.


## Sukkot

On Yom Kippur I am standing before G-d, and I say, "Master of the world, forgive me, I am falling, I was falling so much." Then, when I am sitting in the *sukkah, betsilo demehemnusa, betsilo DeKudsha Brich Hu* [sheltered in the shade of G-d], and I realize that I never fell, because the Rebono Shel Olam, His light surrounds me all the time, and is holding me, a Jew can never fall.

Learn how to walk, learn how to stand. Learn how to fall and to get up. Learn how to fall and to know that a Jew can never fall.

On *Sukkot* we bring seventy sacrifices for the whole world. If I would ask you, "Do you really think that one day, Mashiach is coming, and the whole world will be fixed?" So you will tell me, "Nah, I can't believe it. Listen to the radio, look at the newspaper. You are wrong."

Let me ask you, four weeks ago, did you think you would be so holy? Ahh, the Rebono Shel Olam opened gates for you. And suddenly you are so pure and so holy. Maybe G-d will open gates for the whole world, for G-d's world. G-d created them.

So on *Sukkot*, we say, "Master of the world, *letaken olam bemalchus shin daled yud.* Master of the world, let me have a hand in fixing the whole world."

*"Veyetayu kol leavdecha, vevarchu shem kevodecha, veyagidu roim tzidkecha, veyitnu lecha keter melucha."*

ഇ)രു

# Hanukah

Why is it that I can eat *matza,* but nobody comes running after me hungry to eat *matza* too, but when I place my *menora* by my window, and kindle all the heavenly lights, all the *Yidden* that pass by my window feel the deepest hunger inside their hearts? It is because, as Rebbe Nachman teaches, Hanukah is a light that burns from the inside out, not from the outside in.

I once met this homeopathic doctor, and he told me the difference between a medical doctor and a homeopathic doctor. A regular doctor works from the outside to the inside, but the homeopathic doctor begins with the inside and then goes out.

This, my beautiful friends, is how the Bal Shem Tov wanted to heal the world. He said that it's no longer enough to begin studying Torah from the outside in, when *Yidden* are becoming sick all over the place. Now the world needs to begin studying the Torah from the inside out.

Do you realize that it's possible for people who are 'officially religious' to keep the entire Torah, and still not have the faintest idea of what *Yiddishkeit* is all about? These are the people who keep Shabbos, and yet have still never even tasted what it's all about.

On Hanukah, we must begin to see the outside world, and to see our holy Torah, through that inside light that is burning inside all of us.

Why is it that one person can feel the light of Hanukah, but another person, is sill feeling so cold? *Nebech, gevalt,* right?

I was once at the home of a certain so called 'great' Rabbi. He had a phone in his hand. And so, while he was talking to somebody, his wife brought in the menorah, and, while putting the person on hold, he made the *bracha.* As soon as everybody answered "*amen,*" he got back on the phone and ignored the light and ignored his family. So maybe this Rabbi will go to paradise one day because he did all the *mitzvas*. But, *gevalt*, it's the paradise down here that he's missing.

I want you to listen to this, it's so beautiful. My brother Michael and I are best friends. Imagine that we have a very big fight. So I go to him and ask, "Can you please forgive me?" and he says, "Yeah, I forgive you." But you know, it's no longer the same between us anymore. There is something still missing. You know what's missing? The light between us is missing. There is forgiveness, but there is no more light left between us.

Rebbe Nachman teaches that on Yom Kippur G-d forgives us, but it's not until Hanukah that G-d gives us back the light. So on Hanukah, the light is back between us - and the light is so deep, so intimate.

Hanukah is the holiday of Aaron HaCohen, the High Priest. On Yom Kippur, the High Priest would walk into the Holy of Holies to ask for G-d's forgiveness. But why do we need a High Priest in the Holy of Holies on Yom Kippur, if Moshe Rabbenu already came back from Heaven bringing us the Two Tablets as a sign of G-d's forgiveness? Do I need more than forgiveness?

Ah, *gevalt*: we need so much more than forgiveness. We need intimacy. We need to be so much closer to G-d than forgiveness can bring us.

So Aaron HaCohen didn't go into the Holy of Holies to ask for our forgiveness. He went in after we were already forgiven. Instead, he went into the Holy of Holies to bring down the light of intimacy for his people.

The difference between holy things and ordinary things is very simple. You do not long for ordinary things once you have them. You have them, and the longing is fulfilled. But when it comes to holy things, even if you have them, you still long for them very much. I have Shabbos every week, but how much of it do I really have? How do I know if I truly have the holy Shabbos? You only have the holy Shabbos if you are longing for it all of the time.

On Hanukah it is fire rather than water that we celebrate. Because, like fire, we are *mamash* longing for something so holy and exalted.

෫෬

# "*Ohr Haganuz*," the Hidden Light of Hanukah

## Davening

Every person has two functions. One function is of 'me and the world,' and the other is 'me and me' and 'me and G-d.'

There are two kinds of relationships between people. There is you and me in the world, and then there is just you and me without the world. This is beyond the world, deeper than the world.

How do you know how much you love a person? Are you aware of the world when you are talking to them? If there is still a world, sure you are close, but real true closeness is when suddenly the world stops.

Rebbe Nachman says that, when I *daven* [pray], there is me and the world and G-d. But then, slowly, as I continue to *daven* even more, there is just me and G-d. Then I go higher and higher; I stop to exist. There is only G-d. The deepest secret is, how do I keep it all together.

You know what happens when people go to *shul* [synagogue] on Yom Kippur? Why doesn't the effect last even five minutes after Yom Kippur is over? Because on Yom Kippur, when I'm so close to G-d, it is just me and G-d, but the minute there is a world, G-d disappears. Let's say I love my wife very much when I am with her. But then I walk out onto the street, and already I forget that she exists.

**How do you get it all together?**

How do you get it all together? Here I want you to know something. The Greeks offer us a beautiful world, but that's all. *Yiddishkeit* basically offers us a world; there is only one G-d. There is just me and G-d. So I want you to know something - we lost our children because children want the world. Sure they want to think sometimes that there is no world, just you and me, you and G-d. But where is the beautiful world?

So on Hanukah, the Hashmonaim really got it together. They brought in Hanukah lights. Everybody knows Hanukah is *mehadrin min hamehadrin*, beautiful and more beautiful, and we kindle lights in the house. The house is a place where I'm just alone, where I'm alone with my children. I'm kindling lights by the door and I'm shining into the world. Because the real truth is, the world doesn't tear you away from G-d or from the Torah.

The time for Hanukah lights is at night. Basically, the night is a time when people can get so close, because during the night the world doesn't exist so much. Though there is still a world.

**A hidden light**

The Hashmonaim say, "*Gevalt*, Master of the world, let me kindle the Hanukah lights!" Do you know what is so special about the lights? You are able to see them, and yet it is "*Ohr Haganuz*," a hidden light that you know is not an ordinary light or just a candle burning. It is full of secrets, full of mystery, full of the deepest depths. It means that even while I see something, I'm always aware that there is something deeper, so much deeper, the part where the world doesn't reach.

When I love someone very much, I see them, they are there, but I also know there is so much more.

## Mother and children

The Torah says about our Mother Sarah, *"hinei beohel* [behold, she is in the tent]." The mother fixes for her children their relationship to G-d without the world. There is something between a mother and her children that is so close that it has nothing to do with the world. The father is supposed to give over to his children how to believe in G-d while in the world.

Everybody knows that the woman is the house, as it says about Sarah, *"hinei beohel* [behold, she is in the tent / the woman represents the house]." Therefore, on Hanukah, the deepest fixing is *"ish ubeiso,"* a man and his house - *mamash*, the husband and wife together. It is the world and yet it is without the world, beyond the world.

## Can't take your eyes off it

It is so beautiful that you can't take your eyes off of it, and yet you know that you don't really see it because it is so much deeper, and the deepest depths is that all your children are also kindling lights.

You don't have to make sure that your little boy of seven puts on *tefillin*, but your little boy, as well as your little girl of five - are both kindling Hanukah lights. Because though perhaps what you see is seven years old, but the part you can't see is ancient, eternal, forever, beyond time and space. On Hanukah you put it all together because you are truly close to your children when you know that what you see is only a small part of what they really are.

You know the Greeks say, "The world is only what you see." On Hanukah, we say, "Yes, we see a world, it is beautiful, but *gevalt* there is so much more!"

Our Holy Sages teach us, "We are not permitted to make any use of them [the candles] except watching them." We look at the lights and see everything nobody sees.

You know, friends, Israel is the same way. Everybody knows that on Hanukah we fix our eyes. We fix the sin of the ten spies [who were sent by Moses to the Holy Land]. Because what was wrong there? The spies looked at Israel and saw only what they saw. They didn't see that which can't be seen. But when you see what you can't see, then you look again and you see a different world. And everybody knows that on Hanukah, when you kindle the lights, suddenly, every house becomes a different world. Suddenly every house is Israel, every house is the Holy Temple, and every child that kindles the lights is the High Priest. Good Yom Tov.

ഇൗരു

# Purim and Holy Pride

On Purim, suddenly the whole world is filled with the way the world was before G-d created the world. On Purim, a great light is shining from such a high place, higher and deeper than all the other holidays in the world.

## Holy pride

Rebbe Nachman says something very deep. The world knows of either humility or pride. The truth is you need both, but you have to know when to use them.

Even anger is a very holy thing if you know when to use it. All the emotions in the world are very holy, because G-d gave them to you. You just have to know when to use them.

So the world thinks, "Either you'll be a *shmendrik* - you are always humble - or you are always arrogant." But both are wrong.

On Purim we get so high that we don't know the difference between Haman and Mordechai. This means we don't know the difference between arrogance and humility, because both are holy. On Purim we are on the level that we know exactly when to be humble and when to be proud.

The truth is, to be a servant of G-d, you need a lot of pride.

Rebbe Nachman says, even to pray to G-d takes a lot of pride. That means I am standing before G-d and I am demanding, "Please G-d, listen to me!" This takes a lot of pride, but this is holy pride.

## Holy humility

Then you must have holy humility. Not *shmendrik* humility. Not stupid, senseless humility, which is what we mostly have. You must have holy humility.

The people who have holy humility are the strongest people in the world.

If you know exactly where to use your humility, then you know exactly where to use your pride.

Rebbe Nachman says, you have 50 units of humility and 50 units of pride. If you use up your pride in the wrong place, then it is used up. You have a certain amount of soul strength to be proud, and a certain amount of soul strength to be humble. For example, if I have 50 cents, if I use it up on the wrong thing, then when it comes time to buy the real thing, I won't have it.

On Purim, this great thing is shining so that we know exactly when pride stops being evil, and when humility stops being out of reach. Everything is holy on Purim, because I know exactly when to be humble and when to be proud.

## The greatest evil in the world is sadness.

Why is the world not becoming better? Or, why am I, as an individual, not becoming better? Because I am filled with sadness.

Maybe I am sad because of something I did yesterday, or maybe I am sad because of what I want to do tomorrow. It doesn't really matter. In the meantime, I am filled with sadness, and this is the greatest evil in the world.

All the secular teachings of the world, do they fill you with joy or with sadness? Do you ever see kids walking out of secular school saying, "*Gevalt*, what I'm learning!" It doesn't turn them on. Secular learning doesn't put joy into your heart. All the teachings of Amalek, all the teachings of evil, fill you with sadness.

## Good manners

Rebbe Nachman teaches very strongly that just as there are holy good manners, there is also such a thing as good manners that have their roots in the evil of the world: Good manners with absolutely no meaning. The Germans, when they sent the Jews to the gas chambers, would say "*bitte*, please." So they think these are good manners? It has absolutely no meaning. A murderer says, "Please step over here, I want to knock your head off." Why does he pretend to be civilized? So there are good manners whose roots are in the evil of the world, and then there are real, holy manners. When someone walks through the door I might say, "I'm glad to see you" because of good manners, but it has no meaning, or I can say it because I really mean it.

On Purim, we get drunk. According to good manners you shouldn't get drunk, but what kind of manners are they?

It depends on what level we are when drunk... On Purim we are holy drunk, really holy. On Purim, if you are not on the highest level, you really have no right to drink, but... I have really been privileged to see people really high, holy high, on Purim. In Bobov, the Rebbe sits there and he drinks *mamash* one glass of wine after the other. *Mamash* high. I mean, not drunk, but so high! *Gevalt*!

On Purim we break down all the good manners of the world. We are real. And if you are real, you can be drunk and still be real, still be holy. And if you are on the level of evil manners, you can be sober, not drunk at all, and give a speech in Madison Square Gardens and say the most obnoxious things in the world. So therefore, on Purim we are breaking down all the levels of manners, and we are drunk, but we are just on the highest level.

## A holy drunkard sees only One

What is the difference between non-holy drunk and holy drunk? A non-holy drunkard, if he sees ten people, he says he sees a hundred; if he sees a million, he says he sees ten million. A holy drunkard sees only One; nothing else.

## The war between good and evil

There is a great war going on, the war between good and evil. One day a year we don't fight evil. One day a year there is no evil in the world. One day a year we reach the level of after the war. This is on Purim.

You have to know that only the people who are taking part in the war all year long can know what Purim is. If you don't fight evil all year long, but then on Purim you suddenly say, "I want to jump into Purim," what do you understand? If evil looks good to you, you have nothing to celebrate. On Purim we celebrate that there is no evil. But if you like evil, then you have no part in it.

So how do you fight evil? It says, "Remember what Amalek did to you...." You have to remember that there is evil in the world. You have to remember. So the question is, do you remember or do you forget. Imagine, yesterday I was bad, so I *mamash* promised myself that I'll be good. The next morning it is already forgotten; I forgot my promise, I forgot how bad I felt when I did wrong. If I would only remember a little bit. Purim is the great holiday of the people who remember. They are the ones who are fighting this great war against evil. They really do remember.

## G-d's love is beyond our minds

There are two kinds of love that G-d has for us. One kind of love is kind of contracted. Let's say, for example, that I like someone because he does everything I tell him to do. Or, on the other hand, I can like someone not because he does everything I want him to do, but, even if he doesn't do everything I want, I just love him anyway.

On Yom Kippur, G-d is loving us because we say, "G-d, we did wrong, we want to be better, we confess, we promise we'll be good, we'll do everything you tell us to do." This is very sweet and holy, but it is not the ultimate.

On Purim, G-d is shining His great love into us, His great love that has nothing to do with our doing His will. He just loves us. Like, "I don't care what you do, I still love you. I do care, what you do, but My love is beyond that." And this is beyond our minds.

Therefore we have to be drunk on Purim, because we have to reach that thing which is beyond our minds. We have to be beyond our own mind.

G-d's great love that is flowing down on Purim is not because we did right. It is just because He loves us. This is beyond… beyond every understanding.

Evil can only reach the level of love where we talk about doing G-d's will, so evil can make us not do G-d's will. That light comes from a place where evil can reach. But evil cannot reach that great love that is above and beyond that level, His love that has nothing to do with doing G-d's will.
On Purim this greater love is becoming so strong in the world that there is no evil. There is nothing between us and G-d. Nothing. I can be a drunkard, I can be the most obnoxious person in the world, but who cares? *Gevalt.*

Why is it that when you are drunk you can't stand on your feet, you can't walk? There is a level that your service of G-d is standing before G-d, and walking in G-d's ways. But then there is another level, that even if you are not walking, and even if you can't stand, you're still serving G-d in a crazy way that is even deeper. On Purim we reach that high level that we can't stand, we can't walk, but we are still the greatest servants of G-d.

## Holy imagination

What happens when you are drunk? You get a strange kind of imagination. What is really the greatest thing in the world? The holiest faculty that G-d has given us is imagination. Holy imagination. It depends where your imagination is. On Purim we get drunk and we *mamash* imagine the holiest things in the world. You know what we imagine? We imagine that there is no evil in the world. This is the holiest level a drunkard can reach.

If I am completely drunk and someone tells me, "You know, there is evil in the world," I say, "Evil? I don't know what you're talking about." Not only do I imagine it, the feeling is so strong that I *mamash* believe it. This is the holiest imagination anybody can reach.
This is the way I see it.

## Peace

In former good days, on Purim everybody got dressed up like somebody else. Boys would get dressed up like girls, girls like men. Jews would get dressed up like Indians, like Eskimos, like anything. Rebbe Nachman says something very deep. He says, "Why is there no peace in the world? Because I always think that I am the only one in the world. Only the way I am is right. Men think the only way to be is a man, women think the only way to be is a woman. A Jew thinks the only way to be is a Jew. So on Purim we get dressed up like somebody else. Because I say, 'Maybe this is also good. This is really very beautiful.' So, therefore, Purim is the holiest because there is no evil in the world, so why not get dressed up like someone else?

## Aware of G-d

The hardest time to be aware of G-d is when you eat. Usually, when people eat, they are so much aware of themselves because they are feeding their bodies. It is hard to be aware of G-d when you pray, but it is not that hard. It is really hard when you eat and drink. It's the hardest thing in the world. The more you eat, the less you are aware of G-d. The more you drink, the less you are aware of G-d. On Purim we reach that high level where we eat all day long, we drink all day long, and the way we understand G-d on that day is like never, never before. We understand G-d on the deepest, deepest, highest level. On Purim, the way we understand that there is one G-d is like we don't understand it all year long: It comes from such a high place. And the way we know what we are doing in this world comes from such a high place. The highest place in the world. And this is not by studying, not even by talking, But by eating, by drinking, and by giving gifts to one another.

We have to give gifts to one another, we have to give charity on Purim.

And maybe we also get dressed up like someone else, because it is from a completely different place.

## Great light

On no other day is the great light shining that we *mamash* so much want to get close to G-d again. Not only do we want to do G-d's will, not only do we want to do what is right, not only do we want to fulfill our mission in life - one day a year, *mamash* we just want to be so very close to G-d. And if we want to be close to G-d, we can eat and drink too. We can be half drunk, and eat all day long - it doesn't matter. If *mamash* our heart is burning up, that we just want to be close to G-d, then whatever we do is on the holiest level in the world.

Tremendous light is coming down when I want to be close, when people want to be close to each other, when I want to be close to G-d.

The greatest evil in the world is that we keep away from each other. But on Purim, the great light is shining so that everything is close.

## Newness

Evil is always new. Imagine, if you do something wrong, you swear to yourself you'll never do it again, right? So how come evil comes to you again the next day? The answer is very simple. Evil is really new all the time. Evil has a newness. How do we fight evil? With even more newness! With the utmost newness in the world. On Purim, G-d gives us this tremendous holy newness, *mamash* the ability to really start all over again. On Yom Kippur, holy as we are, we still talk about what we did yesterday. So it's still not completely new. On Purim, we don't talk about what happened yesterday. We don't even talk about what will happen tomorrow. We are just here.

Why aren't we the kind of *Yiddelach* [Jews] that we ought to be? Because we have this evil that comes to us and says, "It is another world now. Okay, when Moses stood on Mt. Sinai it was very sweet, but now it's another world." So evil wants to cut us off from G-d, because of the newness of the world.

The greatest miracle is that everything is new [that there are constantly new inventions], that so many new things are happening. Evil wants to utilize this holy newness against G-d. The most beautiful thing in the world is that the world is always new, that new things are always happening. Evil wants to take this newness and use it to tear us away from G-d. Purim is the day when we take all this newness and we say, "Because of this newness, I want to be a servant of G-d."

## Hold on just a little bit longer

Why am I a little bit bad? Because, *nebech*, I wanted to be good at one time or another. So I started praying so hard, and it looked to me as if G-d didn't care; He didn't answer my prayer. I had tried so hard. For years, I try to be better and it does not work. The greatest thing is that, on Purim, I suddenly realize it isn't true; I was becoming better. G-d heard every prayer. On Purim I realize that I am so close to G-d, I know He was listening all the time. Imagine, I talk to someone on the telephone and I think the other person hung up. Then I realize I wasn't even talking on the telephone, I was talking to him in person. He was actually standing right next to me the entire time.

We were supposed to be in exile for seventy years after the destruction of the First Temple. Crazily enough, we didn't know when the seventy years began. We thought that the seventy years began with the year when we didn't have a king anymore, the year when our king was taken into captivity - and so we thought that the seventy years were supposed to be over. So Achashverosh comes and tells us, "The prophecies aren't true; you were supposed to leave after seventy years, and the seventy years are over." But the truth was, the seventy years only began with the destruction of the Holy Temple. The story of Purim only took place in the sixty-ninth year. So this is the story - Amalek always comes to you and says to you, "Don't you see, the prophets told you something, G-d told you something, and He didn't keep His promise." But on Purim we realize, "It's not true. G-d keeps his promise, all the prophesies are true, G-d hears me, G-d knows me. I am on the way, I just have to hold out a little bit longer.' So Purim gives me the strength to hold on just a little bit longer."

**Maybe this is the way G-d is talking to you**

Purim was initiated by Mordechai and Esther. Two people. A lot of people say, "If I would hear this directly from G-d, I would believe in it, but if I hear it from somebody else, I don't want to believe in it." This is an evil trick. Because how do you want G-d to talk to you? Maybe this is the way G-d is talking to you. You can walk on the street and someone says something to you. Don't say, "No, I want to hear it directly from G-d." This is G-d telling it to you!

Remember the story about Elijah the Prophet? A man is waiting for Elijah the Prophet, and a beggar knocks on his door. The man says, "No, I can't talk to you now. I don't have time for any beggars, I am waiting for Elijah the Prophet." And so he sends the poor man away. This poor man was actually Elijah the Prophet in disguise.

The evil of the world is that we always say, "If G-d would tell me to make peace in the world, I would do it, but if only people talk to me about doing it, I won't." This is G-d's word - G-d is talking to you!

The holiness of Purim is that this is the first holiday that was initiated by two little *Yiddelach* [Jew] - Mordechai and Esther. We believe them. We know this is G-d talking to us. The moment we listen to other people, and we know that G-d is talking to us through them, then there is so much love in the air.

There is so much fighting in the air because I always think that when someone is talking to me, he is the one talking to me, and I don't want to listen to him. **If I would *mamash* believe that in every word I hear, everybody is just giving me a message from G-d, then there would be no evil anymore.** So Purim is the great holiday when *mamash* we listen to each other, we give gifts to each other, we drink, and we know that everything we hear is a little message from G-d.

**Beyond consciousness**

What are the roots of peace in the world? Are they on the level of consciousness, or are they beyond consciousness? It is even much, much deeper than unconscious, beyond subconscious. This is what Purim is about. We celebrate one day on which there is no evil in the world.

You have to know one thing; real peace doesn't come from anything which you can understand with your mind. If it is this kind of peace, then, if you can make peace, you can make war. If I can love you, then I can hate you. I can be good, I can be bad. Purim is the one day when I am consciously unconscious. I am consciously so high that I know that everything is beyond, beyond the whole thing.

On Purim, when I give you a gift it is because I love you, but I also love you beyond consciousness. I am giving charity to a poor man not because I understand I have to give charity; I am just giving. Everything has to be beyond my intellectual understanding. This is the day when there is no evil in the world.

Can you imagine if you would be consciously unconscious! What a strong consciousness and what a strong unconsciousness. If I am unconsciously unconscious it is not so good. If I am consciously conscious it is also not so good, because I don't reach. I have to be consciously unconscious, or unconsciously conscious.

Where is all the newness of the world coming from? Why was my grandfather riding on a donkey, and I am in a 747 jet? Because people consciously invented all kinds of things; they were working with their minds. The whole newness of the world is always with the mind, right? On the unconscious level there is no newness happening in the world. Purim is the great holiday when all the newness in the world is happening on the unconscious level. This is where the newness is really coming from. It is not the 747 which makes the world new, it is something much deeper than that. Maybe it is coming out in a 747, which is OK, but the real newness of the world is coming from that which is beyond conscious. Tremendous things are happening every minute to the world. I can't pick them up with my consciousness, but I need to know where they are coming from. I have to know the marketplace. The marketplace from which they are coming is much, much deeper than anything. The great thing which happens to me after Purim is that my consciousness is so strong, that my consciousness becomes a vessel for everything that was unconscious before, that was beyond my consciousness before, deeper.

The Kotzker Rebbe was the greatest mind in the world. So the Pshischer Rebbe called on the Kotzker on Purim, and he gave him a cup of wine, which, the story goes, was from here up to the ceiling. The Pshischer Rebbe says, "For you, to get rid of your consciousness, wow, you really have to drink a lot!" It is the people who have strong minds who really have to struggle a lot to get out of [beyond] their minds.

With your mind, you have to, annihilate your mind. Don't annihilate your mind with something which is beyond your mind. The great thing about Purim is that your mind knows that your mind becomes a vessel for that which is beyond your mind.

## Stories

Just one more sweet little thing. Everything we understand comes from our conscious, right? Where do stories originate? From the imagination. The truth is, a story comes from beyond, beyond our consciousness, but then it flows into my consciousness. Rebbe Nachman says that when you dream, you always dream stories, not theories. Your imagination is completely free when you dream. You only dream stories. On Purim we read the story of the *Megilla*, the story of Queen Esther. The whole thing of Purim is the story. You have to listen to the story.

Rebbe Nachman says, G-d created man because He loves stories. The whole world is G-d telling a story. It is not, 'He created the world and then something happened.' G-d is telling stories, creating the world, creating people, telling long stories.

People are only friends when they tell each other stories. People have big conventions and they tell each other theories. They are not becoming friends by this. But when people sit and tell each other stories, they really become friends.

### Tell G-d your story

There is such a thing as praying, which is very deep, but Rebbe Nachman says this is not the deepest depths of closeness to G-d. The deepest depths of closeness to G-d is when you can tell G-d your story. Rebbe Nachman would tell G-d stories all the time. He would tell Him, "Listen G-d, this morning I woke up at five o'clock…" and he would tell Him everything he did. A story.

The difference between Yom Kippur and Purim is that on Yom Kippur we tell G-d what we did wrong, but we tell it to Him not in a way of stories, rather, we say, "I did this wrong, I did that wrong." On Purim everything is on the level of stories. Even while I am drunk and I am telling G-d in my heart everything that I did wrong, I am telling it in the way of a story.

The Tree of Knowledge is theories, and the Tree of Life is stories.

Purim is the great holiday of stories, you have to be real good, and high, and drunk, to be able to tell your own story to G-d.

G-d is telling us stories, creating the world, creating people, telling long stories.

The Tree of Knowledge is theories and the Tree of Life is stories.

### No time to wait

When we left Egypt, it was in the middle. In the middle of the night G-d killed the Egyptian firstborn. That means we also have to get out of Egypt in the middle of the night.

### Break loose

Rebbe Nachman says, when do you have to get out of your evil? Let's say right now *mamash* my heart is filled with evil. Do you say, "It is a bad day, I'll wait till a little bit later, soon the evil will wear off." No, you have to get out of Egypt in the middle of the night, right when the darkness is the strongest. In the middle, you have to break loose, right there on the spot. Midnight is a split second. That means something happens at that very moment and you'd better be there. You have to know exactly when. That means there are split seconds in our lives when we have a chance to get out of Egypt - and when that moment comes, we'd better get out.

**Get out**

The prophet said, "We went out of Egypt quickly, and on the Great Day we will go slowly." The meaning is: Until the Great Day is coming, while there is still evil in the world, how do you get out from evil? You can't go slowly. You cannot afford to go slowly. You have to go fast, run! A little bell is ringing in my head, "I have to be better, I have to do this, I have to…" OK, so fast, jump! You have no time to wait. When Mashiach is coming and there will be no evil in the world anymore, then you can take it slow, play it cool. Right now we cannot afford to.

**The greatest slave driver is your mind**

The greatest exile is to be enslaved to your own mind. The greatest slave driver is your mind. Your mind always tells you fifteen thousand excuses. Your mind tells you, "Are you crazy? You'll never make it. You're telling me suddenly you'll be another person, you'll be a better person? You'll be free? What are you talking about? In a world like this? Pharaoh is the king of the world, and you, a little *shmendrik*, you, a little slave, how can you fight the whole world, how can you fight Pharaoh?" Your mind tells you this, not your soul, not your unconscious.

So in Chassidus it says that the last preparation for the exodus from Egypt is Purim. How do you get out of Egypt? You have to get drunk beforehand. How do you know that at this very moment, when your little voice is talking to you, you have got to jump out right away. You have to be drunk to do that.

&)CR

# Purim

**Yaakov and Esau**

Esau was actually the first born, but the real, real first born was Yaakov [Jacob]. The *midrash* says if you put two things in a closet, which do you take out first? The thing you put in second. The *midrash* says that Yaakov was conceived first, and Esau second, therefore Esau came out first. Really in the deepest depths, Yaakov was the firstborn.

Evil comes from the beginning of the world. G-d created the world in such a way that G-d's light is not shining [G-d contracted and hid His light in order to create the world]. Yaakov comes from beyond all that.

Amalek comes from the beginning, because he comes from that place which is void of G-d. But the truth is that Yaakov comes from before that.

On Purim, suddenly the whole world is filled with the way the world was before G-d created the world. On Purim, a great light is shining from such a high place, higher and deeper than all the holidays in the world.

ഇ)രു

## Connected

Esther says to Mordechai, "Gather all the Jews together." You know what the problem with us is? We don't know how much we are connected. We know so very little about how the events in history are connected, but we also don't know how one human being is connected to the other.

One of the great Rosh Yeshivas once said something unbelievable. Someone told him that in Alaska, one Eskimo killed another Eskimo. He says, do you know where this began? Because one *yeshiva bochur* insulted another one. The vibrations traveled until it went to Alaska.

We don't know and understand the connectedness of the world.

## The vibrations

Rebbe Nachman says…

The holy master, the holy of holiest, the deepest of the deep, the *heilege* Rebbe, the *heilege* Rebbe Nachman of Breslev, says: How does war begin? Somewhere…somewhere… somewhere… somewhere on a lonely island, there is a father and mother and children, and they all woke up in the morning. The parents did not say good morning to the children; the parents did not kiss the children. And the children were so broken, "Nobody, nobody knows how to love us." And the vibrations traveled all over the world, and the vibrations traveled from one corner of the world to the other, and at the end of the world people kill each other and hate each other.

So where does peace begin? Where does peace begin… where does peace begin… Somewhere, somewhere, somewhere, on a lonely island, father mother and children wake up in the morning. And the parents kiss the children, and they say, "Good morning, good morning little angels from heaven. Good morning, most beautiful children, thank you for being in the world, we could never live without you." And the vibrations, and the vibrations… at the end of the world, people begin loving each other. People who yesterday hated each other, wake up at the same time, and suddenly there is so much love in their heart that they have to make peace.

## Shalach Manos

I want you to know, my friends, do you know why I don't walk around giving someone a banana and a half of a piece of cake all year long? Because I don't think it was important, and I don't think I am doing anything special, because you have a banana in your house, and cake you also have. Purim... on Purim, when I give someone a banana and a piece of cake, do you know what I am doing? I am wiping out evil from the whole world. I am wiping out Amalek, the arch enemy of Israel, the arch enemy of G-d, and of the world.

What is the greatest evil in the world? The holy Slonimer says that the greatest evil in the world is to think, 'I am all by myself, nobody loves me, nobody is really connected to me, and my actions don't affect anybody.' What is the biggest fixing in the world? When it is clear to me, ah, *gevalt*, it is clear to me that my bananas affect the whole world, my piece of cake turns over the world. You and I, *gevalt* are we connected.

৪৩

# ✍ Pesach Passover ✍

## *Maos Hittim*

### *Yom Tov*

Rebbe Nachman says, Yom Tov stands on the street corner and screams out to the world, "Please know that G-d is leading the world, that there is no nature!" He says that you have to listen with your ears and your heart very closely to hear this screaming. The more you hear the Yom Tov yelling out that G-d is leading the world, the more you feel the joy of Yom Tov. G-d forbid, if you are not so happy on Yom Tov, that means you didn't hear it calling.

How do you get your ears to hear Yom Tov calling? Before Pesach you must give charity, you have to give to the poor. You train your ears by hearing the cries of those in need. Then your ears become refined, and on Yom Tov you can hear G-d telling you, "Know, there is only one G-d." But if your ears are not open to the crying of the poor, then your ears are deaf and you cannot hear G-d calling either.

## *Noam Elyon*

Rebbe Nachman talks about something called *Noam Elyon*, a kind of holy sweetness which flows down from Heaven.

This sweetness is so whole, that if your mind isn't whole and if your emotions aren't whole, then you can't taste it. You don't have a place in which G-d can give you the taste of this holy sweetness.

Matzo is the simplest bread in the world, just flour and water. No salt, no pepper. Rebbe Nachman says that on *Yom Tov* the *Noam Elyon* flows from Heaven in simplicity. If you are not whole, you cannot receive it. The matzo we eat gives over to us its simplicity, its wholeness.

Matzo tastes so good because it is a piece of the sweetness of *Noam Elyon*.

What makes us so perverted? We put so much work into our little piece of bread. What do people do for the few rubles they make? They put their whole heart and soul into it, and each time they do, they become more and more slaves. The matzo we eat on Pesach doesn't take much time to make. We put the least amount of time into our food, and the rest of the time we have is for doing great things, to be free.

# Don't Take any Time

This is a Torah from Rebbe Nachman. Sometimes our children ask us questions, and we can take our time in answering. Sometimes if we take our time, we will lose them. Rebbe Nachman says, if our children ask us, "Is there one G-d?" and we say, "Let's talk it over," - we've lost them. If they ask for advice, what should they do, what career they should have, we can say, let's talk about it. If they ask, "Are you a Jew?" if you have to think about it, that's not good. He says, Seder night is when our children ask, "Is there one G-d?" And our answer has to be right away. Don't take any time.

I remember once reading a book written by one of the outstanding Jewish leaders of one of the other religions. This outstanding leader wrote in the forward to his book that when he was a little boy he once asked a Rabbi if there is one G-d. The Rabbi said, "Let's discuss it. Come to my house and we'll discuss it." He then quoted from here, and he quoted from there. The boy said, "I'm just asking one question, is there one G-d or not?" He couldn't get an answer out of the Rabbi. The next week, the little boy met a swami and asked him, "Is there one G-d?" The swami said, "Yes, there is."

Seder night is when I tell my children there is one G-d. There is one Torah. There is Eretz Yisrael. I have no time to waste. It has to be fast.

When someone is drowning, imagine if I would say, "Let me call a Rabbi and ask if I should save this person, because I heard that last year this person ate ham on Yom Kippur." I call one Rabbi, and the line is busy, so I call somebody else. All these things are cute. In the meantime, the person is drowning.

You know the problem with us *Yidden*, you know why Mashiach hasn't come yet? Because we waited, we waited so long. How did Moshe Rabbenu get us out of Egypt? Right now is the time - "*bachatzot halayla*," in the middle of the night - right now, don't think, just go. This is "*mochin degadlus*," a high mind. It is not 'not thinking.' It is clearer than thinking. It is clear to me. It is on such a high consciousness level, a deep level.

When I see somebody drowning, where do they grasp me? Do they reach for my head? They reach for somewhere else; they touch the deepest depths of my understanding, which triggers something so holy.

So, Seder night, everything is fast, but it's so clear, and it's so good. "This I do not say other than when matzo and *maror* are placed in front of me." Everything is clear. I can tell my child, "This is matzo, this is *maror*." "I am a Jew, there is one G-d."

You know, friends, we are living in a world where the devil would like so much to be able to take advantage of the great moments which we have. Seder night, every Jew wants to have a Seder. So, what does the devil do? He brings chicken soup and kneidelach. Sometimes I ask people, "How was the Seder?" They answer, "Oh, the food was unbelievable." When you ask about the Seder, they are not thinking about the Haggada, they are thinking about the food.

I was in India three years ago. I asked one boy, he was a Hindu who didn't want to come back; I asked him what he knew about *Yiddishkeit*. He said, "Once a year my family got together for a Seder. The spokesman of the Seder was my uncle, who told over all the dirty jokes he had heard all year long. One night I got up and said, "I don't think this is what the Seder is all about." My uncle said to me, "Look who's talking. You haven't even finished Hebrew school yet. What do you know?" So I thought that, if all *Yiddishkeit* can offer me is a night with dirty jokes and chicken soup, who needs it, who wants it?"

When my daughter's teeth hurt, I send for the best dentist. When my children are sick, I call for the best doctor. When it comes to *Yiddishkeit*, the soul of the soul, the eternity of all eternities of my children, would I subject them to the lowest people in the world, who don't know anything?

This is a Torah from Rebbe Nachman. He says that, basically, the downfall and the ultimate slavery in Egypt were brought about because we ate from the Tree of Knowledge. Eating from the Tree of Knowledge causes you to eat your bread with sadness. The beginning of the Seder is that we eat *karpas*, we eat a little vegetable, and, a few moments later, we are on the level of eating bread with *simcha*, with joy. Matzo is on the level of eating bread with joy. From the beginning of the Seder, to the matzo, we are fixing everything from the Tree of Knowledge. And it goes so fast, so fast.

*Chametz* is that everything takes a long time. This is the downfall of mankind. The world says, "We have to wait for peace. It takes time until it comes." Always waiting, waiting. Matzo is the symbol of alacrity [not waiting] in the service of G-d; today is a great moment - don't wait.

# Crossing the Red Sea

Why do we talk so much about the trial of Yosef? Rav Nachman of Breslov says that each time you do something wrong, you hate one person. Each time you do an *aveirah* [sin], you hate somebody. And whom do you hate? Somebody you know. It's clear to me that people who hate people who aren't religious, have a problem. What's their problem? They did an *aveirah*, and, therefore, they hate somebody. They hang their *aveirah* on someone who doesn't keep Shabbos.

Hatred comes from an *aveirah*. Take Rabbi Levi Yitzchak of Berditshov. Why didn't he hate anybody? Because he never did an *aveirah*. Why did the Bal Shem Tov not hate anybody? For the same reason.

Now I want to say the deepest depths. If you see a Jew who hates another Jew, the problem is not the Jew who doesn't keep Shabbos. The problem is the Jew who thinks he keeps Shabbos. He must be doing *aveirot* [sins] left and right when nobody is looking. Rav Nachman says that if you learn Torah and you don't understand it, then, obviously, you don't love Jews, because if you love Jews, then the Torah loves you. The Torah does not allow you to understand it if you don't like Jews.

I want to say something very deep. If Yosef would have sinned with Potiphar's wife, he would have hated his brothers. There would have been no way for him to forgive his brothers for selling him. But he was so strong that he didn't sin, and so his heart was completely void of hatred. As much as he had a right to hate them - he didn't.

Can you imagine the 'splitting of the Red Sea' that Yosef was going through when he saw his brothers? The storm that must have been going on inside of his soul! "*Gevalt*, you are my brothers - *gevalt*, what you did to me!" Then, when the moment came, when he was approached by his brother Yehuda, when he stood next to Yehuda and he suddenly realized: Didn't my mother change for her sister Leah? So why can't I change for my brother Yehuda? I will do what my mother did. "And Yosef could not restrain himself [Bereshit 45:1]."

Yehuda was ready to give up *Olam Haba* [the World to Come] for his brother. But splitting the Red Sea is even higher than that - to actually turn yourself over inside - this is something else. So between both of them, both Yosef and Yehuda, together they both built the house of, the family of, G-d.

What happens to most of us when we have a *gevalt* moment? We go back to where we were before we had it. Jews go to *shul* on Yom Kippur, have a wonderful experience, and then go back to the way they were before Yom Kippur.

"The Sea returned to its original strength [Shemot 14:27]:" You know how the Sea went back? Not to where it was before it split. It went back to the 'splitting all the time.' The Sea is still connected, every second, to its splitting.

All of us have moments when we give everything up [we sacrifice everything]. But then we forget them. They are not incorporated - not connected - to our daily life. This condition that G-d makes with us, of the splitting of the Red Sea, has to be in every second of our lives. Every minute, every second. [When G-d created the Red Sea, He made a condition with it that it would split for the children of Israel.]

Everybody knows that the Temple was destroyed because we hated one another. When we crossed the Red Sea, the Jews saw a vision of the Temple, of Mashiach. What do we need to make us stop hating one another? If only every Jew would say, I'm ready, for the sake of another Jew, to be something else."

## Disagreement

Why are people fighting each other? Fighting comes about when two people do not receive each other on the level of Haninah Ben Dosa. You and I can have completely different ideas, but why do we fight each other? So, Rebbe Nachman says the deepest Torah in the world: When people have a disagreement in Eretz Yisrael [the , it is the sweetest thing. It has a heavenly sweetness. If I say something, and someone has a different thought, what difference does it make? The Torah is so big. But in exile, in *chutz la'Aretz*, when people disagree, they are really fighting. The Gemara tells us that the Temple was destroyed because of *sinas chinom* [unprovoked hatred]. You know what that means? Rebbe Nachman says that the moment that you fight, you are already in *chutz la'Aretz*, you are not in Eretz Yisrael. The Temple can't exist outside of Eretz Yisrael.

## *Geula Shleima:* **The Fixing of Fear**

It says at the beginning of *Parshat Beshalach, "Vayehi Beshalach...* sadly it was that Pharaoh let the Jewish people go." The commentaries ask, Why "sadly?" The Ishbitzer Rebbe says, there are moments when you have the opportunity to get everything in the world, and the saddest thing is when, at that moment, you limit yourself to one thing.

That night when G-d brought us out of Egypt, we had everything in our hands to bring the redemption. At that moment, we could have done thousands of additional things, but we were just happy to get out. It's heartbreaking, why did we limit ourselves to something small? We could have eliminated everything at that moment, and fixed everything. We always take less at the wrong time. The moment when the Gates are open, don't limit yourself to something small.

What will happen when Mashiach comes? What's hatred about between nations? Hatred comes from our missing something that isn't ours, something we didn't take.

**Fear**

When G-d took us out of Egypt, you know what was wrong? We were still afraid of Pharaoh. When we left Auschwitz, we were still afraid of the Nazis. This is engraved fear. The miracle at the Red Sea is that G-d took fear from us, for a moment we were free.

Fear paralyzes us. The less fear, the more free we are, the more we can grow.

Our Torah says that the lowest, simplest person in the world, when he crossed the Red Sea, had higher vision than Ezekiel the Prophet. We were ready for the highest. For one moment, all of Israel had the same vision as Moshe. Why don't we have the same vision as Moshe all the time? It's because of fear.

If I'm absolutely free inside, I'm not afraid of anything.

By the end of Pesach we reach the level of infinite Prophecy and infinite riches. The Egyptians brought all their gold and silver with them, and the ocean spat it out.

There's high oneness and lower oneness. The high oneness is like on Rosh HaShanah, when I fall down before G-d. There is only G-d: I don't exist. Low oneness is there's you, and then there's me.

Why does a seed have to disintegrate before it becomes something? What remains of the seed is the deepest depths, a vessel for everything. When we stood at the Red Sea, at that very moment we were in a state of the deepest disintegration. On the one side Egyptians, on another side the Sea, and on the third side, wild animals. At that moment we were at the deepest place of recognition, and it was the children who saw G-d first when they crossed the Red Sea. We were disintegrating, but obviously not yet enough. We were still afraid of Pharaoh, we were still too afraid to be prophets.

What's the first sign that someone's a slave? No self-confidence, fear.

Why isn't Mashiach coming? We're still a little afraid of it.

Rebbe Nachman says that you can't taste the hidden light of the world unless you first get rid of fear, because fear paralyzes us mentally and physically. At the Red Sea we learned not to be afraid, to trust G-d in the deepest way.

We are so afraid of loving people. The only ones who aren't afraid are our children. Seder night is the fixing of fear. How do we do it? We make children the center.

On the first day of Pesach a sin offering is brought to ask G-d to forgive us for not bringing Mashiach sooner. We might have, but we were afraid to.

At the crossing of the Red Sea, all of Israel went to *mikva* for the first time ever. It was just before Mount Sinai - our conversion - therefore we all went to the *mikva*.

The end of Pesach is the highest *mikva* in the world. Most people don't keep Shabbos, don't keep Yom Tov, because they're afraid to. Even when they keep it, it's not done on the level of *Kriyas Yam Suf* [crossing the Red Sea]. Only after we cross the Red Sea can we receive the gift of a Shabbos without limits, a Yom Tov without limits. Shabbos and Yom Tov are gifts from the inside, inside, inside of heaven.

The way to fight evil is by becoming infinitely holy.

When we get out of Egypt, Pharaoh is still there. There is still evil left in the world. If we know that there is still evil left in the world, how can we sing? But when we crossed over the Red Sea, there was no evil in our world, so now we could sing.

In order to sing you have to be free. Okay. The slaves from Africa used to sing to tell you that no matter how much you tried to enslave them, they were still free. Singing comes from the world of freedom. When you sing, you are telling evil, "You don't have dominion over me."

In Judaism, the walking, the journey, is so important. Judaism becomes precious because of the long walk. The holiness of it is that it teaches you that you are always on the road. Teachers have to teach you the holiness of walking, and they have to walk with you. The Bal Shem Tov says that a teacher who doesn't walk with you, doesn't know your soul, and is not a real teacher.

ഇൗരു

# Rosh Chodesh

## Teshuva

*Rosh Chodesh* [the new month] is basically the essence of *teshuva* [returning to G-d]. Shabbos is not so much *teshuva*. Shabbos is *mamash simcha* [joy] and *oneg* [bliss].

*Rosh Chodesh* is *mamash teshuva*. Why is it *teshuva*? Because the moon begins to shine again at the new month. What is it when a person does *teshuva*, what happens to you? You are beginning to shine again. You were *mamash* dead before. And suddenly you begin to shine again.

So how do you begin to shine?

There is something very special in always becoming more, and more, and more... *Rosh Chodesh* is not that suddenly the moon becomes more than last month. *Rosh Chodesh* is that the moon *mamash* stopped, there is no more moon, and then it begins again.

Most people don't do *teshuva* because they always think; "The way it is now is the way it will be all the time."

*Teshuva* is that, at a certain period, I *mamash* say, "No, it can't be like this anymore." And I *mamash* am getting off my high horse. I am getting less, and less, and less, and less. And at that moment when it is clear to me that I am *mamash* like dead, that the way it is now *mamash* can't continue, at that moment I begin to shine again.

Shabbos, therefore, does not need the *Beis Din* [Rabbinic court] to announce it, though *Rosh Chodesh* does need the *tzadikim* [holy people] to do it. Because, there is a certain torah which I can learn, such as, if someone tells me, "Hey, you know, you have to buy kosher meat. You have to *bench licht* [light Shabbos candles] at 5:25 p.m.," that is something I can learn. But then there are certain things that are so deep, that unless I see people *mamash* doing it, I wouldn't know how to do it. So *Rosh Chodesh* has to be announced by the *Beis Din* of seventy one. The *Beis Din* of seventy one were obviously the biggest *tzadikim*, and they were the ones who *mamash, mamash* do it. They *mamash* have already reached the highest level, and yet, they are thinking all the time, "*Oy*, I didn't do anything yet."

It is not that they think, "I have to do more." There is something very holy in: "I want to always be more." That is one thing; but that is not what *Rosh Chodesh* is all about. *Rosh Chodesh* is that I am *mamash* like dead, *chas veshalom*. Nothing is there.

The Gemara says, *"En haTorah mitkayemes ela bemi shememis atsmo aleha."* It has a lot of meanings. The ordinary meaning is that the Torah is only with someone who *mamash* completely kills his own ego, his own personal desires, for the Torah. This is one meaning. But Rebbe Nachman says another meaning:

*Mamash*, he has to make himself like dead. It means to feel like everything I did so far is nothing. *Mamash* nothing.

## The moon

When G-d created the world, the sun and the moon had the same light. So the moon came to G-d and said, "Two kings having the same light? It doesn't go." So G-d says to the moon, "Ok, you become smaller." And not only does the moon become smaller, but the entire moon is constantly coming and going.

The world always says that G-d was punishing the moon for the *chutzpah* [audacity] of saying that. But obviously G-d was not punishing the moon. If G-d was punishing the moon, why is Dovid HaMelech [King David] likened to the moon?

The answer is that there is a light like the sun which is always the same. It is very holy, and very beautiful. But the moon realizes that it has got to be *mamash* deeper; *teshuva* is deeper than all of this.

## The Mittler Rebbe of Lubavich

The Mittler Rebbe was, so to speak, the expert on *teshuva*. Someone came to the Mittler Rebbe and said, "Rebbe, I heard you are an expert on *teshuva*. You wrote so many volumes of *teshuva*, can you please teach me how to do *teshuva*?"

He said, "You know, the truth is, though I wrote so many *sforim* [holy books], I still don't know how to do *teshuva*."

On one hand, this is a Torah teaching which you can give over to somebody, and then there are Torah teachings which you have to bring down to the world, they are not here yet.

I can't tell you, "Ah, this is the way to do *teshuva*." like a cook book. "You put in a little *teshuvale* here, a little *teshuvale* there, and you take a *bal teshuva* spoon, and then you make *teshuva* soup." It doesn't go this way.

*Teshuva* is something which doesn't exist in the world. It is not part of the world.

Being part of the world means that it exists, and I do it or don't do it. *"Teshuva kadma leolam"* means *teshuva* doesn't exist yet, it is not there yet.

So the moon was saying to G-d, "It has got to be more than this. There has to be something from beyond. Something from beyond the world."

**The deepest knowing**

And therefore the *Beis Din Hagadol*, only they knew something which, so to speak, doesn't exist yet. "*Tachlis hayedia shelo neda* [The deepest knowing is not knowing]." Knowing how to make *Rosh Chodesh* is not the deepest knowing, it is, like, the deepest not knowing.

What is the sun? The sun is G-d's light. And I can walk around all my life, and I think, "I really know all about G-d." And even if I do know a lot, I may be the biggest Kabalist, and the biggest *gaon* [genius], knowing every word of the Torah. Let's say, I know a little bit about G-d. Still *Rosh Chodesh* is when it is clear to me that I have no idea what G-d is all about. I don't know anything.

Everybody knows that Torah *shebechtav* [written Torah] is the sun, and Torah *shebalpeh* [oral Torah] is the moon.

How do I get to Torah *shebal peh*? I am learning a *passuk* [passage], and last year I thought that I knew what it says, and this year it is clear to me that I don't have the faintest idea. I am learning Gemara, I learned this Gemara a hundred times, I know every word by heart. Suddenly something happens to me; it is clear to me that I don't know anything. *Mamash* nothing.

ഇ)രു

# Shabbos

The Talmud says, Shabbos, the *heilege* Shabbos, is a gift from heaven. And you know, my beautiful friends, it is possible to keep every law of Shabbos, but the gift of Shabbos, the sweetness of Shabbos, the *oneg* Shabbos, the holiness of Shabbos, you have to ask for, and you have to pray for. We all need it so much. We all would like it if in the Holy Land everybody would have Shabbos, but what we have to do is to give each other the gift - the gift of Shabbos. We have the power, G-d gave us the strength, to make Shabbos so holy, so beautiful. I bless you and me, we should give over Shabbos to our children, to our neighbors, and maybe one day, one day the whole world will be filled with Shabbos, with bliss, with sweetness. The whole world will be Shabbos.

The holy Master Rebbe Nachman says: You know why there is no peace in the world? Because you can only make peace when you have so much joy. You cannot make peace with anger. *Shabbos shalom umevorach* [A peaceful and blessed Sabbath]. Only with sweetness, with bliss, with holiness, will we bring peace into the world.

ഇ)രു

# On *Bentshing Gomel* - Shabbos

On four occasions we have to *bentsh gomel* [say a special blessing thanking G-d for helping us]. One occasion is when someone had been lost in the desert, another one is when someone had been in prison, the third is when someone had been sick, and the fourth is when someone crossed the ocean by ship, or, now most people say, if one flew over the ocean.

What is the whole question of being in exile or being free? Being in exile means I am not in the place where I am supposed to be. Free means I am in the place where I am supposed to be. The two don't have to be different addresses. If I am sick, I am really not in the place I am supposed to be, because I am supposed to be well. If I am crazy, G-d forbid, I am also not in the place I am supposed to be. If I am lost in the desert, or in prison, or in the waves of the ocean, I am not where I am supposed to be.

The Gemara says that evil is a strange ingredient. If you put some in the cake or the soup, like salt or pepper, it really tastes good. If you overdo it, however, you feel there is something in the soup that doesn't belong there. So a certain amount of evil is important. Evil has something good about it, a certain fire, a certain battle. If I would do everything without free choice, if I would just want to do it, it would be nothing. If I had free choice and I did it, then it does something to me. Rebbe Nachman says, the whole idea of evil was created only in order to give me free choice. Evil was never in the world for me to do evil, it was only put there so that when I do right - it can be done on a different, higher level. If we do wrong, that is completely out of place.

Every Jew, every person, is in exile in his own way; we are not in the place that we should be, and all of Israel is also not in the place where they should be. This is only until Shabbos comes. When Shabbos comes, then, suddenly, something happens and we become free. That means we get rid of that part of us which is the wrong ingredient, we are back in our place, everything is right again.

The first reason for *bentshing gomel* is due to having been lost in the desert. What is in the desert? In the desert, nothing grows, nothing happens. The strongest exile might be to be a desert person, to do nothing, like a desert where nothing grows, where nothing is built. What is this exile of desert? It is laziness. Actually, this is the utmost of evil. Laziness comes from gravity. Gravity pulls us down, makes everything heavy so that we don't have the strength to do it. Rebbe Nachman says that *yesod heafar*, the element of earth, is such that holy earth makes everything grow, and unholy earth makes everything heavy, just by the gravity of it, nothing else.

There is no way out of laziness. You just have to stop being lazy. There are no two ways about it. Do you know what lazy means? Food is in front of you and you are too lazy to lift up your hand. There is food all over, holy food. You are dying from hunger, and food is right there in front of you.

How can you get rid of laziness? you can't take it out of yourself alone. There are certain things that you can get rid of on your own, certain sicknesses for which you can take medicine, and there are certain other sicknesses for which you just have to see a doctor. There is a sickness called laziness and you can't get rid of it on your own. There has to be a great light from Heaven to cure you. This is Shabbos. Suddenly, when Shabbos comes, we get rid of all this heaviness, all this gravity. We stop being a desert, and we are ready to build again.

The second person who has to *bentsh gomel* is a person who has been in prison. What is a prison? I am in one room and I can't get out. What is so bad about being in prison? I have a bed, and they feed me, so what is so bad? I can't move. This is not being lazy, it is something else.

Imagine meeting someone who says something to me that really hurts you. The person didn't mean it, and it is just a stupid thing. It is possible that you could be very stupid and be bothered by it. You could walk around for weeks and be in prison all the time, thinking, "Why did they say that?" First of all, ask why they said it, maybe they didn't mean it.

Everyone has his own little prison. He is hung up on one little thing, and he can't get out of it.

This is not laziness. This is complete darkness. Laziness is not darkness, it is just laziness, and nothing happens. But this is darkness, because whatever good happens to me, whatever great things I can do in the world, whatever good and holy things people tell me, are spoiled if I am still thinking, "Why did that person say that?" This is possible, and it puts darkness into everything. Shabbos takes you out of that darkness.

Then comes the third example, the person who was sick. There are two levels of sickness. There is one kind of sickness in which you are simply sick. Then there is a stronger kind of sickness which is that even when they give you the best food, you think it tastes bad, and when they give you the lowest, rotten, most evil smelling food, you think it is tremendous. It is possible that your sense of taste is completely gone, but that you are still alive. But then there is an even lower level, G-d forbid, where you are just about dead. Then comes Shabbos. Every Shabbos, G-d gives us one holy word to bring us back to life. Within those twenty-six hours of Shabbos, either you or someone else tells you one holy word, and this one holy word can really get to you, if you only have enough sense to hold on to it.

The person who *bentshes gomel* for crossing the ocean represents the whole world, and the way people in the world treat each other - going up and down like waves in the sea. You are living in the world, and the vibrations of all the lies in the world really gets to you, it makes you go up and down, knocks you off. The Bal Shem Tov says, the body is a ship, and the soul is in the ship. The body goes up and down: one minute super holy, one minute absolutely at the lowest point - just like the waves. It is not that we are not holy - we are holy, but the whole problem is that the next minute we are low down again. We are both the holy of holiest, and we are the unholy of the unholiest. We don't know where we belong. It is like a ship in the ocean that can't find anchorage.

Then comes Shabbos, and on Shabbos we are in a place where the whole world can't reach us. We can really find our place, back on the shore.

ഇരുന്നു

# Sit Your Mind Down
*Likutei Moharan Tinyono 10*

*Ma shehaolam rechokim meHaShem yitbarach veainam mitkarvim eilav yitbarach. Hu rak mechamas sheain lahem yishuv hadaas.* Why is the world so far from G-d? Why aren't they getting closer? Because they don't take time out to think.

**Because their mind isn't sitting...**

*Yishuv* means to sit, and *daas* means mind. When you want to think of something that needs strong concentration, you sit down, so that your mind is more at ease. People never give their minds a chance to sit, so to speak, so it is always standing.

Why don't they do that? If they would give their minds a chance to sit and think, then they would think: What do I gain by all of this?

*Vehaekar – lehishtadel leyashev atzmo heyteyv: Ma hatachlit mikol hataavot umikol inyanei haolam haze?* [The whole thing is to think, "What do I gain by all this?"]

There are some kinds of desires that have to do with my body, and there are some kinds of desires that are outside of me - like honor - and success - that are not directly connected to me physically, but are still also connected to me. And what do I gain from all this?

If people would think about this, then they would realize that they are not gaining anything from all the things they desire. Then most probably they would get closer to G-d.

Rebbe Nachman says... *Ach da, sheal Yidei mara shchora ei efshar lehanhig et hamoach kirtzono, veal ken koshe lo leyashev dato.* Why do you lose control over your mind? Because you are sad.

According to the Bal Shem Tov, according to Chassidus, the greatest sin in the world is to be sad. So Rebbe Nachman says, What is so bad about being sad? Because when you are sad, then you have no control over your mind, and if you have no control over your mind, then you cannot get your mind to sit down and think straight.

*Rak al yedei hasimcha yuchal lehanhig hamoach kirtzono, veyuchal leyashev dato.*

Only when you are happy, when you are full of joy, then you can control your mind and get your mind to sit down and think straight. So, therefore, it says, "*Ki b'simcha tetzeu* [Isaiah 55] With joy you go out from exile."

**Tie joy to your mind**

It is not enough to be happy. You have to tie the joy to your mind. It is possible that every part of you is joyous and your mind can still be in exile, can still be sad. So you have to take your mind, and tie your mind to joy.

In other words, a free person is one who is master over his mind, who can take hold of his own mind, and pin down his own mind. To think, "What is happening to me, what is the purpose of my life?" A slave is someone who is not a master of his mind, who cannot take hold of his mind. So the only way to get out of slavery is with joy.

**How to become happy**

But how do you come to joy? What do you do when you are full of sadness?

*Vlavo lesimcha hu al Yidei ma shemotzay biatzmo eize nekuda tova.* The only way to become happy is if you suddenly look at yourself and you realize, "I really am not as bad as I thought." What makes us so sad? We look at ourselves, and we give up on ourselves. If we would at least start thinking, "*Gevalt*, I am not as bad as I thought, in fact I'm doing a lot of good things."

Rebbe Nachman says, it can't be that your whole life you never did someone a favor. So you did one person a favor! Isn't that enough reason to dance on all the streets of the world all your life?! Just yell: "*Gevalt*, I did someone a favor! It's the greatest thing in the world!" because, who are you? You are just a little human being, flesh and blood, and you did someone else a favor!? *Gevalt*, one time in your life you did someone a favor!

Rebbe Nachman says, it is impossible that in your entire life you didn't pray at least once. So you prayed once! You spoke once to G-d! What do you need more?

And then Rebbe Nachman says, isn't it enough that you are a grandchild of Abraham, Isaac and Jacob? Isn't that the greatest honor in the world? Even if you are lowly and rotten to the core, but you have such a great grandfather!

And then he says, regardless, as bad as you are, you stood at Mt. Sinai. You were at Mt. Sinai! So why aren't you rejoicing with that? As bad as you are, you were at Mt. Sinai. You heard G-d's voice! It's the greatest thing in the world!

Then he says, there is a very special thing in the Gemara called *bedicho daatey*, that my mind is laughing. Not only do you have to be happy, you have to hear your own mind laughing. You tell yourself; "I am so bad." and your mind is looking down at you and laughing; "What, are you crazy? You did someone a favor one time, tremendous! *Schmendrik*, what are you *krechtzing* [complaining] about?" You have to be in such a state of joy that you hear your own mind laughing.

And if you hear your mind laughing, then you are on the level that you can really pin your mind down and say, "Listen, if I did something good at one time, OK, so now let's think; what am I doing with myself? If I'm so happy that I am a grandson of Abraham, Isaac, and Jacob, OK, so what am I doing with myself?"

## Why can't I control my mind when I'm sad?

If you are completely filled with sadness, if you look at yourself and you give up, then you just cannot penetrate into your head.

Rebbe Nachman says that I'm far from G-d because I never take the time to really think, "What am I doing with my life?" And as long as I am sad, I just cannot take hold of my mind, to sit down, and say, "OK, tell me exactly, what are you doing?"

## In a nutshell...

Rebbe Nachman says that people are far from G-d because they don't let their mind sit - they don't have *yishuv hadaas* [a settled mind]. They don't sit with their mind, their mind is standing all the time, it is always in a rush.

As long as you are sad, you cannot control your mind. So in order to control your mind, you have to be happy.

So, how do you become happy? You have to realize and remember that you must have done something good once in your life. And even if you never did anything good, your grandfather Abraham did something good. And even if that doesn't help, you yourself at one time stood at Mt. Sinai. So one way or another, at one moment in your soul life, or your physical life, you must have done something good. So this is enough to make you happy. You start from there. Then you become a master over your own mind.

And then, not only does your mind have to be free, your mind has to be laughing at you. You know what laughing means? It is a very light thing, completely free, without weight.

This is the way I look at it... The mind, in order to think, has to go places. If it has too much of a load on it, it can't go anywhere, it is too heavy. Sadness is a very heavy weight. When you are laughing, you are free, no weight. So Rebbe Nachman says, as long as the weight on your mind is so heavy, your mind can't go anywhere. But the moment you take off the weight from your mind, to the extent that your mind is laughing, then you can go anyplace, you can go to Heaven. You can go back to G-d.

ഔൽ

# Praying in the field
*Likutei Moharan Tinyono 11*

*Da kesheadam mitpalel basode, azai kol hoasavim kulam ba'in betoch hatfila, umisayin lo, venotnin lo koach betfilato. Veze bechinat shenikret hatfilo sicha.* Rebbe Nachman says… I want you to know that when you pray in the field, every blade of grass comes and helps you, and gives you strength to pray. And, therefore, he says, prayer is called *sicha*. The little grass in the field is called *siach hasadeh*, and prayer is also called *sicha*. So, he says, prayer is actually called 'little grass from the field.'

It says of Yitzchak, "*Vayetze Yitzchak lesuach besade"* [Isaac went out to pray in the field]. Or, to pray *with* the field. He went out in the field in order that all the grasses of the field should help him pray.

Therefore it says in *Devarim* [Deuteronomy], and we say it in the *Shema*, "*Vehoadomo lo titen et yivula* [If you deviate from G-d's way, then the earth will not yield its produce]." What does it mean? Rebbe Nachman says that it means that the earth will not join you when you pray. Because, he says, even if you are not exactly in the field, but since you need the field for your food, and everything comes from the field, regardless, the field is with you all the way, and helps you pray. Therefore, he says, '*Yivul*' is the initials of *Vayetzey Yitzchak Lasuach Basade*. Meaning, the fruit of the field, '*Yivul*' is made up of the same letters as 'Yitzchak went out to pray in the field.'

( "יבול" – ראשי תיבות: ו'יצא י'צחק ל'שוח ב'שדה)

ଓଓଔ

# Simplicity
*Likutei Moharan Tinyono 12*

**Because if you are overly clever…**

*Keshe'adam holech achar sichlo.* When a person goes after his own understanding and his own little wisdom.

*Yuchal lipol bitoutim umichsholim rabim.* He can fall down to the lowest depths and make a lot of mistakes.

*Velavo lidei raot gedolot,* And he can come to a very bad place. A lot of evil people led the world astray…

*Vehakol haya al Yidei chochmatam vesichlam.* And it looked like it wasn't so bad; they had a lot of sense, but they trusted their own sense.

*Veikar hayahadut hu rak leyleych bitmimut ubipshitut.* Rebbe Nachman says that the most important thing in *Yiddishkeit*, of service of G-d, is to go with wholeness and with simplicity.

*Ulehistakel bechol davar sheoseh, sheyihiyeh shom HaShem yitbarach. Vlivli lhashgiach klal al kvod atzmo. Rak im yesh bazeh kvod HaShem yitbarach yaase, veim lav – lav, vaazai bivadai lo yikoshel leolam.* The most important thing is that whatever you do, you should think if G-d is there. Don't be overly clever. And don't think so much about your own honor. The most important thing is to think whether or not it will bring honor to G-d. And then you will never go wrong.

*Veafilu keshenofel, chas veshalom, lisfekot, veyesh shenefilato Gedola meod meod, rachmana litzlon, shenofel lisfekos vhirhurim, umharher achar HaShem yitbarach.* Even if you fall down into so many doubts, and even if you doubt G-d, and you think that everything of G-d is wrong, and everything which has to do with G-d is wrong,

*Af al pi ken hanfila vhayirida he tachlis hoaliyah,* It doesn't matter, because if you stick to this, you can get out of there also. There is no place that you can't get out of - if you stop thinking that the world begins and ends with your mind.

Do you know how much wisdom it takes not to be overly clever?

Let's say I can understand everything in the world, but in order to understand that I cannot understand everything - this is even deeper than my mind. This comes from one level deeper than my own mind. A car can go so far. An airplane can go higher. But the car doesn't know that the airplane can go higher. I, however, am not the car, so I know that the car can go far, but the plane can go higher.

Listen *Yiddelach*, this is one of the deepest Torahs Thoughts of Rebbe Nachman, so let me just translate it, and then we can delve into it.

## The roots of the whole creation

*Ki da, ki shoresh kol habriah hu hakavod... nimtza shekvodo yitbarach hu shoresh kol habriyah.* You have to know that the roots of the entire creation is honor, because whatever G-d created He only created for His honor. Because it says, "since everything was created for G-d's honor," that means that G-d's honor is the roots of the whole creation.

*Ve'af al pi shekuko echod, al kol zeh behabriah yesh chalokim.* And he says, although the whole creation is one, still, there are all kinds of parts of the creation. And in every creation, a little bit of a different kind of honor is manifest. And the honor which is manifest in that part of that creation, is the roots.

**Ten Sayings**

We all know that G-d created the world with Ten Sayings, and then the Gemara asks, "Why didn't G-d create the world with one saying?" The Gemara answers, "In order to give reward to those who maintain the world, and to punish those who destroy the world."

Every one of the Ten Sayings has its own honor. And therefore it says, "*ubeheychalo kulo omer kavod* [*Tehillim* 29] in His little palace, everything is honor." Because it says, "*melo kol haaretz kevodo* [the world is filled with His glory, His honor]."

But, yet, Rebbe Nachman says, every honor has certain borders; this is how far this particular honor goes, and then, at that point, begins the next honor.

But then there has to be some place where the people who disgrace G-d are. The people who are completely against His honor are also living. So, from where do they receive their life? They must receive their life from a place that is even deeper than honor.

So then he says: "*Shehu bereshis mamar sutoom* [there is a hidden kind of creation] and the honor of this saying is so completely hidden, that nobody can understand it - you can't even think of it, but I am telling you it is so."

**Even if you feel very far from G-d's honor, the moment you start asking, "Where is G-d?"...**

There are places where you feel that the world is filled with G-d's glory. But then, if you fall down to a place where you are not on the level of G-d's glory, of G-d's honor, anymore, then you receive life from the place that is even deeper than the whole creation, which was not even said. And, since it wasn't even said, it therefore has no honor, it is deeper than honor.

**Wherever you are, when you start asking...**

If you fall down to the lowest depths, and you doubt G-d, and you are just against the whole thing, but you then, deep down, start asking, "Where is G-d?" you then connect yourself to the hidden word which is deeper than honor. And then you bring forth this deepest depths which is beyond honor.

Sometimes you fall into a place which is like a small chain reaction. It goes round, and round, and round, and you can't get out of it. You start doubting, and doubting even more. When you want to go back, you always run around in circles, and you never get back to the center. How do you get out from the ring, and get to the center? The only way is, you have to cry and ask, "Where is G-d?" You ask, "*Ayeh mekom kvodo* [Where, where is G-d]?"

When you are in the lowest depths, and there you start asking for G-d, then you make G-d manifest even in the lowest depths.

This is what it means to repent. To repent means that you begin to ask, "Where is G-d? Where is G-d's glory?" Because you look at yourself and you know that you don't bring any glory to G-d, you don't bring any honor to G-d. And this is the greatest honor you can give to G-d - that you ask, wherever you are, "Where is G-d's glory?"

And, therefore, the Gemara says, if someone asks you, "Where is G-d?" tell him, "G-d is right in Rome." Because even there, with all the pagan worship, G-d is right there, but He is hidden. But the moment you look for Him, you can find Him even in Rome.

(OK, to tell you the truth. I don't really understand one word.)

**What is honor?**

What does it mean that honor is the roots of everything in the world? What is honor? What is so deep about honor? What does honor mean?

G-d created the world with Ten Sayings. G-d said, "Let there be dry land, and the ocean, let there be animals, let there be man." But in fact, G-d created the world in one word - *bereshis* - and then He said each one of the Ten Sayings in detail. So sometimes you receive life from the Ten Sayings, and sometimes, if you already lost the Ten Sayings because you destroyed your own honor, and you are full of doubts, and you don't know where you are anymore, then you receive life from the word *bereshis* which is the *mamar sutoom*, the hidden word which is not manifest.

When I see animals, I know G-d said "Let there be animals," so I see G-d. But yet this one word that G-d said and so created the whole world with it, this one word I don't see. It is invisible, it is completely beyond. That means that this honor is not visible. In order to honor something, I have to see it. I may not have to see the whole thing, but I have to know it is there. But this is so deep that it is not even there. So when I lose contact with all the Ten Sayings of the world, then I receive life from that hidden *mamar*, from that hidden saying. And how do I receive life from that hidden saying? When I ask, "Where is G-d?"

So Rebbe Nachman says, according to this, it is something very deep. When I know where G-d is, I am receiving life on a pretty high level. But if I fall down to the lowest depths and I don't know where G-d is, I am full of doubts, then, in a certain deep way, I am receiving life from an even higher source. That means that if the Ten Sayings didn't get to me, I need a stronger medicine. That means I am receiving life from that thing which is hidden. And this is my chance to reach the highest level in the world.

So, therefore, Rebbe Nachman says, when you fall down, and your heart is full of doubts, on the contrary, this is *mamash* the time when you can search for G-d there. Then you can get to the roots of the whole world, to that kind of honor which is even deeper than the honor of the world.

This is what he says, I don't understand it yet, but it is just a beautiful thing to know that it is so.

The only one who knows what Rebbe Nachman says is Rebbe Nosson. Rebbe Nosson says, "I hope you are listening to what Rebbe Nachman says, because you have to realize that this is the deepest depths of the world, and I don't understand it myself."

## Don't give up

The most important thing is, don't give up. Because even if you are in such a place and you absolutely don't see G-d because it is so bad where you are, and so dirty, and you are so far gone, and you think you have no way of getting back to G-d - but if, for just one split second, you ask, "Where is G-d?" and you *mamash* cry, *"Gevalt!"* then because of your asking for it, at that very instant you are reaching the very highest level in the world. You are penetrating and breaking open this hidden word which gives life to all the other words.

## This is the only advice

You have to realize, Rebbe Nachman says, that this is the only advice, and this is the only straight way, not only for those who are not so holy, but even for the holiest people in the world. Because the most important thing is to realize that you are not permitted to stand on one rung. You have to keep on going and going and going. And before you go higher, you have to fall down.

At that very moment while you are falling, you have to be far from G-d, because if you were close to G-d you could not walk, as the holy Bal Shem Tov says; how does a mother teach a baby to walk? If the mother would hold the baby's hand all the time, the baby would never learn to walk by himself. The baby has to fall a hundred times, and then, slowly, slowly, the baby gets up and walks a step by himself. Then when it can walk one step, the mother walks back two steps. The more steps the baby can walk, the more steps the mother walks back. So with us: the more steps we can walk, the further G-d is walking away, in order to teach us to walk.

## Roots of creation

Rebbe Nachman says that you cannot become a new person until you reach the roots of creation.

The root of the whole creation is this hidden word, *Breishis* [in the beginning], with which G-d created the entire world. You cannot reach the root until you ask, "Where is G-d?" If G-d is manifest to you, that means it is already creation, since G-d is manifest in the creation. How can you reach the roots of creation? When you ask, "Where is G-d?" - that means the whole creation doesn't mean anything to you, it didn't reach you. And then you can reach the roots of the roots.

In order to understand this, he says, you have to know that you have two ways of serving G-d: There is one way of serving G-d; the whole earth is filled with his glory. And this is when you are aware of G-d, and you know the Ten Sayings, and you see everything in the world.

The second way is when you ask, "Where is G-d?" Why is it when a person does wrong, suddenly he has no place in the world? It really goes hand in hand. When you are not aware of G-d's glory, when you don't see G-d, then you *mamash* have no place in the world. Because at that moment, you are really not receiving life from the Ten Sayings, so you are really not part of the creation. You really have no place until you start asking, "Where is G-d?" Then you start receiving life from the roots of creation.

**Before the Great Day**

Before Mashiach is coming, when we come to the end of the exile, then the hiddenness will be so strong that really everything will be hidden. This will be the last thing, when we will really have to make G-d's glory shine into the world. So, in order to really make His glory shine, we really have to ask for Him. And we will not ask for Him until He will be completely hidden. So Rav Nachman says, as much as G-d was hidden all the time since the creation of the world, it doesn't compare to the way He will be hidden before Mashiach is coming, before the Great Day.

And, therefore, before Mashiach is coming, we will get our biggest chance.

And, therefore, before Mashiach is coming, most of the world will seem to be so 'clever,' suddenly everyone will be an intellectual.

This is the final stage of this asking "Where is G-d?" Because how do you come to ask, "Where is G-d?" When you put your mind aside. If your mind is completely perverted and turned upside down fifteen thousand times, then you need to *mamash* forget everything you know, and ask, "Where really is G-d?" You have to ask this in really the most simple way.

We need to get out of all of this so called knowing, intellectualizing.

The greatest covering up of G-d is that I think I know.

Before Mashiach is coming, we have to go through the strongest breaking through of the greatest covering up of G-d. Suddenly the whole world will be filled with great intellectuals, and, Rebbe Nachman says, all the people will give great speeches, they will even publish books, and they will speak in all the languages of the world, but woe to them! Woe to their souls. Because a little boy who believes in G-d knows more than all of them. G-d should save us from them.

Rebbe Nachman says, if they would at least speak in the name of lies, it wouldn't be so bad - but they speak their lies in the name of truth. What's going on here?

So, therefore, he says that the only thing you can do at this point is ask, "Where is G-d?" And if you ask where He is, you will see that He is right there.

### Beis HaMikdash

When did we start building the holy Tabernacle? According to our tradition, if we hadn't made the golden calf, we would never have built the little Tabernacle in the desert. That means, in a certain way we brought G-d's holiness closer to the world because of the golden calf. Because after we made the golden calf, we started asking, "*Gevalt*, where is G-d?" We were crying so much for it, until we found a place for Him.

When you ask, "Where is G-d?" - when you ask, "Where is G-d's glory?" - that means that you don't know where G-d's place is. And so then G-d reveals a place. And this is the holy *Beis HaMikdash*, the holy tabernacle.

So it is the same before Mashiach is coming. We will ask, "Where is G-d? Where is G-d's place? Where is the place of His glory?" It will be such a strong asking, until, so to speak, G-d will have to build the Holy Temple.

Because, obviously, we didn't really find G-d's place yet, because otherwise the holy Temple would not have been destroyed. It must have only been a temporary residence.

If you really fell down to the lowest, and you really think, 'G-d can't be there because I'm too far gone,' then you actually have a chance to reach the highest.

Just like before Mashiach comes, when it looks like G-d is completely absent, it's then that we have to break through - then we will really find the place of G-d in the world.

### No place

G-d revealed Himself to us in the desert, because in the desert there are no clear paths. In the desert you don't know where to go, you don't know where you came from. You don't know where your place is, and you don't know where G-d's place is. It is completely place-less. And there you start asking where G-d is, and you get close to His revelation. Because only when you have absolutely no place in the world, and you really ask where G-d is, then G-d can talk to you again.

When G-d told Abraham to sacrifice Isaac, he didn't tell him where to go. He didn't tell him the place. So Abraham was walking around for three days looking for the place. Because, when do you reach the level that you are ready to sacrifice your soul to G-d? To reach that level you have to look for the place.

## Beyond

There is a way that I'm sitting down by myself, and talking to myself, and I can straighten myself out. I can do this if I can realize for one moment that, "I'm not as bad as I thought I was," so that I become enough of a master of my own mind, that my mind can begin to laugh.

And then, there is another level, if I can't do that. What do I do then? I have finished trying all the tricks. I can't do more. Then all I can do is yell, "Where is G-d? There has to be G-d somewhere!" And then, if I cry, "G-d has to be somewhere," then G-d will be revealing Himself to me from beyond, beyond.

ഇറ

# Singing

Why is it that when someone talks, the more you look at him while he's talking the more you can understand what he is saying, but when someone is singing, when you close your eyes you hear the *nigun* [tune] better?

And why is it that when someone is talking, *"trei koli lo mishtama* [you can't hear two people's voices at once]"? But with *neginah*, singing, the more people who sing together, the more beautiful it is.

Rebbe Nachman says: Words are on the level of the *asarah ma'amaros*, the Ten Pronouncements with which the world was created. Therefore, when someone talks, he's using worldly tools. Singing, however, comes from the world which is beyond Creation. If I sing one thing, and you sing something else, it can become harmony.

When someone talks, you look at the person. But when someone is singing, you close your eyes, because singing is so heavenly. The less you're in this world, the less you're looking at the world, the more you know what to sing about.

ഇറ

# Alone

Rebbe Nachman talks about meditation, but meditation is not really the right word for what he describes. He speaks about being alone. And when is a person really alone with G-d? When he is praying. When I study, I'm also alone. There's the way I understand what I study and the way you understand it differently, but this being alone in study doesn't compare with the being alone in prayer. The real aloneness of a person is when he *davens* [prays], as much as the words I say are the same words.

But then Rebbe Nachman adds, that the deepest kind of aloneness is *tefillin* [phylacteries]. I put them on my head, and I connect myself to G-d. And I put *tefillin* on my arm, and no one knows what's going on.

## The only place you can go is to G-d

Sometimes you really have trouble, and you feel rejected, everybody in his own, individual way. So where do you go? You really have absolutely nowhere to go. And so then, if you reach that level where you know that the only place you can go is to G-d, then you get a little close to the Oneness of G-d.

What is the holiness of the Jewish people? That they are *mamash* alone in the world, historically. Why does it come out that we are alone on the world level? Because the holiness of a Jew is that he is alone with G-d. Since the whole holiness of the Jew is that he is alone with G-d, so when it reaches the world, it comes out that he is alone. The Torah says; the Jew lives alone. Six million Jews, the world didn't help. With the state of Israel, the same thing. I'm not talking about individual people, but the world as a whole; they just don't know how to react to us.

But it's really good, because we don't really need them - they need us. Yet, on the other hand, Rav Kook says we are connected to the whole world, because we have a mission to the whole world. But our mission to the world is only when we can teach the world this aloneness with G-d. Because the holiest message we have is that every person is alone with G-d. The Alter Rebbe says, "I know that one and one is two, but do I know that this is my finger? It's a different kind of knowing. If I know G-d like I know this is my finger, then I'm *mamash* alone with G-d. It's deeper than heart or soul knowing, it's the deepest kind of knowing there is. Then we really know we're alone with G-d."

This means that it didn't start with the world hating us, but with our being alone, which is very holy. Like a great fire coming down from heaven... Abraham, Isaac, Jacob... alone.

ഇരുൽ

## Questions and Answers asked by students in the class

**Question:** What if the last time I really had a feeling about G-d was a long time ago, before the university and before reading philosophy?

**Rebbe Shlomo Carlebach:** So that's good, that means you're on the way to being higher. It's very strange, but if you have a hundred dollars, and I want you to have two hundred dollars, so I give you a hundred dollars more, right? But Chassidus says, when you have a hundred dollars and G-d wants you to have two hundred, He takes away your hundred and He gives you two hundred. So for one second you have nothing, and then He gives you two hundred. G-d never adds, He always takes away, then gives more.

**Question:** This is the only place where people believe in G-d; even traditional Rabbis don't talk about G-d.

**Rebbe Shlomo Carlebach:** You have to learn Rebbe Nachman, that's the only way. Rebbe Nachman really believes in G-d.

සාමය

## Tallis

The *Tallis* is supposed to make you cover your face; really cover yourself completely. The way they are making *tallesim* today, like Band-Aids, it's really a joke.

## Minyan

Rebbe Nachman says, if you're really alone, then you're closest to people. If people who really know what alone means get together with other people, they are really together. Why is it that when we learn we don't need a *minyan*, but when we're *davening* [praying] we need a *minyan*? Because when we are learning, we're not that much alone, but when we are *davening*, and we're *mamash* alone, then we really get together.

People who don't know what alone means can't relate to someone else on a deep level. So, on the contrary, when we *daven*, people can *mamash* get together and become like one.

Ten people *mamash* change the whole thing of *davening*; ten people can say *kaddish*, and nine cannot. When you're learning, there can be five, or one or two - it doesn't change anything. But when ten people get together to *daven*, something happens; they really get together.

සාමය

# Joy

What's the problem with the world? Yes, everyone can say something else, and it all may be true, But the problem with the world is that people think that if someone is really, really happy, it's not normal. Imagine if a person walks around, and he is absolutely blissed out [blissfully happy]. You'd begin to doubt if he was normal - and maybe he really isn't - but who cares. Right?

The truth is, our holy master, Rebbe Nachman, says, "You cannot live without joy." Yeah, you can exist - but live? You cannot serve G-d without joy, you can't do anything without joy.

Listen to me, sweetest friends, this is very, very beautiful. You know, one of our holy Rabbis wrote a book called Tanya. It's one of the deepest kabalistic books with 52 little chapters. And in those days, it was a custom that when a Rabbi comes out with a book, he asks Rabbis to give him permission to print it. So he sent his holy book to the Rebbe Reb Zusia, one of our Holy Masters, and asked him to give him permission to print it, and the Rebbe Reb Zusia said, "I can't believe that you can take such a great G-d into such a little book."

Now listen to this. I want you to open your hearts, friends. How can I, a little human being, take the great G-d into my heart? Well, the answer is very simple. When I'm absolutely filled with joy, I'm infinite. When I'm filled with joy, I have no boundaries. I'm infinite. When I'm infinite, I'm a vessel for the infinite G-d.

Friends, I want you to know this, and maybe I told some of you a thousand times, and I told this to myself two million times; that the world thinks we can make peace, and then we'll be happy. But the answer is just the other way around. There'll never be peace unless we're happy.

A heart which is filled with joy has no place for hatred. It doesn't belong there, it just doesn't go in! Even if you try, it doesn't go. It doesn't go in.

## There is one G-d Who takes care of everything

Why are we sad? Because we always walk around thinking that things are wrong. Why do I think that things are wrong? Because I have a feeling that I am running the world. And since things are not the way I think they should be, that means they're wrong. But let's face it, I'm not the master of the world!

If it's clear to you there is one G-d, if it's clear to you that there is one G-d Who takes care of everything, if it's clear to you that one G-d is taking care of the most lonely leaf driven by the wind, so what are you *kvetching* [complaining] about?

There's a *midrash* that says that there was a ship in a storm, and everybody was very, very, very worried. Yet there was a little boy sitting on the deck, sunning himself in the sun. And the storm is raging, tossing the ship up and down. People ask the boy, "Aren't you afraid?" and he says, "No, because my father is the captain."

Rebbe Nachman says, every light needs a vessel. G-d's great light, in order to shine into us, needs a vessel. The name of that vessel is joy. There is no other vessel. G-d's infinite light needs an infinite vessel. Now listen to this, this is the deepest depths. The truth is, there is a light which is beyond vessels. It's even beyond a vessel.

I want you to know something very, very, very deep. You know, when you kiss somebody, you close your eyes. And this is automatic - I watched my children, and everything that children are doing without being taught - that means it comes from heaven; it wasn't taught.

Listen to me, sweetest friends. There is a light beyond vessels. When you love somebody very much, not only do you have vessels for this great love, but it's even deeper than that, it is beyond everything. As long as joy has vessels, I have it and you don't have it. But if my joy is beyond vessels, I can walk on Fifth Avenue, and anybody who meets me wants to dance from joy.

To explain: first of all, when you open your heart and you are filled with joy, this means that G-d's great light has a vessel - joy. But then afterwards, you work your way up, and that vessel itself is suddenly bursting, right?

In the story, the boy says, "G-d is my captain, G-d will take care of everything." This means you're still a little bit interested in vessels. This is still a little bit logical, right?

On the level of beyond vessels, I really don't know anything. But on the level of 'in vessels,' if you say about someone I love, "She's terrible," I say, "No, she's very beautiful." If you say, "No, she's ugly," I say, "No, she's beautiful." If you say, "She's terrible," I say, "No, she's good," because I love her within vessels. But if I love her beyond vessels and you tell me, "She's the most terrible girl in the world," really, who cares? I just love her. She's terrible? *Mazal tov*, she's terrible. She's ugly? Good. Who cares? I just love her. Who cares?

You see, the lower level is that I believe in G-d so much that everything is good. But then there is a higher level: I really don't care. I do, and I don't. Because if there is one G-d, what else do I need? What do I need?

And here Rebbe Nachman moves into a third subject that I want to share with you.

You know, the way I look at G-d is the way I look at people. And the way I look at people, is the way I look at G-d. If I walk around thinking the world is terrible, and that G-d is not doing such a good job, that's the way I look at people, and, mostly, at least a little bit, at myself too. "G-d doesn't do anything for the world, I'm not doing anything for the world, nobody's doing anything for the world." You know what the primary thing is? It has to be clear to me; not just that there is one G-d, but it also has to be clear to me that G-d is doing so very much for the world! I'm doing so much for the world. Every human being is making the world more beautiful!

But now Rebbe Nachman says. If I really, really, am filled with joy, then the smallest good and holy thing that I see in another human being, blows my mind [is exceptionally astounding to me]. It blows my mind… because I'm so much in tune with goodness and holiness.


**Tasting**

It is one thing to be good, and another thing to have a taste of goodness. It's one thing to be happy, and another thing to taste joy. A lot of people don't mind dancing a little bit, hopping around a little, but do you taste your own joy?

Have you ever been at some weddings? There's a little bit of happiness, but do you know where the happiness is? On their nose, on their head, on their ears... but their tongue is still bitter.

And listen to this, sweetest friends; people who never taste joy can't help but saying bad things about other people. Because their tongues are still filled with evil. If you taste joy with your tongue, it's good, right? If you have a decent meal, you're not going to eat something terrible afterwards, right? Do you know how good it tastes to say good things about another human being? It tastes so good. Do you know how good it tastes to give some courage to another human being? Not just that it's good and sweet and holy - it TASTES so good! *Gevalt*, does it taste good.

You know my most beautiful friends, when people get married, they drink wine under the *chuppah* [wedding canopy] - do you know what this means? It's not enough just to be married - do you taste the marriage? It's not enough to love each other. Do you taste it on your tongue? Do you taste it?
And here I want you to know the sweetest thing in the world. When you kiss somebody, do you know what it means? I have a taste in your soul. I have a taste in your holiness. I have a taste in your sweetness, in your G-dliness.

You know what one of the greatest blessings is? To be above everything. One holy Rebbe said that what we really want is not for G-d to give us everything we need. We want G-d to lift us up while He is giving it to us.

You know, friends, when you love somebody very much, and you give them the smallest thing in the world, you're lifting their soul with it. You know, friends, when someone loves you very much and they give you a glass of apple juice, is it just apple juice? They're lifting your soul to the highest level. Do you know that everything that G-d gives us has the power of lifting us up to the highest level? Every moment of life that G-d gives us is so uplifting! So special!

If a person wants to test himself: Am I getting closer to G-d? As simple as it is - are you getting closer to people? Are you getting closer to your wife, to your children? Do you love people more? And the holy

Vorker says: If you want to know if you love G-d, it's very simple. When you see another human being, and you can control yourself and not speak to him, then you're very far from G-d. But if every human you meet and you see just blows your mind; "*Gevalt*! I can't believe it. I can't believe it! Another human being made in G-d's image is walking around in the world! Master of the world, I didn't think You would do so much. *Gevalt*!"

I want to bless you that you should blow your mind over your children. And above all, above all, I want you to taste the holiness of your own children. We are living in a world where… parents think their children are "good." Some Jewish mothers think that, "My son is a genius." But they never tasted their children. Never tasted the depths of them. Never tasted what their children are really all about.

You know, friends, what we need most? We need good parents, holy parents. We need holy fathers and holy mothers. We need holy teachers. Not only teachers who teach you what you don't know, but teachers who blow your mind with how much you do know. Because most children know everything anyway. The holy Rizhiner says, "All children need is someone to show them the alphabet. The words they'll get on their own." Sometimes we are so eager to teach them words, that we take away from them all they remember from Heaven - all those holy, beautiful words.

You know, friends - I'm sure you know it anyway - we are living in such an enlightened generation. People know, without knowing, the deepest depths of G-d's teaching. We're living in a world of the highest Kabalists in the world. And the saddest thing is that they buy a little paperback book on 'Kabala,' and - forget it! It ruins your whole insides. Friends, I want to bless you and me that we should only read books which don't destroy that inside knowledge which we have. That we should only open books which we want to kiss after we learn from them, because they're so infinite and so deep, they give us such a deep taste of what G-d is all about. (There are some books written by people who are not even religious who claim to teach kabala. They do not compare to the books written by holy *tzadikim*.)

You know, friends, it's not enough to believe in G-d. Do you know what G-d is all about? You need to know what G-d is all about! It's not enough to be good. Do you know what good is? The Tree of Knowledge lets you know; 'this is good and this is bad.' But you don't know what good is! You have no taste.

৪০ল

## Teaching Rebbe Nachman in Prison

This is my favorite prison story. I don't want to say anything bad... In 1969 a lot of young people were into stuffing themselves with drugs. In a city, about two hours away from New York, the grandmother in a very wealthy family died, and she left about a million dollars to her grandson to be given to him on his 21st birthday. But the parents - and he's also the president of a temple, and the mother is the president of Hadassah of New England, very 'outstanding' people - felt the son wasn't ready for the million dollars.

And it's still better if she has it in *her* pocket, than in his pocket, 'since she loves him so much.' It was *mamash* ugly.

Okay, the boy was smoking a little hashish sometimes, you know. But he has his head on his shoulders as much as his father. You know what they did, on his 21st birthday? They called the police on him and had him arrested. The boy was so heart-broken. His parents got wild! They put him in solitary confinement.

His girlfriend called me up. And she says, "I want you to know, you don't know my boyfriend, but he knows you. He was once in the House of Love and Prayer." And, "The rabbis in that city all know his father, he's the president of the temple, how would they go against him? He just needs someone to talk to."

I had to leave the next morning - I had a plane at 9 o'clock to Paris, I had to be there. I said to her, "I'll tell you something. If you can arrange for someone to drive me from New York to the prison right now, I'm ready to sit with him all night. And then arrange to drive me tomorrow morning straight to the airport."

Anyway, she came and picked me up to drive me to the prison. But I didn't know that in order to go to prison, you need a written statement from the lawyer. Now basically, a Rabbi can go into prison any time, but I had no identification that I'm a Rabbi, and I didn't have a letter from the lawyer.

In prison, everybody sleeps at night. I'm getting there at about eleven o'clock, and this *nebech, nebech* sad little guard sitting there in prison, half asleep. I knock. And he says, "What's going on here?" I say, "Listen, my dear friend. I am a Rabbi, and I have to see one of my parishioners. His name is this... he's in solitary confinement, and it's a question of life and death. This boy needs me."

"Uh," he says to me, "Do you have identification?"

I said, "What do you mean? Are you crazy? Look at me! What do you think I am, a garbage collector or a shoemaker? I am a Rabbi, and I wanna see him!"

*Mamash*, I put the fear of G-d into him. He says, "Okay, okay, okay!" (ha, ha)

I want you to know. What the saddest thing was, his parents sent food to him in prison, and he refused to eat their food. He just said, "I have nothing to do with you anymore." I had a coat, and I had filled my pockets *mamash* full of all kinds of food, falafel, vitamin pills - just for him. And the guard didn't investigate what I have. I had also brought a lot of Rebbe Nachman books.

The guard brings him out... And this boy was such a high person. I want you to know, I spent four hours with the boy. We didn't talk about the word "prison," about parents, about hashish, about anything. I was *mamash* just learning Rebbe Nachman with him for four hours.

Every few minutes one of the guards came in, listened a little bit, and walked out.

I had to make my flight. So at about 3:30 a.m. I finish. I gave him all of the food, and he hid it in a little coat of his, and we walk out. And here is where the story really begins. The guards are sittin' there, right? I said to the boy, "Tell me something." (I said this in front of the guards.) "Tell me the truth brother. Are those guards still human beings, or have they lost everything? Is there hope for them?" So he says to me, "You know something? I think there is hope for them."

So I said to the guards, "You know something? It seems I came all the way here to spend a little time with you here in this prison. This young man and I were just learning the deepest secrets of the Torah. Why don't you all join us for a few minutes?" *Mamash*, we made a circle: the prisoner, humble me, and the guards. We were singing a little bit, and I was teaching them Rebbe Nachman's Torahs, and they were *mamash* crying *geferlach* [profusely]. They were *mamash* crying. It *mamash* got to them. It was the most unbelievable thing. It was like after Mashiach has come. Naturally, we then hugged each other, and I kissed them. They locked the door. I walked out. I look back, and the prisoner and the guards were standing there waving. Unbelievable! Listen, I'm telling you, it was like after Mashiach has come. I couldn't believe it. Couldn't believe it.

ജ♢ര

# A Letter to you from Rebbe Nachman

This is a letter that Rebbe Nachman wrote to Rebbe Nathan, Rebbe Nachman's greatest pupil. This letter is also written to you. He wants you to read the letter in such a way that you know it was written to you. So he says, "I want you to read the letter and say your name and your mother's name before you read it." He says, "I'm begging you, really say your name, and your mother's name, because it will be good for you." OK, it's way out. If you want to be completely with it, why don't you also say your name and your mother's name while reading it. OK?

*"You, Shlomo ben Naftali, [say your own name] my sweet close friend and pupil, I'm crying out to you. I'm begging you, stop for a few minutes, and listen to what I have to tell you, because I'm talking to you about your eternity.*

*I want you to know how much work I put into my own self, until I was able to tell you too, to come close. Do you know how many miracles happen to you? How many wonders, till you got a little closer to G-d?*

*Therefore I'm begging you, the most important thing is, don't fool yourself, and don't let anybody else fool you.*

*Don't you know, there is nobody else who can fix your soul. Only you can fix your own soul. And all the levels that you want to reach, only you can reach them.*

*And, therefore, the only way of getting to this is - you have to be alone, and you have to talk to yourself. You have to talk to G-d. And you have to mamash tell Him everything.*

*Maybe it sounds simple, but if you could only do it with complete simplicity, mamash like a child. Do it really with all your heart.*

*Do you know how much your soul is missing, yearning to talk to you? Do you know how much you are missing yourself? Can you imagine; you're living so long in this world, and you never spoke to yourself? If you could only hear the way your own soul is missing you, then nothing in the world could be between you and your own soul.*

*And when you talk to your own soul, then you can judge yourself in such a holy way, a deep way, a high way, and just with a few words, you can fix your own self. Your nefesh, ruach, neshama [soul].*

*And you can fix the world until all eternity, because every person has to know that, "The whole world depends on me." Because if the world didn't depend on me, I wouldn't be alive.*

*I want you to know one thing. I'm yelling out to you, to let you know, that because your whole eternity depends on it, therefore it's the hardest thing to do. Because everything which is not important is easy to do. But that thing which is really important is almost impossible, even if it's so very simple. You'll have ten thousand excuses, and fifteen thousand questions. In the meantime, you won't do it.*

*Therefore, my holy brother, my holy sister, have compassion. Don't stand before G-d without anything. Don't stand before your own self in shame.*

*And please, don't you know, the life of your children and grandchildren till the end of generations depends on you.*

*I know you're ready to die for G-d. But I'm not asking you to die for G-d. I'm asking you to take off a few minutes."*

*Oy*! Better sing a little song after this. It's too heartbreaking.

⪔⪕

# Holy Words

What is called holy? What is a holy word? A holy word is if with every word I utter I'm completely, completely given to that word. Not that I just utter those words. It's like I'm giving birth to those words. Even deeper than that; I am completely one with that word.

If that word is that holy, then that word is written on me. And then I'm as holy as the holy Torah, because the holy letters are written on the parchment. And people who have those holy words written on them, they're just so very holy.

## If you are completely one with the words you utter…

This is so deep…. If I, and the word I utter, are two, it's not holy. It may be good, and sweet, and cute, but it's not holy. Holy words are when I'm completely one with the words. It's written on me. That means I could say to you, "Look at me, the word is written on me."

## Missing something

In a certain deep way, my body is really finite. And my soul is really infinite. Infinite. What's infinite? When I want something, when I'm missing something, it's infinite.

This is something very deep: In general, many times we are closer to people when we miss them than when we are in front of them, right? Because when we miss them, it's on an infinite level. But when we're standing next to them, it's finite.

When I am here and you are far away there, our two infinite parts are relating ok, but the question is, are we relating on a finite level also.

But the real, real deep relationship is when the finite and the infinite are so much together that I can stand next to someone and still miss them. Or, I can miss them from very far away and still love them at the same time.

## What is my soul, really?

So what is my soul? My soul is completely missing. What's my soul? I'll tell you something very deep. Most people, the moment they have what they need, they stop having a soul. Most people, the more they have of what they need, the less you can feel their soul. Why is a poor man so precious? Because he needs so much, and he has *nebech* nothing, so his soul is shining more strongly, because he misses something, he needs something. But the moment you have something and you stop missing it, then your soul isn't working anymore.

So, sadly enough, without getting involved, many religious people, from the moment they're a little bit religious – i.e., they keep a little bit of Shabbos, they wear a little *yarmulke* – their soul stops working for them, because they think they have everything. They're not missing anything. This is not real soul service. The soul is… my soul has to be completely such that even whatever I do shouldn't cut off the wings of my soul. Because my soul is infinite. G-d is infinite. Everything is infinite.

## Listen to your soul

In order to bring forth this holiness of my soul, my real soul, what I'm missing all the time, I have to listen to my soul telling me what my soul is missing. Because the moment my soul tells me what my soul is missing, then this becomes really *mamash* real.

A lot of people have something in their heart, but it's not real enough to fight against this 'what they have,' which is so strong.

Listen. Where do your words come from? Words come from a very deep place in your heart. Words don't come from that place of 'what you have,' words come from that place where you're missing something. And you talk out of that part of you which is missing. It's missing something…

So when you meet people with very dirty language, you know that they *mamash* are only missing dirty things. Because words come from that part of 'What are you missing in life?' 'What are you waiting for?'

So, therefore, with every word you utter, something really happens to you. Something happens to you at that moment that you speak. Not only does something happen when you do something, but when you say a word, something happens. When you say holy words, then suddenly my soul wants something more holy, something deeper. If you say something stupid, then, in a certain way, your soul gives up and says, 'Forget it. Forget it.' G-d forbid.

## Yearning

Holiness depends on how much you're yearning for something. Imagine I meet a poor man and I give him a nickel. That's a sweet act, a good act. But the thing is, while I'm giving him the nickel, how much am I yearning to give him something. That's how holy the act is.

If, while I'm praying, I want so much to pray, that's holy. But not if while I'm praying I say, "Alright, I'm praying already, so that's it."

If while I'm learning, while I'm studying something, I want so much to understand what I'm learning, I want so much to become one with it, that it should *mamash* become a part of me, that's how holy the learning is.

Rebbe Nachman says that with missing something, or yearning for something, you don't know how far you can get, you can reach the highest.

And he says, there were people who had such holy souls they could have reached the highest. But they didn't reach it because they didn't yearn for it enough.

### Heart

What am I living from? What gives me life? My heart. What's my heart? Even physically, my heart is yearning; it is going, beating all the time. Yearning for something. Inhaling, exhaling. What happens to my heart? You know, we always think that my heart is living from the inhaling. It's not true. My heart is living from the in-between inhaling, exhaling, inhaling, exhaling. In between. You know how things are, you say, "I really need just a little bit of fresh air." Then you get a little bit, and you say, "*Oy*, it wasn't good enough. It wasn't good enough. I've got to do something better." Sadly enough, if the moment you do it, you just think, "I'll do it the same way, I'll breathe the same way as I did before." That means you're old. You're dead. Can't you imagine if we could be on the level that each time we take a breath we would think, '*Oy*, I didn't do it....'

Ꙍ

# Maturity of the Mind
*Likutei Moharan 53*

Abraham and Sarah were the strongest in converting people, because they didn't physically have children yet. They realized, 'Why don't we have children yet? Because our minds aren't ready. How do we make our mind ready physically? By having a lot of children spiritually.' It's a *gevalt*.

Therefore, Rebbe Nachman says that at the moment when Abraham reached the 'highest quantity of converting,' then he had Yitzchak.

*Tzadikim* are running after people to talk to them about G-d because they want their minds to reach the utmost level of maturity. This is the deepest depth there is. And, therefore, the old *tzadikim* are the ones with the ability to bless people who have no children that they should have children, because the *tzadikim* have the key for children in their hands: because they have so many children spiritually, so they are on the level that they are able to give others maturity of the mind. It's very deep.

That means, if a *tzadik* blesses you to have children, he doesn't just bless you that you should have children, he blesses you that your mind should be on the level that it becomes real. What does it mean to be mature, to have this holy mind of having children? It means that your mind and G-d's mind become one. Because your mind, the human mind, can know one thing and yet do something else. But G-d's mind is that it becomes real.

ഇൗൽ

# Three Things Widen your Mind

The Gemara [Talmud] says that three things make your understanding wider, three things widen your mind.

There is such a thing as understanding everything, and then there is the wideness of everything. It is possible to understand everything in such a narrow way. I can understand and I know something, but it's so narrow. And then there are some people who have the holiness of un-narrowness. They understand the same thing as others do and they say the same thing, and they mean the same thing, but they don't mean it in a narrow way. It's very, very wide.

The Gemara says something very strong. You need three things in order not to be narrow. You need a beautiful wife, you need a beautiful house, and you need beautiful vessels.

### A beautiful wife

Besides that this is really true on a physical level, there is something to it physically. But Rebbe Nachman talks about this on the highest level, he says the soul is called the husband, and the body is called the wife. What makes your mind wide? When your relationship to your body is on a very high, holy level, on a beautiful level. If you look down on your own body, and you want to destroy your body, it's a very bad scene. That means your mind isn't wide. You see, if my soul is big enough to make place for my body, that means I have a beautiful 'wife,' that means you are very deep. Your relationship to your body is completely balanced.

### A beautiful house

Then Rebbe Nachman asks, what does 'my house' mean? Rebbe Nachman answers, the most important part of the house is the door, because, if you can't lock the house, it's not a house, it's still on the street. So he quotes the Gemara which says, "Woe to the one who has a house that has no door." What is a door? The door is the way I walk into learning Torah. I have to tremble. The door to everything is a trembling before it. That's the door. This is very deep. If I meet a friend, and we become good friends, it's like building a little house. If I don't tremble before him, the house has no door. You can walk in and out, and you don't even feel that you're walking out. So there needs to be this holy trembling. When I learn Torah, I study it and I tremble before it. It has a door. Open it. Close it.

**Beautiful vessels**

Rebbe Nachman says that the holy vessels I have are holy pupils. I pour my light, my mind, wide and strong, into vessels.

**Three things widen my mind**

1) I know what to do with my body.

2) I have a holy trembling with what I'm learning, with what I'm eating, with everything around me.

3) I have someone to talk to. Someone to put my light into.

ഇറ

# Five Levels of Understanding

Rebbe Nachman says that there are five levels in understanding.

The first level is I know a lot with my mind. I have a lot of information. I know a lot.

The second is, I know the way things were before they were created. On that level. Not only the information, what's going on, but I also know those things before they were created.

The third thing is… you see, we always think, "What is the purpose of this, what is this doing." The third level is that I understand things that have no purpose.

The fourth level is that nothing matters to my mind. The fourth level is… (This is so deep that I can't even understand it.) He says, it doesn't matter to my mind if it's there or not. On that high level, it doesn't matter, right?

The fifth level, he says, is that my knowing it, doesn't make it less possible.

*(I don't understand this, I can only translate it. This is way out, you know.)*

He says like this: The first thing is that I know a lot. I know a lot. The second thing is I know them even before they were created. The third thing is my mind is so deep that I can even encompass things which have no purpose. The fourth thing is that it doesn't matter to me if they're there or not. And the fifth level is, that my knowing them doesn't make them less possible. If you understand this folks, you're on a pretty high level. He says if you reach that level then your mind is G-d level.

ℰᑐᑕℛ

# Light and Vessels

The entire *Likutei Moharan* was not written down by Rebbe Nachman. It was written by his pupil, Rebbe Nathan. But the thing we are learning right now is actually *mamash* Rebbe Nachman's words, it was written down in his own words. And you can feel that this is on a completely different level as much as Rebbe Nathan understood what Rebbe Nachman said, but this is *taka mamash*, the depths of this is unbelievable.

**Lights without vessels**

Many people walk around in this world, and they're broken, right? The reason is because a lot of people have a lot of lights, but they have no vessels to hold their own light. Most kids have a lot of light, but they don't have the vessels for their own light. They don't know what to do with it.

So they have one of two options: Either they force their light into the little vessel that they have, or they decide to lead a life of vessels and disregard the light. If they have small vessels, so they have a little light. Like some 'straight' people, they have a little light, and little vessels, everything is straight [normative]. Or, they decide to live on a 'light level,' that means they have no vessels, and so they're broken all the time. But it's also not good, because the world is made up of light and vessels.

Imagine if I *mamash* believe that I should walk on the streets every day and give gifts to everybody. That's my light. But then, I can't, right? So there are two ways I could go. I could walk around giving gifts, but then I stop doing everything else, I leave my wife, my children, and I just walk around on the streets giving out gifts. It's a very holy thought. It's a very holy light, but I'm ending up being crazy. Or, I think, "No, I can't, because right now I have a job, I have got to support my wife and children." And so I abandon the light. Either way is bad. Either way is bad. You see, the world does not yet know the secret of light and vessels. Either they have vessels, or they have light. They don't know the secret of light within vessels yet. There's no one to teach it to them. Because what most people teach is all vessel talk, and not even good vessels. The whole thing is, the secret of Torah is, G-d speaking to us on Mt. Sinai is, the most important thing is that we have light within vessels.

## The words of the Torah

The most amazing thing about the words of the Torah is that those words are vessels for great light. And real holy teaching is not something that makes you crazy, real holy teaching is that it makes your light deeper and your vessels stronger.

The Bal Shem Tov would always say to people, "I bless you that your body should be strong enough for your soul." Everybody can make himself crazy, anyone can make his soul shine like an atomic explosion, but what's going to be with your body?

So a lot of people, and most religions, only have lights, but no vessels. So what do they tell you to do? They tell you; "You want to be holy? Leave your wife and your children, and go to live like a monk." Hare Krishna kids, they're holy kids, they have great light, but no vessels. Because this is not the world you're living in. You don't walk around with a shaved head asking everybody for a penny. It's very holy, but this isn't where it's at. And even with higher things, this is also not where it's at.

## Hidden holiness

What's wrong with standing in a grocery store and selling herring? It's very holy if you know how to sell it. But this is a hidden kind of holiness.

Obviously if you're standing and praying it's very holy. But to sell herring, or to be a mailman.... It is a very holy thing to bring a letter to somebody. Though you could say, "It's the most awful thing in the world." but it can be the holiest thing in the world. Do you know what it means to deliver a letter to somebody? *Gevalt*! You can work for Western Union and say, "It's really bad, brother." Or you can do it thinking, 'Gevalt, it is the greatest privilege in the world to bring somebody a message. It might change their whole life.'

Whatever you do, you can do it on the highest level, or on the lowest level. It depends on whether or not your vessels and your lights are strong.

## Yerushalayim

The holiness of Yerushalayim is not that there is no light anywhere else. The whole world is full of light. Yerushalayim is a vessel for this holy light.

Every house could be a holy temple, but it isn't, the vessels are missing. After all, how can a house be a vessel if it's not really a house, right? The holiness of Yerushalayim is that this holy little house is a vessel for this light.

Everybody could be a high priest. Aharon HaCohen was the one who made vessels for it.

**Strong vessels**

Moshe Rabbenu was the one who had strong enough vessels to go up on Mt. Sinai, talk to G-d, and come back to tell us about it.

I can also go up to Mt. Sinai, but I'll blow my mind. They'll carry me down crazy. If I would have a revelation like Moshe Rabbenu's, *mamash* hear G-d talking to me, though perhaps I could have that revelation, but I'd crack up and loose my mind. Crack up completely.

With Moshe Rabbenu, not only was his light holy, but also he had strong vessels. He came down from Mt. Sinai and said, 'Give me some apple juice.'

The Alter Rebbe and 'the Angel' were sitting and learning together one night, and, it was like heaven and earth were opened up before them. The Alter Rebbe went into the kitchen to get a bagel and he even remembered to put butter on it. Imagine what a strong vessel he was. He didn't forget to put butter on, because this is the way of the world. He wasn't one ounce less holy than when he had the revelation. He was with it completely.

So, today, what we have to do very strong [intensely] is not only to have holy lights, but we also must have very holy vessels.

I'll tell you something very very strong. On a level 'between people,' many times people love each other from afar, which means the great light is shining, but when it comes to meeting each other, they have no vessel. They don't even say hello to each other. Have you ever seen this? Sometimes you want to meet someone, you love them so much. You want to see them. But then when you're standing in front of them, you don't know what to say. Because we have no vessels. And sometimes it's so good, because we have the light and the vessels. Sometimes I want to tell someone I love them, and the light is so strong I don't know how to say it. That means that I have no vessels. Yet sometimes the way I love someone is with vessels that have no light. That is also meaningless. The secret of the world is light and vessels.

**Chaos world**

In Hassidus there is such a thing as *olam hatohu. Olam hatohu* means the world of chaos. What's chaos? Everything is there, but it's not in its right place. Imagine, you can take the house you're living in and turn it over. Turn over all the furniture, put the dishes in the bed, the bed in the fridge, and then someone will ask, "Is anything missing?" "No, everything's here." But what are you doing? You can't live like this, because the light and the vessels don't mix. Everything has its proper place.

**The fixed world**

Then there is *olam hatikun*, the world of correction. The fixed world.

The top *tikun haolam* [fixing the world] man is Yaakov Avinu [our forefather Jacob]. Esau is *olam hatohu*. Do you think Esau didn't have great lights? He was learning by Yitzchak [he lived in the house of our forefather Isaac]. Do you think that when you learn by Yitzchak you don't blow your mind from the great light? Do you think that Esau didn't know that it's the greatest thing in the world to do somebody a favor? This great light was tremendous. But he had no vessels. He could walk out from Yitzchak's house and immediately kill somebody. He had no vessels to hold on to this great light. So Esau is *olam hatohu*; you know everything - it's not that you don't know - but you have no vessels. So it's nothing. It's meaningless.

Yaakov Avinu is *olam hatikun*. Yaakov learned with Yitzchak, and every word had a vessel. Yaakov Avinu was able to spend 21 years being a shepherd, and be the holy of holies. Yaakov Avinu could talk to his father-in-law Laban, the biggest thief in the world, and Yaakov remains Yaakov and Laban is still Laban. Most of us, if we spend a lot of time talking with a big thief, something would rub off on us. Yaakov sent the strongest message to Esau, he says to him, "I was with my father-in-law Laban, the biggest thief, but I didn't learn anything from him. Don't think it rubbed off on me."

If, thank G-d you have a good healthy body, and you are able to walk straight, and you see a cripple, do you start limping because he's a cripple? Thank G-d your feet are ok, your body's ok, so you walk straight. But imagine if you're also a cripple. If you see another cripple limping, you'll think, "Maybe that's a good way to walk, I'll also walk like him."

If my vessels and my light are completely in touch, if my light is with the vessels and the vessels are with the light, then I won't be influenced by somebody else. But if my light and my vessels don't go completely together, then with every little thing, I'll think, "Maybe this is the way." "Maybe that is the way."

Listen, if I know what it means to be a Jew, then I can see the holiest people in the world, I love them, I respect them, and everything, but I am a Jew. But if I'm not so sure about my being Jewish, that means my Jewish light, which is hiding in my soul, doesn't have any Jewish vessels. Then every little thing I see, I think, 'Maybe this is right. Maybe this is wrong.'

Let's say somebody is married, and yet, every woman he sees on the street he thinks, "Oy, I should have married her." That means there's something wrong there. It means the light and the vessels, the man and his wife, never got together properly. Because, ok, this other woman is very beautiful, but she's not his wife.

If the light has a vessel and everything is in its place, then it's just such a beautiful world. *Olam hatikun.* That means the fixed world.

Today, such great lights are shining, and each generation has deeper lights. And the last generation didn't make vessels for this great light. Do you know what happened in the last generation? They threw out all the lights, and just had little vessels. They have, like, small whiskey shot glasses, and we need big bottles.

I have a light and I need at least 20,000 bottles for it. So imagine my father comes to me with a shot glass and he says, "Pour it in here." So I do one of the two things. Either I give in, or, *nebech,* I don't give in. What I really have to do is, I have to make new vessels.

## A great light will shine

"A great and new light should shine upon Zion. And we all should be blessed and privileged that we should have this great light." Rav Kook says, what does it mean? If the light is shining, so how could I not have it? What does it mean that I should have the light? It's a very deep translation. He says that a great light should be shining, and I should have vessels for it. We should all be there. Because if the light shines into the vessels, then something also happens to the light, because the light without the vessels is very painful to the light, because light needs vessels.

Imagine if I want to tell somebody "I love you" but I don't know how to say it. I don't have the vessels. It hurts so much. I want to do something, and I don't know how to do it. I want to be a Jew, and I don't know how to do it, it hurts, right?

If you know how to do it, not only do you do it, but then your light becomes much deeper. A very, very deep thing.

Imagine if I want to keep Shabbos and I don't know how to do it. If I know how to do it then the Shabbos is much deeper, it's real. Everything that has a place is real, meaning to say that the light cannot reveal itself in all its greatness and depth unless it has a vessel. Without a vessel, it's a light, it's true, the light is shining, but not with all its fullness. The moment the light is shining with its fullness, it must have vessels. It has to be in a certain place.

## Where do I get vessels

There is a *passuk* in the Psalms, "*HaShem Yikalkelecha,*" and so the sad translation is, "and G-d will feed you," which really doesn't blow my mind. So G-d will feed me, so? You don't have to be King David to make such a statement. G-d is feeding the whole world. It's very sweet. The Zohar Kodesh says that it means, "G-d will give you vessels." It comes from the word *kelim – Yikalkelecha* - He will give you vessels.

## Shabbos

The whole idea of Shabbos is that Shabbos is the day of vessels, G-dly vessels.
In the craziest / paradoxical way… during the week we have vessels for this world, not for great lights. But on Shabbos, by not doing anything, we get these great big vessels, because on Shabbos G-d gives us vessels. If you make a vessel, you have to work to make it yourself, but on Shabbos, the light is so deep,

you cannot make a vessel for it by doing anything. It's such a deep light that your vessel is 'not doing anything.' This is a way out / amazing vessel. A G-d vessel. Shabbos is the day that not only does G-d give you a great light, but by not doing anything on Shabbos, you also make the vessel. We always think Shabbos is only light. But it is also vessels. But the vessel for Shabbos is, 'not doing anything.' Can you imagine, such a great vessel…

Let's put it this way, there are vessels for words, that are made by speaking the words, and there are deeper vessels for words, that are made by not saying them. That is also a vessel for the words. So the vessel for this great light for which I have no vessels, is made when I'm not doing anything on Shabbos. Then my vessels become strong because on Shabbos G-d not only strengthens my light, He also strengthens my vessels.

And, above all, the most important thing is that I realize that I must have vessels, one way or another. Buy them. Get them in a pawn shop. I don't know how. But imagine if I know that I really need a Coca Cola - I'll walk around until I find it.

Maybe we have the lights, and throw them out.

Maybe we have the vessels, and fill them with herring instead of with wine.

For example, the straight people / conformists. Their lights and their vessels fit, but it's not the truth. You know what they did? They cut off / truncated their lights, and only left a little flashlight. Because real light always gets deeper, it demands more vessels. The first sign that you're really living on a little bit of a light level is that you're looking for more. If you don't look for more, then you're just living on a level of vessels, dead vessels.

This is not only the idea of Rebbe Nachman. This is the top / epitome of Kabala, the top concepts of mysticism. Because the whole creation of the world is based on the fact that G-d put His light into vessels. If this concept is not understood, it is as if you speak English and you don't know what "yes" and "no" mean; you're off. If you want to know anything, you have to know the secret of vessels and lights. Because this is the beginning.

**Surrounding light**

But then you have to realize that there are lights which have no vessels. Which have no vessels… But if you have light and vessels, then you are strong enough to also carry the light which has no vessels. This light which surrounds us. You know, sometimes you meet people who have a great surrounding light. I mean, there's something, you don't know what it is, and they don't know what it is themselves, but it's a great light. But this is only with the people whose light and vessels are strong, then they have this surrounding light.

Imagine a box that is five miles long. If my head is strong you can put it on me and I can carry it. You'll say, "It's protruding on all four sides!" But that doesn't matter, because I'm fairly well balanced, and so I can carry it. In the same way, if my light and my vessels are strong inside, then you can put a big light on me, one which is bigger than I am, and I can carry it. But I have got to have a strong head. *Oy!*

## If you're filled with something holy

Remember what the Gemara said, that G-d is different than human beings. Human beings can only fill an empty vessel. But G-d can fill a full vessel. You see, if you're filled with holiness, then you always have space for more holiness. But if you're filled with nothingness, then you're so full that nothing else can go in. You know, there is a full emptiness and an empty emptiness. You can be filled with emptiness.

Why do we really die? Because deep, deep down we really don't think we need our body forever. We don't yet know the holiness of the body. So we really think, "My soul is so holy, it really has got to keep on going. But my body? It is not important, so it only needs to stay for a few years." This is the difference between the Tree of Life and the Tree of Knowledge. The Tree of Knowledge knows right and wrong. It looks down at the body because it knows, 'This is right and this is wrong.' It wants to get away from evil, so what does it tell you to do you do? 'Knock off the body.' And deep down, deep down, you think, "You know, it is pretty good. If I would have to live with my body for a thousand years it would be a bad scene / not so pleasant, who has strength for so long?" The Tree of Life responds, "I really know the holiness of the body, of really wanting to stay forever."

Before saying *kriat shema*, we say, "Let us walk upright into the holy Land." The Hebrew word *komimiut* is a double upright, two uprights. In Hassidus it is explained: The uprightness of the body, and the uprightness of the soul. Right now we don't really let the body rise to its full stature because we don't think that the body is so good. Because we are like Adam, putting the blame on somebody else. Everything I do wrong, I say, "It was the fault of my body, because my soul is so pure." So I put the blame on somebody else, I put all the blame on my body.*

---

*Do you know the famous story of the holy Rizhener Rebbe. Someone came to the Rizhener and said, "I'm very holy." The holy Rizhener asked, "Why are you so holy?" The man answers, "Because I am rolling in snow every night, and I am fasting." So the Rizhener says, "Come, I'll take you to the window, and I'll show you 'something holy'." There was a poor horse standing out in the snow, because his driver was a drunkard sitting in the bar drinking like mad. The holy Rizhener says, "What do you think of that horse in the snow? It's so holy. But the owner is sitting there drinking. You know," continued the holy Rizhener, "your body is rolling in snow, but you yourself…."

ഔയ

# Living Words

If you hear something, and it really affects you, and something really happens to you, it means it's really living, and anything that is *mamash* [really] living is growing.

The Bal Shem Tov says, not only can you hear living words, but you can even hear living letters. One living letter, and it makes a whole explosion in your heart.

Yet from dead people you can hear entire sentences, and it has no meaning.

He says, everything is put into the earth; dead bodies, and seeds. When someone puts something into you, it's like putting something into your soil. If he puts in dead words, he makes your heart into a cemetery, but when he puts in holy words, it's like a seed, it's growing.

ℰ◯℞

# Happiness and Prophesy

This is an awesome Torah teaching: You know why people are not *b'simcha* [happy]? Because really, let's face it, they have never done one thing in their lives which gave them joy. So Rebbe Nachman says, what do you do? You should do one *mitzvah* [good deed] with so much joy that you think to yourself, "Even if I never ever do anything else, it's worth it to live 100 years, even just for this alone."

Rebbe Nachman says that the Bal Shem Tov makes it clear that when you do somebody else a favor, the joy should be so *gevalt*. When you do somebody else a favor, it should be clear to you, "It's worth it to suffer 100 years of this world just for the privilege of doing somebody else a favor."

But then Rebbe Nachman adds, if you do one *mitzvah*, one good deed, with so much heart, then you *mamash* reach the level of prophecy.

Remember, prophecy, the spirit of prophecy, only rests on you when you're filled with joy.

The Gemara says that there is no prophecy outside of Israel. It's only because, after the destruction of the Temple, we never reached the level of enough joy to have real prophecy anywhere else.

**Decrees**

Sometimes you can feel it; that in heaven, there's something going on but it's not decreed yet. And sometimes (G-d forbid) it's already written in a decree.

Do you know that, even a decree in heaven, when they're still dealing with the decree in heaven, you can still change it.

You know, after the Germans went into Poland, people asked the Belzer Rebbe, "Can't you do something? Can't you pray?" He said, "It's all over, the decree is closed. I can't do anything anymore."

But that is also not true. Because, everybody knows that by praying you can change everything in the world. The only difference is, the way you pray before the decree comes out and is finalized, and the way you pray after the decree comes out - I mean, you better pray about two billion times stronger.

Rebbe Nachman says, G-d forbid, when the decree is already called out in heaven, then you cannot even pray anymore, because the gates are closed. So you have to go through the back door. And the back door is, that you tell stories.

## Stories open the gates

*"Someone who attains this degree of joy will be able to know what decrees have been passed against the world, whether the decree has been sealed yet or not, and against whom judgment has been passed. And through this he will know how to pray for the world, because after the decree has been sealed the Tzadikim have to clothe their prayers in story form."* (Likutei Moharan, Torah number 5)

And the stories open the gates.

This is one of Rebbe Nachman's deep Torah teachings. Imagine a girl loves someone very much, and she gives them the key to the door of her house. Later, she gets very angry, and she takes the key back. Yet the only thing is, she never takes away the key to the back door.

Rebbe Nachman says, the key to the back door is always open, it's never closed.

## With all your heart

So Rebbe Nachman says, and this is so important; imagine I'm so sad, and I can't get out of it. So I say to myself, "Is there one *mitzvah*, is there one thing that I can do?" So I decide, "I want *mamash* to do this one *mitzvah,* this one good deed with all my heart."

Do you see how deep this is? Rebbe Nachman says, what is called 'with all your heart'? 'With all your heart' means that even if I never ever do anything else, I bless G-d that I was alive to do this one thing.

So Rebbe Nachman says that whenever you're sad, think; "Is there one thing in the world I did, or I want to do, that can *mamash* keep me alive forever?"

But then Rebbe Nachman adds, if you do something *b'simcha* [with joy], then *mamash* you're so full of prophecy that you know how much you have to pray for something. You know if the decree is sealed already or if the decree is not sealed. If the decree is sealed, it means it is not enough just to pray, you have to go through the back door.

**Praying with all your heart**

How do you know how happy you are, how much you are *b'simcha?* If you can *mamash daven* [pray] with all your heart, that means you're *mamash b'simcha*. Because when you're half sad, you cannot put your whole heart into praying. Because when you're sad, you give up. Sadness is: 'I don't believe in prayer – that it can really change everything.' The minute you don't believe in prayer any more…
The *heilege* Bal Shem Tov says: I was only privileged to reach such a high level because I *daven* with all my heart.

Remember that Rebbe Nachman says, "You know what 'with all our heart' means? It means, with every ounce of energy you have."

Praying is not an act, it's a state. *Mamash*, I am *mamash* praying.

ഇറ

Do you know what praying is? Rebbe Nachman says praying is living. I receive life when I'm praying. People always think I'm praying <u>for</u> something. Praying <u>is living</u>. This is life. When am I closest to G-d? When am I doing my 'inhaling' for the whole day? When I'm praying.

ഇറ

# Imagination

The truth is, you cannot be a prophet without the utmost, unbelievable, most infinite imagination. A person who has no imagination can never be a prophet. You can be the holiest person in the world, but if you don't have any imagination, it doesn't work. Really, what is a holy soul? Someone who has great imagination.

Like Rebbe Nachman; Just to make up the story of the Seven Beggars takes the holiest imagination in the world. Or the story of The Master of Prayer. It takes way out imagination, right?

I'm not knocking it, but what is the difference between the great holy Rabbis who only knew Gemara and those who were the great Kabalists? Imagination. The more your imagination works, the closer you feel to the secrets of the world. The real truth is that to learn Gemara properly you also need imagination, the most way out imagination is in every word of the Gemara. But this is if you are already on the level, because then it also becomes a secret.

The holiness of the soul is really the holiness of imagination. What is a person who is really tied into this world imagining?

What is the whole thing of believing in the Mashiach or not believing in the Mashiach? It is a question of imagination, right? A person says, "Listen, I see the world. People believe in money, people believe in war. You will tell me that suddenly some day the Mashiach is coming on a donkey, he'll blow a little trumpet, and the whole world will come running, and everybody will say, *ich veis*, "*Shalom Aleichem!*" It's crazy!" It's a question of imagination. If you have a good imagination, why not? That's all there is to it. Why not?

Why are we dreaming at night? Because at night the only thing which we have is imagination. And the greatest vessel for dreams is imagination.

Rebbe Nachman says the most way out thing [amazing statement]; the strongest imagination that you need is to believe that G-d created heaven and earth. And to believe that, you really need imagination. You look at the world, and you see a solid world - you need the strongest and holiness imagination to see that G-d created heaven and earth.

Rebbe Nachman says that all the holy *Tzadikim*, all the holy people, had this strong imagination. And if you have this tremendous imagination, not only can you receive dreams, but you can interpret dreams - and even uplift someone else's dreams.

ഇൻഈ

# Dreams

What's a dream? The truth is, that when you're sleeping and your soul goes up to heaven, you're on the level that you can receive things that you cannot receive when you are awake.

Rebbe Nachman says: All the things which G-d is sending down to this world, they are on the level of a dream, it's not real / actualized yet.

How do you conceive of this thing which is coming down from heaven? You conceive of it only on the level of a dream. But then, it still has to come down into this world, and this depends on you.

You have to realize that this light which is coming down from heaven has no vessels, yet you're the vessel for it. So something's coming down from heaven, and the way you receive it, that's the shape you are giving to that light. And whatever level you are on, whatever you really are, that's what will become of the dream.

So, therefore, the vessel of the dreams are your thoughts. And it depends on the holiness of your thoughts. If your thoughts are holy, then your thoughts are vessels for dreams and the great light. If all day long you have evil thoughts, so then at night, though something's coming down from heaven, but since you're full of evil and hatred, everything is wrong, not with the dream, but with you. You're taking this dream and turning it around, making the dream bad.

But then, everybody knows that if you have a dream that's very disturbing and you don't know what to do with it, so then you need to ask three friends, or at least one, telling them, "I had a dream and I don't know what to do with it." These friends have to tell you, they *mamash* have to say this; "It means, you saw a good dream, you saw a good dream, you saw a good dream."

The ultimate vessel for a dream is not so much your thoughts, as it is your words. So, as much as the dream, the great light from heaven reaches your thoughts, but when it reaches your words, then it becomes real. And the words are so holy and so real that if your friends love you, they make vessels for that dream, even if your vessels weren't so good and you destroyed this holy light, the friends get in there and they reshape your dream, and make it into a good dream.

Therefore, Rebbe Nachman says something really strong / powerful. Everybody knows that on the High Holidays, and in Jerusalem every day, when the priests are giving us their blessings, we have a little prayer to say while they say the blessing, "G-d bless you and keep you." Then we have to say a little prayer, "G-d, I had a dream and I don't know what to do with it. Please let it be a good dream."

Then Rebbe Nachman adds something that is just so beautiful. Blessings are dreams, blessings are dreams. If someone loves you very much, they make those dreams become real. So the priests loved Israel so much that they had the power of reshaping the dreams with their words, of bringing the dreams down to the world in a positive way. So, therefore, when someone blesses you, this is the time to ask that your dreams should be good.

Therefore, he continues with something very, very strong; the truth is that the holiest Jew in the world was Joseph *hatzadik*. His whole thing was dreams. He became a king through dreams. He got out of prison because of dreams, he interpreted the dreams of the baker, and he became a king because he interpreted the dreams of Pharaoh. What's the specialty of Joseph? Joseph was the utmost conception we have of holy thoughts. His words were so pure that he could *mamash* interpret dreams. He could take the dream of Pharaoh and feed the whole world with that dream.

Why do we dream at night? Because at night, the only thing which we have is imagination. And the greatest vessel for dreams is imagination.

Rebbe Nachman says the most way out / amazing thing. The strongest imagination that you need is to believe that G-d created heaven and earth. You look at the world and you see a solid world, you need the strongest and holiest imagination to believe that G-d created heaven and earth.

Joseph, who had the utmost purity of thought, was the one who knew that there really is one G-d. Rebbe Nachman says that all the holy *tzadikim*, all the holy people, they had this strong imagination. And if you have this tremendous imagination, not only can you receive dreams, but you can interpret dreams, and even uplift someone else's dreams.

He says another sweet beautiful thing: What is a stronger imagination, imagining a great theory or imagining a good story? Rebbe Nachman says that the soul is only stories. Because the fact is that when you dream, you don't dream about a theory; when you dream, you dream stories. Maybe in the story of the dream you spoke a story, because the real imagination is a story.

There are two kinds of stories. There are stories that put you to sleep when you listen to them, and there are stories that wake you up.

So Rebbe Nachman says, the difference between the dreams and the stories of holy people, and of the not-so-holy people, is that the dreams and stories of the unholy people put you to sleep. That means that while they are sleeping, they are dreaming of stories that put them even more to sleep. And the *tzadik*, the holy person, dreams in a way that wakens him up, and wakes up the whole world.

The truth is that everybody has to know that a dream comes from the highest and deepest secrets of the world. That means that even in the dream of the lowest creature in the world, it too is full of the greatest secrets of the world and the mysteries of life. But the only one who is really in tune with this is the holy person, who has holy imagination.

Let's put it this way, how far can you go without holy imagination? You can dream of killing the world. Holy imagination is completely infinite; not only can you see the destruction of the whole world, but you can imagine that there is still one G-d after all that.

So, therefore, Rebbe Nachman says that before you go to sleep, this is what you have to do, and what you have to ask for. The most important thing to ask for is, "Please let my imagination be so pure that my imagination will be a vessel for the dreams I'm dreaming."

Think about it one more time. You know what's happening at night? The new day is coming down. What gives you the strength to live another day? The dream you had last night.

The question is: What did you dream about? How did you receive that dream? If your imagination is way out and you can imagine that there is one G-d, then the next morning you wake up and your imagination is so holy and you are so full of life that you have a story for the world which will wake up the whole world. Your dream can bring the world back to life.

Because the truth is that Joseph was so holy, not only his first dream that he would be the king of the world and that he would feed the world and bring it life, but even his lifting up of the dream of Pharaoh, this low creature, Joseph was able to lift up his dream and via this dream he fed the world. That means Joseph was on the level of the highest imagination.

There are a lot of people who are imagining G-d, but they are imagining Him on the level of theory, which is not real. It's not a dream. It has to be on the level of a story, and then you come to the world and you tell them that there really is one G-d.

You see, there are people who are imagining the Oneness of G-d without a story, yet the real people are imagining G-d on the level of a story.

ℰℭℛ

# Wisdom of the Heart

**In the beginning**

Before G-d created the world, everything was infinite.

But G-d wanted to reveal His kingdom.

And there is no king without people.

And so He needed to create a world with people who know that there is a King.

But you cannot understand G-d without certain knowledge, certain emotions, certain kinds of vessels to understand Him. Because there must be emotions of love, of strength, of beauty, of eternity, all kinds of deep emotions.

Because you only know G-d via your heart.

And the moment you have emotions, it is already finite.

G-d put aside all the great lights, and there was left an empty space, and in this empty space He created the world.

You know, G-d is infinite. But we cannot understand G-d in an infinite way. We can only understand G-d in a finite way, because we are finite people.

So G-d had to create finite vessels to create the world.

'Finite vessels' is that we can know G-d in a finite way.

## Wisdom in your heart

What is the vessel for all the vessels for those emotions in your heart?
There is wisdom in my mind, and there is wisdom in my heart. The wisdom of my mind is very good, but it's nothing. It's deep, but it doesn't get there. You cannot know G-d just with the wisdom of your mind.

You have to know G-d with the wisdom of your heart.

Because the heart is the deepest depth there is.

## Good and Evil

Then G-d created two things: There is a good voice in your heart, that means your heart is a vessel for good, and yet your heart is also a vessel for evil.

So G-d created you and gave you a heart and all those deep things, and with all those emotions you should know that there is one G-d.

But what happens if you have evil thoughts? Then you're defiling this holy depths of yourself which G-d gave you in order to understand Him.

I want you to know something very deep. *"Metumtam"* in Hebrew means "closed up." What happens to you when you're evil? You're closing yourself up from G-d, from the world. Something happens to you, you're covered up. Like you take a bottle and you close it; you can't put anything in anymore.

To be holy means to be completely open, that everything is flowing into you.

But when you're doing wrong, you're just closed up, and nothing happens.

But then you also have to know that the truth is that, the heart basically a great fire, there is a great fire burning in the heart.

And the heart is so big that the heart wants to know G-d in an infinite way also.

So, therefore, King David said, "I make a little hole in my heart: *libi chalal bekirbi."* The same way as G-d made an empty space in His heart, in His world for you, so you have to make, like, an empty space for G-d, to understand Him in your heart.

And this is because then, if you make a little empty space, G-d can shine all these vessels of holiness, of emotions, into you. Then you will know how to serve G-d.

But if you think evil things all the time, your heart is closed up, and then you cannot use the same heart to understand G-d.

So the moment you think, 'I want to serve G-d,' that means that, at that moment, you make a little empty space in your heart, and G-d can reveal Himself to you there.

## What does it mean to pray?

If someone asks you, "What is it to pray?" that answer is that to pray means to make an empty space in your heart with words. Every word you utter, you make a little depth in your soul, a little empty space in your heart.

You know what praying is? Praying is that G-d is revealing Himself to you. We always think; 'I'm asking G-d.' It's not true. Prayer means that G-d is revealing His kingdom to you.

And with every word you utter, you make a little empty space in your heart and G-d can be there.

## Don't overdo it

But then when you make a little empty space in your heart, don't overdo it, because otherwise you'll burst.

So in a certain crazy way, you have to yearn for the infinite, but if you're infinite, so then G-d cannot tell you / reveal Himself to you. So you have to yearn in an infinite way for the finite. Because what does it mean to have holy thoughts? That means that the holy thoughts, like, make G-d a little bit finite in order to bring Him closer to your head.

## Yerushalayim

You have to know that Yerushalayim [Jerusalem] is a house of prayer.

There is a high Yerushalayim, and there is a low Yerushalayim. There are two houses. There is a high house and there is a low house.

What is a high house and what is a low house? The low house is that, in a finite way, you are making a way for G-d, and through this finite little house, G-d is shining the infinite on you.

Everybody knows that you are a little part of G-d. And where is G-d? G-d is in your heart. If G-d is in your heart, that means your heart is infinite. And, therefore, like, the flame in your heart is *mamash* infinite, and in the most infinite way you're burning up; "I want to know what G-d is."

But sometimes you're burning up so much that you cannot do anything. Because every act you are doing is a finite act. And, therefore, it's really hard / frustrating. You know, sometimes you want to be so infinite, but this isn't how it is in this world.

It's very strange. If you come to somebody and say, "Would you like to know G-d in an infinite way?" He's ready. But if you ask him, "Would you like to know G-d in a finite way, and put on *tefillin* every morning?" and he says, "No." why is it? Because, basically, you're yearning for the infinite, right? You'd like to know G-d in an infinite way, which is really true. But you have to realize one thing. You are living in this world, and you will not know G-d unless you do the finite things.

G-d promises you that into this finite thing that you do, He will pour in the infinite. This is the vessel.

So the same way as G-d made empty space for you, you have got to make yourself empty.

'Empty' means that for one minute, you stop being infinite. That's very strong / powerful. Everybody wants to know G-d in an infinite way. But you can't. So you have to make yourself finite. That means taking your infiniteness away from you, making yourself empty.

'Empty' means that in that place, you're not infinite. That is the place where G-d is really living. And this is the secret of creating the world. And this is the secret of serving G-d more and more and more.


**Questions and answers asked during the teaching**

*Question:* *Shlomo, there's something bothering me about what you said about your heart bursting.*

**Rebbe Shlomo Carlebach:** If I'm serving G-d in an infinite way, I'll blow my mind, I'll get crazy the next minute. Why do a lot of kids become a little bit religious and then they *mamash* get crazy. It's a holy thing, because they're really yearning for G-d in an infinite way. But they didn't keep it. They didn't make an empty vessel in their hearts.

*Question:* *That's what you mean when you taught us about 'annihilation,' isn't it?*

**Rebbe Shlomo Carlebach:** That's pretty good. You are *mamash* top. It is one of the ways, but it's a very strong thing.

Annihilation means to make an empty space. To go against your being infinite, and let G-d do the thing. It's saying to G-d, "I'm ready for You to let me know You on Your terms."

Listen to this: What's the whole thing of having good thoughts or evil thoughts? Good thoughts mean, "I want this world to be right." What's the greatest, greatest holiest thought? "I want this world to exist. I want me to exist. I want G-d to exist in this world."

So the way for G-d to exist in the world is - there has to be a little empty space.

**Question:** *How do you divide the finite regarding the acts of deeds that you're talking about like tefillin and tzitzis, from the finite of making money? Does that come from the same source?*

**Rebbe Shlomo Carlebach:** Do you mean what Rebbe Nachman says, that the most empty space is money? But this is G-d's empty space. G-d emptied Himself. Wherever I make money, G-d isn't there because I think I'm doing it; 'It's my power,' right? Money makes you powerful. This is one spot where G-d isn't manifest. It's empty space. And you have to fill it with G-d again.

But the empty space Rebbe Nachman is talking about here is that you want to serve G-d so much... Listen, I can walk up to a person, and love them so much that I *mamash* kill them with my loving. Coming on too strong, you know, cool it.
And the same way if we come to G-d, saying, "Listen G-d, I want to serve You in an infinite way, blow my mind." So G-d says, "Cool it brother."

But the thing is, if I cool it completely, I become dead, and that's bad too. There has to be some of both.

**Question:** *What bothers me is that, if you're really speaking in terms of actually the way it is, as long as both are the same areas, money and tefillin and tzitzis, it's not so great.*

**Rebbe Shlomo Carlebach:** No, it's a different thing because I'm talking about <u>your</u> empty space, and <u>G-d's</u> empty space. <u>G-d's</u> empty space is money. <u>My</u> empty space is *mitzvas* [good deeds]. I don't know if I'm making myself clear.

**Question:** *There's a good finite and there's a bad finite. It's not all just...?*

**Rebbe Shlomo Carlebach:** There has to be finite, but this finite has to be such a holy finite that it doesn't cover up the infinite. It has to be infinitely finite.

And this is the house above and the house below.

## Married couples

You can see this even on a human level, for example, with married couples. Imagine, a lot of people are very close before they get married. And then, when it comes to the finite thing, waking up in the morning and talking to each other, it does not work out so well. Because they're very good together on the infinite level, but on this empty space level they don't click.

And then there are a lot of couples who are tremendous on the finite level, but they're dead, right? Everything goes clock, clock, clock, but there is nothing between them. This infinite thing isn't between them.

So this is called the low house and the high house.

And the same is in the service of G-d. Everybody just wants to have a revelation of G-d; 'I'm ready to be Moses on Mt. Sinai.' But are you ready to be Moshele the water carrier and kindle lights at the proper time?

### *Teshuva*

What happened to you when you sinned? Why did you do wrong? Basically every child wants to serve G-d in the most infinite way. The only area where you failed G-d is that you couldn't make this empty space within yourself.

So *teshuva* [returning to G-d] is that you're connecting the infinite to the finite again.

Because you are doing *teshuva* so strongly, therefore the dividing wall between the infinite and the finite is less. Obviously. A *tzadik* is a very holy person, but you see in him the finite more than the infinite. And in a *bal teshuva*, the holiness of a person repenting is that this infinite fire is *mamash* obvious. It's *mamash* burning in an infinite way.

### Shabbos

Therefore, Rebbe Nachman says, this is the whole thing about Shabbos. Shabbos is - the holiness of Shabbos is, the vessel is - that you're yearning for G-d in a most infinite way, and even the Shabbos is infinite too. That means that all the *mitzvas* that you are doing, they're all finite *mitzvas*. They're very holy, but, they're also cutting me off a little bit from the infinite. So it's hard. But Shabbos is not doing anything. So on Shabbos, Shabbos itself is a vessel for the infinite. So that means on Shabbos my infinite and my finite are together.
It's top.

*Question: But you do things on Shabbos in a finite way.*

**Rebbe Shlomo Carlebach:** What do you do?

*Question: Pray.*

**Rebbe Shlomo Carlebach:** But the *mitzvah* of Shabbos is praying? The *mitzvah* of Shabbos is Shabbos.

Listen, on Shabbos you also eat, and you also sleep. But this isn't where it's at. This finite is more on the top level of infinite.

There's a strong difference between eating matza and eating on Friday night. Matza, you have to eat matza, it's an act that has to be fulfilled, and the piece of matza has to be that long or that short, and that thin. On Shabbos, even if I eat *challah* - it has to be kosher...

*Question: It has nothing to do with Shabbos.*

**Rebbe Shlomo Carlebach:** It has to do with Shabbos, but it's still infinite, because on Shabbos the *mitzvah* is the <u>bliss</u> of Shabbos, and you have to eat in order to keep up your level of bliss. But you know, you're not fulfilling the *mitzvah* with the chewing like you do with the matza. You're doing the *mitzvah* by being in the state of bliss.

So, therefore, he says *Bereshit* is '*B reshit* - 2 beginnings.' There is a beginning of the infinite and a beginning of the finite.

*Question: What do you mean by "beginning?"*

**Rebbe Shlomo Carlebach:** When G-d created the world, *bereshit* is the first word in the Torah, it means 'at the beginning.' And the Zohar HaKadosh says, *Bereshit* means '*bet - reshit,*' two beginnings.

*Question: Would you clarify what you mean about two beginnings?*

**Rebbe Shlomo Carlebach:** I don't know exactly either. Rebbe Nachman speaks about the two beginnings, the finite beginning and the infinite. This is how G-d created the world. The infinite has to be completely intact and they both have to go together. That means if for one thing you're just becoming a finite *Yiddelah* [Jew], you're off, right? And if you're just infinite, you're a very holy *Yiddelah*, but you're not the way you should be. You have to be both. Two beginnings, finite and infinite.

*Question: Can a finite vessel receive the infinite?*

**Rebbe Shlomo Carlebach:** There are vessels that can receive the infinite. This is the whole thing of Torah and *mitzvas*, that in finite vessels you receive the infinite. But if you don't use those vessels, then either you're completely nothing or you'll go out of you mind.


**What is a real person?**

A real person is someone who really integrates the infinite and the finite in a million ways. But most people, either they're completely infinite, or they're finite. Either way is bad. That means that even whatever you do, you must have the strength to do it in a finite way. Why aren't most of us better? Because we'd like to be the holiest man the next morning, but when you woke up the next morning and you're not the holiest man, so you give up. Because you have this infinite yearning, but you don't have the strength just to be finite. Don't be the holiest. Just be a little bit holy.

It's like one Rebbe said: Everybody would like to be the greatest scholar in one night, but this one night they also want to sleep.

Especially when it comes to the service of G-d, it's a very delicate thing. You have got to have this infinite yearning because, if you don't, you're not with it. You've got to be infinite.

The doing has to be finite and the yearning has to be infinite.

Rebbe Nachman says something in addition at the end. That's why the custom is that a *kallah* [bride] gives her *chassan* [groom] a *tallis* [prayer shawl]. Because a *tallis* is infinite, to let him know that their house will be a combination of the finite and the infinite. This is a *gevalt*.

*Question: As you become more infinite, or aware of more of the infinite, do you become less finite?*

**Rebbe Shlomo Carlebach:** No, on the contrary. I'll tell you something very deep. If you love somebody very much, then you're also ready to do them little favors. They both become deep, because if you're really with it, then you know that the finite is also infinite. And if you're bad, then to you the infinite is finite.

This is completeness, this holy depth. The combination of the high house and the low house….

Then you can say, when I pray it has to be in a completely infinite way. And yet it also has to be finite. The holiness of the prayer book, it's the most finite thing in the world, those words were written up two thousand years ago. But the way I'm praying, it has to be in an infinite way.

You see what it is, today a lot of people do 'creative services.' And it's a beautiful thing. I wish we could make up prayers, but why does it fail? You know why? Because creative service means I'm praying in an infinite way, but they're using the most finite language there is. Because they don't have the holiness to know the secret of saying finite words which contain the infinite. I heard this reform rabbi saying a creative service as part of a meeting of the Sisterhood. It was sweet, basically sweet. He wants to say something; but the way he said it is not even finite anymore, just stupid. Because between finite and stupid there is a very fine line.

What makes a good doctor? A good doctor, if he looks at your nose, and he is in a certain way infinite, then he can *mamash* see the way the nose is connected to the foot. And the way the connection to the foot is connected to the brain and the brain to your whole personality. Infinite ways. And if he's a finite doctor, he'll look at your nose, and he'll say, "I'll give you a spray for your nose."

It's the same way between people. Someone can tell you a little thing, but if you're on the infinite level, you can hear everything out of this one little word.

Rebbe Nachman is saying, basically, that since your heart is the place where you fathom G-d, it's infinite. It's infinite. Because if it wasn't infinite, how could G-d be there? But since you're living in this world, G-d gave you finite vessels to understand His infinity.

Rebbe Nachman says the heart is there because real wisdom is in your heart. It's much deeper than the mind. The mind receives from the heart.

ℰᏝ

## Still be Holy

A High Priest who finds a dead person is obliged to bury him and so he defiles himself for this dead person. However, even though he becomes impure, he is still the High Priest. The High Priest does not stop being a high priest for one second.

Rebbe Nachman asks, "What do you think I would do if I did the most awful thing?" He answers, "Do you think I'd stop being what I am? I'd still be the same thing. For five minutes I'd cry for what I did wrong, but that's it."

You know, the question is: Are you that holy that you can even stop being holy and yet still be holy? If there is such a word. I don't exactly know how to explain it. I don't have the right words.

ℰᏝ

## Silence

Rebbe Nachman says...

This is just so deep. It says, '*Haaretz hadom raglav.*' *Haaretz*, the earth which you're walking on, *hadom*, is the silence, *raglav*, of my feet. The earth is the silence of my feet.

*Halacha* [the body of law in the Torah], every law of the Torah, is not called "law," it's called *halacha*, walking. Everybody says, "I want to be a *halacha Yid* [religious Jew]." *Halacha* doesn't mean you're connected only when you're doing an actual Torah law. Even when you're not doing it, you also have to be connected. And the not doing can be on the highest level. If you know that you can do better and you didn't do better, that's also being a *halacha Yiddele*, because at least you know you should be better.

There are two levels of walking. Imagine if you want to do *teshuva* [return to Torah Judaism]. You want to do *teshuva* so badly. You want to become a better *Yiddele* [Jew]. What is your relationship to G-d until you become better?

Imagine if in the middle of the night, you wake up and realize, "My whole life I never put on *tefillin*, but tomorrow morning I'll put on *tefillin*." You have to wait until sunrise to put on *tefillin* [that is Torah law]. Let's say sunrise is at 4:20 a.m. What is your relationship to G-d from 1:00 a.m. until 4:20 a.m.? Or imagine you realize you've never sat in a Sukkah in your whole life, and it is now just August. What can you do, *Sukkot* is only in October. What are you going to do?

So this is what Rebbe Nachman teaches us, the deepest depth in the world; that while you're waiting for it, you're also doing it.

## Running and returning

Rebbe Nachman says that I'm doing *halacha* [walking] in two ways: Running *ratzo* [running up to], and *shov* [returning back down], which means I'm looking at myself and I realize how far away I am. It's a two way street, going back and forth... Going back and forth.

## Walking on silence

*Haaretz hadom raglav* [The earth is the silence of my feet]. Now listen to this, this is the deepest depths of the world. Is there anybody more silent than the earth? You're walking on the earth, and the earth doesn't make any noise, even though you're walking on the earth.

This literally, means you are walking on silence. What are you really walking on? What you're really walking on is silence. On waiting. On waiting and waiting.

## What's the *aleph* [א]?

Rebbe Nachman says that everybody knows that an *aleph* "א" has a little *yud* "י" up there on top, and a little *yud* "י" below, and a little *vav* "ו" in the middle.

Now this is one of the top Torah teachings of Rebbe Nachman, just to give it to you in a nutshell. *Aleph* is very deep. It's just way out.

A person has to know that first there has to be a little *yud* up there. The little *yud* up there, this is my doing.

Rebbe Nachman says that the upper *yud* is *keter* [the *sefira* 'crown']. This is the utmost waiting.

The *vav* in the middle, he says, is like when a person is put to shame, his face changes color. Your soul is changing, your heart is changing - all the changes you're going through, *mamash* going from top to bottom, it turns you over a thousand times [the face changes color from red to white, to red, to white]. That's the *vav*.

And then the little *yud* below is your silence.

You have to be *mamash* ashamed very deep. You know, friends, it is not that you're just sitting there and waiting. It is not that you say, 'You know, I went to a lecture last night and I heard a very important thing about Sabbath. It's a ritual and a beautiful thing, and I think I like it, and I also think it's also good for my children, because, you know, they must have something Jewish to hold on to. But - I don't want to overdo it - it goes without saying. But I think the Sabbath would be a sweet thing to begin with. But since today is only Monday, so I'm waiting until Friday night.' Waiting is not that you just don't do anything. Waiting is that you're turning over a thousand times; you are so ashamed you didn't keep last Shabbos. You are so ashamed that I didn't do it all this time, that *mamash* you are turning over a million times a second, *Gevalt*! This is the *vav*.

The *vav* is *emet* [truth]. Why? Because it goes from all the way up, to all the way down to the lowest, it has no end. The truth is, a *vav* has no end, it's just a long line. This 'being ashamed' has to be with truth. Listen, if you say to G-d, "I feel kind of ashamed I wasn't a better Jew, but You have to understand my circumstances." *Bobkes* [it's nothing]. You see, the thing is, it has to be real. It has got to be real.

The whole thing of an *aleph* is that there's a little *Yiddele* [*Yid*, meaning Jew, is a similar word to *yud*, the Hebrew letter, י] up there, my little *neshama* [soul] is up there. My *neshama* knows so much. My *neshama*, this is my *kavod*, my honor. This is the deepest depths of me. This is what connects me to G-d. This is me before I was created. This is me after I was created. This is the deepest depths of me. What is my deepest depths? What is my real connection to G-d? Not the things have done, my real deep connection to G-d is all the things I want to do.

Listen friends, this is so deep. If someone asks you, "What makes you into a *Yiddele* [Jew]?" A *Yiddele* is not what you did yesterday. What makes you into a *Yiddele* is that you're waiting for next Shabbos. What makes you into a *tefillin Yiddele*? It's not that you put on *tefillin* this morning. What makes you into a *tefillin Yiddele* is that you're waiting with great shame, "*Gevalt*, Rebono Shel Olam [Master of the world], this morning I put on *tefillin*, but it was nothing - my heart wasn't in it, my soul wasn't in it, I didn't *daven* [pray] properly - but I am waiting for another chance tomorrow."

But now listen to this: What is the lower *Yiddele* [*yud* י]? An *aleph* א looks like a little *yud* י (on top), a *yud* י (below), and a *vav* ו in the middle. What is the lower *yud*? The lower *yud* is my silence... listen to this, this is the deepest depths of it. What is my silence? My silence is that even while I didn't do it, I know that despite everything, I am a Shabbos *Yiddele*, I'm a *tefillin Yiddele*.

If someone comes to you and says, "What kind of a *chutzpah* [audacity] is this, that you say you are a *tefillin Yiddele*? You never put on *tefillin* in your life."

You say, "No. I'm waiting. I never *davened* [prayed] in my whole life, and yet I will say, 'I'm the greatest *davener* in the whole world'."

"How come you're the greatest *davener* in the world, you never opened your mouth to *daven*?"

"Because I'm waiting to *daven*."

## Honor

A person has to give *kavod* [honor] to G-d, and a person has to give *kavod* to himself. What does it mean to give *kavod* to yourself, to honor yourself? It means that you're in touch with that which is higher than you.

You know what it is? It's really so deep friends. What is happening with most people? They *mamash* dishonor themselves.

We want so much respect it's just *gornisht* [nothing], doesn't go. Why do most of our children, *nebech*, no longer respect their parents anymore? Because the parents lost touch, they're not honoring themselves anymore. What does it mean to honor myself? It means to wait, to wait to be better.
You know, children are real.

## Why did Yitzchak honor his father so much?

If Avraham would have ever said a lie to Yitzchak, he would not have been able to tell him, "I'm taking you up to the *akeida* [altar, the binding of Isaac]." because Yitzchak would say, "Listen father, one time you lied to me, maybe this is a lie also." So that means Avraham never told him a joke [He never said, "I was just joking when I promised you…."]. Maybe Avraham was laughing together with Yitzchak because Yitzchak is laughter [Yitzchak comes from the word *Tzchok*, laughter], but he was not just joking around.

Can you imagine how much Yitzchak respected Avraham that when he was told, "I'm taking you up to the *akeida*," Yitzchak accepted what his father said.

And remember, Yitzchak was also a prophet. And the truth is, it is written that, after a prophecy is revealed to one prophet, then all the other prophets also know about it. It says in the Zohar HaKadosh; Yitzchak had a question to G-d, "If this is a prophecy, then why didn't I know about it?" But this was part of the test. Can you imagine?

But what was so holy about Avraham? The holy Slonimer Rebbe said that Avraham was saying to G-d, "Ok, I'm not so much of a Jew, but maybe Yitzchak will be an *emes Yiddele* [a true Jew]." Can you imagine how much holy waiting he had?

The deepest depth of connection between parents and children is when the parents want so much to be *emes* a *Yid* [a true Jew]. But then they're afraid, "Maybe I won't make it?" So they pray so much, "Please G-d, at least let my children be an *emese Yid*." Children know this. The first sign is if the parents want their children to be more of a *Yid* than they are. And that is because the parent wants to be more of a *Yid* himself.

This 'more,' this waiting, this is the high *yud*. This is the *kavod*.

Imagine if all parents were waiting to be better parents.

I'm still looking to find those parents who say, "I wish I would be a better father or a better mother." Do you know how much their children connect to them? In the most unbelievable way.

But most parents say, "I'm the best father or mother in the world, I hope my children realize that." That's the end, there is no connection any more, no *kavod*. The high *yud* is missing, so it's a cut off letter. Have you ever seen a letter where the top is missing? It's meaningless.

## The sun and the moon

Rebbe Nachman says, this is the secret of the sun and the moon. The sun is the high *yud*. It's the greatest light in the world. The highest light in the world is; 'I am waiting.' Because do you know what kind of a Shabbos you have if you're waiting for the Great Shabbos?

But then there is another little light, the little *yud*, and this is the moon. The moon represents that even while you are in absolute darkness, while you never kept Shabbos yet, you still know that you are connected to Shabbos. You are connected to everything holy. This is the moon. It's a sweet little light, it doesn't expel the darkness. It's still dark, and there isn't much you can do with it. It's just there. Even if you never kept Shabbos in your whole life, you're still a Shabbos *Yiddele*.

What's the holiness of a *Yiddele*? How are we able to last so long in exile? Because we have the moon. How does a *Yiddele* exist in the darkness of the night? He knows; "All the *mitzvas*, every holy word in the Torah, even if I didn't learn it yet, even if I didn't understand it yet, I'm connected to it."

Imagine if you can't even read Hebrew and someone asks you, "Are you connected to every letter in the Zohar? Are you connected to every letter, every word in the Gemara?"
You will say, "I can't even read Hebrew." But it doesn't matter. It doesn't matter. Every word, every letter, you are connected to it.
Someone will ask you, "Do you know all the 613 laws?" You will say, "I barely know two or three."
The truth is that you are connected to all of the 613 laws.
Someone will ask you, "Are you connected to Rabbi Akiva, to Rebbe Tarfon, to Rebbe Assi, to Abaya, to Rava?" And you will say, "I never heard of them."

It doesn't matter. This is the holiness of the moon. The holiness of the moon is that you're connected to everything.

But you know what the most beautiful thing is? That this holy connection has so much power, that it makes you new all the time. If you walk around and say, "*Gevalt*, it's so dark, I have no connection yet," then you still have a little moon in your soul telling you, "*Gevalt, Yid*, you still have connection to everything."

Then you become a new moon.
And after you become a new moon you realize, "*Gevalt*, I know so much more about *Yiddishkeit*."
Then you realize, "*Oy vey*, I know so little."
Then it's a new moon again.

ಌೕಌ

# *Haneor Balayla*

This Torah teaching from Rebbe Nachman is just so important: Rebbe Chanina, the son of Chachinai, says, *Haneor Balayla* - if you're up at night and you walk along your way alone, and you turn your heart to nothingness - *l'vatala*, means, if you translate it properly, to nothingness, to unimportant things, that means you are walking around with stupid thoughts. Then you, so to speak, just bring about your own death with your own hands, because you *mamash* deserve, G-d forbid, that you have no right to live. This is written in *Pirkey Avos*.

**The simple meaning**

Now the simple meaning of this is... Imagine that you want to get angry at somebody very much. But this person is not around. So you just make up your mind that if this person walked in the room now, you'd grab him and *mamash* tell him 'where it's at,' what you think of him, and then you'd definitely throw him out - and never speak to him again.

Then something happens when this person walks in to the room, and suddenly you are not so angry any more. You just ask him, "Why did you do that?" in a soft way. The person will just say, "I really didn't mean it," and the whole thing will be forgotten.

Isn't it crazy? This person didn't utter one word, he just walked in to the room. What happened?

Everybody has an inside light and an outside light, a surrounding light. Your whole soul is not within your body. Just a little part of your soul is within your body giving you life. But the truth is, that the essence of your soul is beyond you, beyond your body. It's just there. And this is a very great light, a very great light.  So you might be angry at somebody, but the moment when they walk in and you're standing in front of them, then the light of their soul is shining so much that you can't be angry.  You just can't.

### Your soul is really shining

According to our tradition, everything wrong which happens to you is only because your soul wasn't shining in your surrounding light, because if your soul is really shining, then no evil can befall you, because evil can't reach you.

### Learning Torah

How can you get to be on that level that your soul should really be shining?  You can if you are learning Torah, if your insides are filled with learning, with Torah. Because the whole Torah is really one. One.  If you learn one letter you're really learning all the letters.  If you learn one word, you're really learning all the words.

### A good friend

Do you know what a good friend is?  What does it mean to love somebody very much?  It's very simple.  If you don't love somebody very much, you'll say, "I love you." That means right now, a few minutes after five on Tuesday, I said to you, "I love you." And that's it. So, it is sweet…. But then, sometimes you love somebody so much, you say, "I love you," but it really includes all the eternities of the world.  You can *mamash* hear the echo like you said it about 30 times before and after.

### Learn the Torah on a high level

You know what it means to really learn the Torah on a high level? It means that while you're learning, it's not just this minute. All of you before, and all of you after, whatever happens before and after, is learning. This is only true with learning the Torah. You cannot say you're taking a book on psychology and your whole eternity is learning this book. Because it's just information, it's not soul.

### A holy soul

So if I'm on that level, then suddenly I'm on this tremendous eternity level, so then everything that goes around within time cannot reach me.  It just can't reach me.  People cannot get angry with me.  The little dog in the house wants to bark at me, but it just can't, because it saw a holy soul.

*Here it is appropriate to insert one of the stories written about Rebbe Shlomo Carlebach in the book; 'Holy Brother'.*

Rivkah Haut's watchdog "Ginger" was an integral part of her family for over twelve years. A playful and devoted companion to Rivkah's little girls, an alert and conscientious guardian of the Haut household, Ginger had but one minor flaw; she hated men.

"It was the most amazing thing," Rivkah recalls. "Here was this sweet, gentle, loving playmate of my daughters, who became transformed into a rabid, vicious, foaming-at-the mouth animal whenever she saw a man. The mysterious metamorphosis never failed to astound us. In the presence of men, Ginger grew unrecognizable. She would growl menacingly and move to attack. Even my own husband, after twelve years of living together, couldn't get within three feet of Ginger without fearing for his life. This scenario occurred all the time with men, without exception. The one and only time Ginger deviated from this behavior was when Shlomo Carlebach came to my home for a two-day visit.

"I was expecting Shlomo, but had forgotten to lock up Ginger, as I normally did before a man entered the house. When Shlomo suddenly appeared in the kitchen (my daughter had responded to his knock, unaware that Ginger was loose), my heart sank. I was sure that Ginger would surface momentarily, and accord Shlomo the usual warm welcome she typically reserved for men.

"Sure enough, within a minute Ginger materialized in the kitchen, and stood stock still looking across the room at Shlomo. What happened next I will never forget; I was so startled by what occurred that I think a dish slipped out of my hand and crashed onto the floor.

"What happened was this: Ginger didn't snarl, snap, or bark. She didn't growl or arch her back, readying for attack. Instead, she bounded over to Shlomo eagerly, her tail wagging swiftly and enthusiastically, her throat emitting low, husky whimpers of delight. She acted as if she were warmly welcoming a long-lost friend, but Ginger and Shlomo had never crossed paths before. Shlomo bent down to pat Ginger, talking gently to her, and they developed an instant rapport, becoming fast friends. Indeed, during Shlomo's two-day stay at my home, Ginger stayed at his side constantly, rapturously devoted and completely in his thrall.

"In the twelve years Ginger lived with us, this situation never happened before and it didn't happen again. I'm not mystically inclined, but the experience with Shlomo and Ginger defied rational explanation. I can only suggest that there was something so singular and extraordinary emanating from Shlomo Carlebach that the dog, with its special animal sense, picked it up and responded to it immediately."

෨෦෨

## The simple meaning

The simple meaning is still very high, but this is just the simple meaning. It is dangerous to walk at night. And let's even say; this world - this whole world is like a night.


## Alone

If you are up at night, and you walk alone... do you know what it means to be alone? Imagine you ask someone...

"What do you mean when you say, 'I walk alone? Isn't there one G-d in the world Who is always there with you? "

"No, I cut myself off from G-d."

"You walk alone? Have you ever heard of a *Yiddele* [Jew] walking alone? When a *Yiddele* walks, all the *Yiddelach* [Jews] are with him. Avraham is with you, Eliahu Hanavi walks before you, what do you mean, 'alone'?"

"No, I walk alone. I cut myself off from everything holy in my heart. In my mind I cut myself off from the Torah, I'm thinking about everything stupid."

I'll tell you something very strong. Imagine if every Jewish boy or girl who would, G-d forbid, want to leave our religion, if, in their minds, they *mamash* would have to say good-bye to the Six Million Jewish people from the Holocaust before they left, because they're walking with us all the time, and if they are, G-d forbid, breaking away from *Yiddishkeit*, so they would have to just walk over and say goodbye to the six million. I don't think they'd have the heart to do it. If they would know they have to shake hands with Avraham Avinu, and say, "Listen, so far you were walking with me, *zie gezunt,* good bye." And they would have the *chutzpah* to tell G-d, "You know, G-d, I don't want to be the way You want me to be, I know more about You than You know. Because You think that I know that You think I'm a *Yiddele*. I'll surprise you, G-d, I'm not." It's a bad scene, right?

Anyway, as Rabbi Chanina in Pirkey Avos says, if you cut yourself off from G-d, from all of Israel, and you're learning things that are meaningless, then you *mamash* are hanging death upon yourself.
This is what the ordinary meaning of *Haneor Balayla* is.


## It really is

Now listen to what Rebbe Nachman says, listen to this deepest depths in the world. This is one of the strong principles in Chassidus. There are two levels of lying, and there are also two levels of truth. Imagine if today is Tuesday, and it's now 5:30, and we're sitting here, and I will come up with a lie and say, "No, it is not Tuesday, it's Friday. And we're not in *Yerushalayim*, we're in Hawaii, and it's not 5:30, it's 12:00 o'clock at night." How much am I lying? Not too badly, because it could have been, it could have been that it's really Friday. It could have been that we're in Hawaii, and that it's 12:00 o'clock. It could have been. It just so happens that it isn't. But listen to this; if someone asks me, "Are you a Jew?" So I could lie, and say, "I'm not." But then, instead, I tell the truth, "I am." Listen to this: if I lie and I say, "I'm not a Jew," how much am I lying? Is it that it 'just so happens' that I'm a Jew? I could have been a non Jew, but I 'just so happen' to be a Jew? If someone asks me, "Is there one G-d?" I would say, "Yes, there is." Would I say, "Yes there is," just because I don't want to lie? Could I have said a lie that there isn't, but I'm telling the truth that there is? Everybody in his right mind understands that this level of lying is a different thing. If G-d forbid, I say, "there is no G-d," it's not that there could have not been a G-d, and there is, it so happens that there is a G-d. It's not that it so happens that there is a G-d - There really is one G-d! It's not that it so happens that I am a Jew - I really am a Jew! If someone will ask you, "Is there such a thing as Shabbos?" It's not that there could have not been Shabbos, but there is - There really is Shabbos.

You have to realize that the level of the truth of the Torah, of the *mitzvas*, of everything holy, is a different kind of truth. It's not like Golda Meir was Prime Minister, but it could have been Shazar. It's not this kind of level. It's a different kind of level.

**It is up to you**

Now listen to this. Let me ask you something very, very deep. Ok, the truth is, there really is one G-d. What about the world? It is possible that there could have not been a world, right? G-d didn't have to create the world. There could have not been a world, but it so happens that G-d did create a world. How does that sound? Do you say that the world is also on a G-d truth level? So this is what Rebbe Nachman says, this is one of the holiest things Rebbe Nachman says; to be on a G-d truth level - that is up to you.

**Free choice**

What is your level of free choice? Your free choice is to either be on the level of, 'Yes, I'm here. It so happens that I'm here. I also could have not been here, but I'm here.' Or, I can *mamash* be here, I really am here.

Most of the people that we meet - it so happens that they're here.

Let's put it this way: The holy Bal Shem Tov, was it that 'it just so happens' that he was here? He really was here! Avraham Avinu [our forefather Abraham], he was *mamash* here! You can see his footsteps. He was *mamash* here.

But some people in the world, they 'just happen' to be here. But since you don't want to lie and say they weren't here, so you say, "They were here."

**Really there**

You can go to Athens, hang around for four weeks, and see a lot of things, and maybe you forget you're a *Yiddele*. Then, suddenly, you walk on the street and you meet somebody, you see him wearing a *yarmulke* and *tzitzis* and he will ask you, "Are you maybe going to *Yerushalayim* [Jerusalem]?" And suddenly, something will happen to you, and you remember, *"Gevalt,* I have to go to *Yerushalayim."* You know what happened? You met thousands of people in Athens, and it's nothing. This *Yiddele* whom you met (maybe he was Elijah the Prophet) he was really there. Not, 'he could have not been there,' he really was there. Really there.

**Two levels**

Whatever you do can be on two levels. Imagine, if someone loves you, and you love them. You can say to them, "Do me a favor." So sometimes some of the people do you a favor, but they could also not have done it. But then, if you are so close to somebody, you have free choice, right? But you really don't.

You know, sometimes someone does you a favor, it's 'really there.' It's G-d's existence.

**G-d *mamash* gave us G-d existence.**

When you are born, you're just here in this world; it just so happens that you are here. But to reach this G-d level, this 'really being here,' this is your own free choice.

**How can you sleep?**

So Rebbe Nachman says, *haneor balayla,* you have to be up at night. How can you sleep? How can you sleep at night?

And I'll tell you something even deeper: Night doesn't have to do with time. Everybody has his own night.

Sometimes, you know, when it's very dark in the light of your soul, in your little world, the first thing you realize is, "What's wrong with me? I'm not even here yet. I'm just walking around, I'm not here."

What do you have to do? You have to walk at night, *mamash* alone.

**Nobody can do it for you**

You can have all the biggest and greatest Rebbes, you can study all the books in the world, but to give you this G-d existence, this is just you alone. Nobody can do it for you, nobody in the world.

**Annihilating yourself before G-d**

How do you get on this level, to get to this holy G-d existence level, this truth existence? You have to be there and completely cleanse your soul, to annihilate yourself before G-d. How do you get this G-d existence? If you are completely, completely one with G-d.

What does it mean to be *mamash* a servant of G-d? That means *mamash* you're completely annihilating yourself before G-d. And suddenly you're living on a G-d existence level. It is a completely different level.

*Mitchayav benafsho*

"*Mitchayav benafsho*" - this is just the deepest depth. The ordinary translation is that, G-d forbid, You are bringing about your own death. But Rebbe Nachman says it's just the other way around. He says, "*mitchayav benafsho*" means he then gives his own soul the most, most existence in the world.

You know, '*chayav*' means that, if someone says to you that you're *chayav*, that means that you have to do it. It means *mamash* it's there. "*Chayav*" means you have to, it has to be there. If I have to give you a hundred dollars, you say I'm "*chayav*." I better put the hundred dollars on the table. It has to be there, it has got to be there.

This is just so deep. The truth is, when G-d created the world, G-d had free choice not to create the world, right? So G-d created the world, but the truth is, the way the world is, it could be or it could not be.
Now listen to this, I want you to put your soul into it, it's heartbreakingly beautiful. What does it mean that G-d has 'chosen' us *Yiddelach* [Jews]? There's a whole world, right? The world can be or can not be. But then G-d has 'chosen' the *Yiddelach*. When you're 'choosing' something, it's deeper than free choice.

**Choosing**

I want you to know something very deep. When you walk into a store and buy a shirt. You decide to buy this shirt, so you have free choice to buy this shirt, right? But imagine if you have a chance not to be a Jew, G-d forbid, but then you decide, "I have got to be a little *Yiddele* [Jew]." This is reaching deeper than your free choice. It reaches so deep that you realize you cannot be without it.

'Choosing' means that this is deeper than free choice. This means it's reaching in such a deep place... OK, you have a choice to be a Jew right now. You can walk out of here and do anything in the world. But the truth is that G-d has 'chosen' you and you have 'chosen' G-d.

If someone comes with a gun, sticks it in your back, and he says, "Listen brother, I want you to pray to an idol." You know, you have free choice, you could lie down before an idol and pray. But you say, "Brother, I have no choice. Because I'm so much of a *Yiddele*, I believe in G-d so much, I can't do it."

## The difference between us and the whole world

The difference between us and the whole world, on a very deep level, is that G-d has 'chosen' us. We *Yiddelach* are *mamash* here, right? Why were so many nations here and they left, and yet we are still here? Because we are *mamash* 'here.' The Romans could have been here or not been here. The Greeks could have been here or not been here.

## To give the whole world G-d existence

G-d chose us *Yiddelach*. What's our mission in life? To give the whole world G-d existence. We have got to turn on the whole world. What does it mean to prepare the world for the kingdom of G-d? *Mamash*, that G-d should shine in the world. If the world is on a G-d existence level, then it has to 'be here.'

Let's put it this way: A person who can kill another person, do you know what that means? It is not the person who is killed who is not here, it means that the person who kills isn't really here. Because he is not part of G-d's existence. Because if he would have been part of G-d existence, how can he kill? How can you do something to destroy the world?

The Bais Yaakov says, there are still forces in the world that say, "G-d, why did You create the world? Who needs it? The whole world is nothing, the whole world is a joke." You see, people who hate, people who kill, they're not killing this one person, or hating this one person. They are sinning against G-d's plan, because they think, "Who needs the whole world."

## On an individual level

But now let's not talk about the whole world, because Rebbe Nachman talks about just one person, on an individual level.

Maimonides really says, "I swear to you that any person in the world, the lowest person in the world, when he wants to become a servant of G-d, can be as holy as the High Priest in the Holy of Holies." That's on an individual level.

**Avraham Avinu lifted up the world**

When Avraham Avinu came to the world, suddenly there was one person in the world who was '*mamash* there.' And because of this one person, suddenly the whole world was on a different level. Suddenly Avraham Avinu lifted up the world from that 'free choice' level of 'being or not being,' to the level of '*mamash* being'.

**If you are *mamash* tied to your roots...**

Rebbe Nachman says... you have to understand this very well because it's very, very deep: You have a choice, to plant a tree or not to plant it, right? But then, when the tree is growing, does the tree have choice to run away from its roots? No. It can't. It's 'really there.' How can a tree be without roots, right?

Each time you do a *mitzvah*, each time you learn Torah, you are choosing to be a Jew. It's not only that you're choosing to do this one particular act. You are doing it because you are a Jew. That means that each time you do something, you are choosing to be a Jew, you are affecting your whole life.

**We have to lift up the world**

What is the purpose of us *Yiddelach* [Jews]? What is our purpose on the deepest level of the world? We have to lift up the world to a different level. We have to lift up the world so that the whole world should *mamash* 'be there.'

Sometimes people ask me, "How do you know if somebody loves you?" The answer is very simple: If, in their presence you are 'really there,' if, in their presence, suddenly it's not that you happen to be here, but you're 'really here,' that means they're giving you, for that moment, this holy G-d existence. That means they really love you.

Sometimes you meet people, and they cut you so short they don't even let you have this 'being or not being existence.' They just want to wipe you out. They don't even give you a fighting chance. And then there are some people who *mamash* give you this... 'just utmost of existence.' And you know what we *Yiddelach* have to do? We have to do this to the whole world.

What are you doing to an apple when you make a *bracha* [blessing] over it? Before, the apple was here, it could have not been here, but then you make a *bracha* and you say, "Little apple, I want you to know something; so far you were just an ordinary apple, but now you are *mamash* really an apple."

Imagine, you are walking into a bakery and you buy two *challahs* [loaves of bread] for Shabbos. What happens to those two *challahs*? They are *mamash* there. They are *mamash challahs* for Shabbos. And suddenly, they are different and they taste different.

## Children

I'm thinking about it all the time: What do children need most? You see, old people are already accustomed to this kind of existence, this 'being or not being,' just hanging around existence.

But when children are born, they *mamash* know, their soul tells them, "You are only born in this world *mamash* to be completely here." And they are waiting for encouragement so much, they are waiting so much.

Why do children need love so much when they are little? And they not only need someone to love them… they *mamash* need this *michuyav hamitziut* [real existing], they really need this kind of existence. They want to *mamash* know that they are *mamash* here.

Therefore the Gemara says that the first thing you do when a little boy or a little girl learns to talk is that you teach them Torah. Because the moment they can talk, their tongue wants to exist, and the tongue exists when you say words of Torah.

When a little boy can *shukkle* [shake] a *lulov* [the palm branch waived on Succoth], his hands want to exist, his hands want to shake the *lulov*. Because each time he is doing a *mitzvah* he is *mamash* existing.

On a very simple level, imagine if I feel the same before I'm putting on *tefillin* and after I'm putting on *tefillin*, then it was a very lousy putting on *tefillin*. Because each time I put on *tefillin* something has to happen to me, suddenly I am '*mamash* here'. *Mamash* here.

## To feel it

So therefore Rebbe Nachman says, this is a very, very high level. Although I'm sure all of us have tasted it for a second, because it's impossible not to - maybe on Rosh HaShanah you felt it, maybe one time when you were dancing with the Torah on Simchas Torah and you felt it, or maybe one time when you stood by the Holy Wall you really knew, "I am really here, there really is one G-d."

## Annihilate yourself before the Oneness of G-d

But to be on the level of feeling it all the time, and not only to feel it all the time, but to never cease to turn the whole world on to it, to give existence to the whole world, what do you do to get to that level? He says, for that, you have to *mamash* annihilate yourself before the Oneness of G-d.

If a person comes to you and he says to you, "I want you to know one very special thing, I am 'really here.' I am really on the level of *michuyav hamitziut*. I've got to be here because G-d needs me. But you? Look at yourself! I am telling you, who are you?" It's a bad scene.

If you are annihilated before the Oneness of G-d, it doesn't matter to you if it's an Eskimo, a cockroach, or if it's a little dog, because it is G-d's Oneness. Because G-d created the world with this holy oneness. But it's up to you to bring in this holy oneness, this most existing oneness.

## Meditate

Now we are coming to the crux of the whole thing. People talk so much about meditation today. This *Torale* [teaching] of Rebbe Nachman has changed the lives of thousands and thousands and thousands of people. This is what Rebbe Nachman says:

What does it mean to meditate? To meditate does not mean to just sit there... - I'm not, G-d forbid, knocking off any ways of meditation, I'm sure they're very holy - but Rebbe Nachman says, what does it mean to meditate? *Mamash*, suddenly to become *michuyav hamitziut*. It means you are *mamash*, *mamash* 'there.' And to be *mamash* 'really there,' you have to annihilate yourself before the Oneness of G-d.

How do you annihilate yourself before the Oneness of G-d? You have to be alone. You have to be alone. Got to be alone.

It's a very strange thing, you know, because G-d created the world in such a way that I am I, Michael is Michael, Barbara is Barbara. But the thing is, when you want to reach the oneness, you have to annihilate yourself, not to annihilate Michael, right? Everybody is ready to annihilate somebody else before the Oneness of G-d. But you have to annihilate your own walls. How do you annihilate your own walls? You *mamash* have to stand before G-d and 'be there.'

## Something in the air

Then he says something very strong. Why do you have to meet G-d at night? Because during the day, the 'air' is polluted. Not polluted with gas, you know, Rebbe Nachman wasn't concerned with that. During the day the 'air' is polluted because everyone is running. You know what's happening in the world? What are people doing all the time? They are thinking, "I have to run to make a few rubles [money]."

How low can you think? You think you're here for a few rubles? If you think you're here for a few rubles, you're definitely not 'here,' right? Your only chance to be 'really here' is if you know that you're here because G-d created you, and you have to do something in this world very deep and very holy. But if you run around all day long to make a few rubles, and who knows what you're talking about and thinking about, then you're completely out of it.

How can you walk around in an 'air' which is so polluted, which is so filled with that? And how can you *mamash* penetrate this 'air' and *mamash* be 'here?'

So therefore Rebbe Nachman says, it has to be at night. Because there is something in the 'air' at night. At night there is something very special going on. At night, the lowest creature knows, deep down, "I'm here for something deeper than just making money.' Why are stores closed at night? Because people basically know, "I'm not here to run a store." Why don't business meetings go so strong at night? Why? Because they really know, deep down, "I really shouldn't go to a business meeting, I really should do something else." *Nebech*, not that they know what they have to do yet, but there is something in the 'air.'

**You are afraid to annihilate yourself before G-d?**

Our life level is always on the level of 'being or not being,' because until we reach the level of 'G-d choosing us' or 'us choosing G-d,' which is deeper than free choice, everything is still part of the 'free choice' level.

Many parents don't want to send their children to Hebrew School. They say, "When they grow up, let them make their own choice." They say, "We can't send them to Yeshiva because they'll become too Jewish and they won't have free choice anymore." You know why they say this? Because their whole life is on a level of free choice; 'being or not being,' maybe yes, maybe not. They have never tasted for even one second what it is to *mamash* 'be there.'

Why do most marriages break up so fast? Because they could have married this girl or they could have married somebody else. OK, so they married this girl, but if it doesn't work out they'll marry somebody else. It's all on a 'free choice level,' it's never real. It's not on a 'G-d level' because G-d is not on a level of, 'He could be, He could not be.' He really is!

You see, if someone says, "It so happens, I'm a Jew. But I could also have been a Zen Buddhist." he might be a very holy person, but whatever his service of G-d is, it's not on the level that it could be.

If you keep Shabbos, and you think, "It's also possible for me not to keep Shabbos," then it's not Shabbos, it's not 'G-d Shabbos.'

This is tremendous, tremendous; *mamash* you have to annihilate yourself before this; to know *mamash* 'This is it,' it is deeper than free choice.

We are still holding on to a little bit of free choice, right? This is the last thing we have. We don't realize that not having free choice is much deeper than all of this.

You know, if you wake up in the morning and you have free choice to put on *tefillin* or not to put them on, it's very holy, but then, much deeper than this is that when you are putting on the *tefillin*, it's deeper than free choice.

## A place where people don't walk during the day

Rebbe Nachman says so strongly that, not only do you have to walk alone, but, even during the night you have to walk in a place where people don't even walk during the day. It has to be two things: It has to be at night - the time has to be at night - but also it has to be in a place where people are not walking during the day. Because it's disturbing; you can't reach the level of annihilating yourself before G-d if people walked there who don't know what it is.

And then you're all alone.

And then, *mamash*, you have to cleanse your heart of anything that is unimportant.

And then you have to *daven* [pray]; you don't need prayers from the prayer book, because this is something else.

There are two levels of *davening*:

1. There is a level of *davening* when you pray from the prayer book. It is very, very holy, but this is only after you're 'existing,' after you're a *Yiddele*. After you're 'existing,' you're already part of everything holy, then you *daven* [pray] to ask for your needs.

2. But then there is a deeper kind of thing, that you *mamash* want to be in this world, you want to exist, 'Give me a completely different kind of existence.'

## Make up your own words

And there is nobody in the world who can tell you how to pray. Nobody in the world, not even Rebbe Nachman, not even Moshe Rabbenu, can tell you what to say. This is the deepest secret between you and G-d. There you have to make up your own words.
And sometimes, Rebbe Nachman says, you have no words; you just sigh. What a sigh.

## Cleaned from arrogance

And then, he says something very strong. This is so true. If you ever reach the level of really 'true existence,' then you are completely cleansed from all the arrogance in the world. From any coarseness or any arrogance. Because if you ever tasted this 'real existence,' then you give existence to every person you meet…

What is arrogance? "I am better than you." "I have four PhD's, and you have only three." It's all nonsense, right? Then *mamash* you're above all this nonsense.

Because, he says... listen to these words! The moment you are *michuyav hamitziut*, the moment you are 'really there,' then *mamash* you become one with the whole world. Not just one - you are just completely annihilated before the whole world.

## One with your own soul

And the most important thing is that you are then really one with your own soul. What does it mean that your soul is part of G-d? You see, your soul is 'really there.' But you are created in a way that your whole soul is not shining into your body. That means your soul and your body are only on the level of 'yes or no.' It could be no.

But if you're on the level of *michuyav hamitziut*, then your whole soul is shining into you, your whole soul.

And then, through you, you can lift up the whole world.

## *Questions and Answers*

**Someone in the class asks:**
**Question:** You say that when you're at that level to distinguish between degrees of learning. Wouldn't it be the same thing, then, on that level to distinguish between traditions, customs, and religions? Say like I'm a *Yiddele* and you're a Buddhist....

**Rebbe Shlomo Carlebach:** I'll tell you something very, very deep. You see, many of our Jewish kids make a mistake in one thing. If you completely and to the utmost respect a Zen Buddhist for being a Zen Buddhist, that doesn't mean that you have to become a Zen Buddhist also.

Us *Yiddelach* [Jews], most of our young people have so little pride and so little taste of their own religion.

I'll tell you something very strong. I'll give you a good example. I'm a man. But imagine if I would then say, "I met a woman, and I'm so much annihilated that I've got to be a woman also." No. It is not like that. I'm a man and she's a woman, and I'm not making myself smaller or bigger by this. I am I and you are you.

The truth is, I met a little Zen Buddhist. Let's say I meet Swami Satchedananda, and I respect him a billion percent. And we are giving each other existence, he in his way and I in my way. But this doesn't mean that therefore I have to say, "Maybe he is right."

**Question:** But when you're way up there, and you say Satchedananda, are you even thinking that he has another tradition?

**Rebbe Shlomo:** Sure, why not? Just like I'm aware that this is a man, and this is a woman. Because the holiness of the world is that everybody has to be what G-d wants him to be.

**Question:** But when you're way up there, are you even thinking this is a woman?

**Rebbe Shlomo:** Why not?

**Question:** Well, I don't know why.

**Rebbe Shlomo:** 100%, because if I'm saying no, then I'm not aware of G-d's creation.
You see, on the contrary, the more this is real existence, then the more things are really shining the way they really are.

If you are aware of a woman before you reach holy existence, then you are only aware of a woman; "Ahh, it is a good thing for me, maybe I can do something," you know, on a low level, which has nothing to do with that person.
But if you are on this high existence level, you're *mamash* aware that this is a woman, that G-d made her into a woman, and that G-d made me into a man.

**Question:** Are you even thinking about that when you are up there?

**Rebbe Shlomo:** No, no, you see, I'll tell you what. Most of us sadly enough are so coarse that the moment they think man and woman, they think something else. Listen, if I tell you this is an apple, this is a pear, it doesn't affect you badly. So the same way, if I'm on that level of being completely 'there,' in awe before G-d's creation, so then I'm aware that this is a woman, this is a man, this is a Zen Buddhist, this is a Jew. I'm therefore in touch with what everything really is, because this is the way it should be.

**Question:** Before you were talking about cockroaches. If you see a cockroach and you're really high, you think "what a beautiful cockroach?"

**Rebbe Shlomo:** Right.

What do you think? It may be the highest.

**Question:** Maybe it is the highest, but I'm wondering if the highest is if you don't say this is a beautiful cockroach.

**Rebbe Shlomo:** What else should I think it is? It really is.

**Question:** "This is a beautiful creature."

**Rebbe Shlomo:** Oh, no, no. G-d didn't make a creature, He made a cockroach. Why shouldn't I be aware it's a cockroach? Why shouldn't I be aware of it? If I see a mountain and a valley, would I say,

"I'm so turned on I don't know which one is a valley, which is a mountain?" You see, if I'm on the level of *michuyav hamitziut,* really there, on the contrary, I'm really aware, not less aware.

You see, the sad thing is that in all Eastern religions, they always think that the less aware you are, the holier you are. But for us *Yiddelach,* it's just the other way around.

**Question:** But could it be that if you're on top of a mountain, you wouldn't say, "What a beautiful mountain," you would say, "What a beautiful place this is." And if you are in a valley, you wouldn't say "This is a beautiful valley...."

**Rebbe Shlomo:** But the thing is a valley, right?

**Question:** If He wants distinctions....

**Rebbe Shlomo:** No, no, listen, I'll tell you something. Don't be angry, but this sounds to me...

**Question:** Don't be angry with me Shlomo, because I've been thinking about these kinds of questions so much it's bursting out of me.

**Rebbe Shlomo:** First of all, you are my top holy man. But I'm just telling you what I think. Maybe I'm wrong, but you're asking me. Right?
For me, to be *mamash, michuyav hamitziut* means that I am completely aware.

I'll tell you something very strong. Do you think if I'll talk to an Eskimo, or, let's say I have some Chinese friends - there is something especially beautiful about Chinese people. So the more I'm aware of G-d's creation, the more I'm aware that those people have something that maybe I don't have. So if I say, "We are *mamash* one, I'm not Chinese and you're not Jewish," this is stupid. On the contrary.

The hardest thing is when you really are a little bit universal, and then sadly, we already start thinking that we have to cut everything out. It is not true.

When we talk about when Mashiach is coming, that the world will be one, does that mean that everybody will have the same face, the same nose? G-d forbid! You know, the holiness of G-d's Oneness is that G-d's Oneness will shine out of everybody, but everybody will be what they are.

Without telling you stories, it so happens I mentioned Swami Sachtananda because we are *mamash* soul friends. And it never happened that I am less of a Jew when I am in his presence, or he is less of a Hindu in my presence. On the contrary, *mamash* I am completely a Jew. It is only the little Jewish kids who hang around there, they don't know where it's at anymore. Because those Jewish kids, since their parents never gave them this real existence, so they are still 'free choice' *Yiddelach.* They're hanging about, they never know where it's at.

I don't know if I made myself clear to you, but I really think you know.

I'll tell you something very strong. This whole idea that women have to stop being women because it's not holy, this is a very low kind of holiness. Listen, the Torah is the holiest in the world. Every word is holy. So maybe the Torah should never say, "This is a man. This is a woman." Maybe the Torah should say, "Somebody Avraham. Somebody Sarah." But this isn't it. The holiness of the Torah is that the Torah says, "This is Adam. This is Eve. Man and woman. This was Sarah. This was Avraham." If I ask Avraham, "Tell me the truth, are you a man or a woman?" Would he say, "Wait till later, I'm too high now, I'll tell you later." It doesn't go. Avraham said, "I really am a man, G-d created me a man." And Sarah will say all the time, "I'm a woman."

You see, I'll tell you something. You're 100% right, because the way we are living in this world, the moment you say man and woman, you think of 'something else.' But if man and woman would first bring to your mind that G-d created the world in a most beautiful way, and that there is such a thing as men and women, and it would remind you of G-d and not of something else,... if I'm on that level....

When it comes to man and woman, we are so accustomed to the sad fact that if someone tells us, "man and woman," right away, who knows what he's thinking about....
That means, walls, right away. The way we are living, you think that if I say, "I'm a Jew and he's a Zen Buddhist," that means I make a long wall. Why? There doesn't have to be any walls, and it doesn't make me stop being a Jew.

☙❧

# The Depths of *Mikva* [Ritual Bath]

Rebbe Nachman says: The Kabalists say it doesn't say that G-d created water. It says G-d created heaven and earth. Water is between creation, and before creation. Water makes things grow, water flows beyond space, it's infinite.

Our mistakes come from those times when we disconnect ourselves from before creation. When we immerse in water completely, we connect beyond time and space.

Pure means open, I'm open to receive. Impure means not open to receive, not ready, closed up.

One of the things given to Chava [Eve] in order to fix the mistake of eating from the Tree of Knowledge is going to the *mikva* [ritual bath]. The Tree of Knowledge is knowing and doing things on the outside, though closed up on the inside.

Water is open to the inside.

In Hebrew, *mayim* is water. Before creation, there was only Oneness. After creation, G-d and the world are two-ness. Water has the deepest depths of oneness.

First, I want you to know, there are two kinds of closeness. One kind of closeness is when I'm standing face to face with you; *Mamash*, you look at me and I look at you. This is very close, but it's not the closest. The closest is when I'm so close to somebody that I can't even see him anymore.

In the *mikva*, you close your eyes. When you kiss someone, you're so close to them that you have to close your eyes to really see them on the inside. In the *mikva*, you close your eyes because you're so close, you see so much, so deep.

Rebbe Nachman says that when Mashiach is coming, the world will be filled with G-d knowledge like water in the ocean. When Mashiach is coming it will be like being under the water of the *mikva*, so very deep, so awesome. Mashiach knowledge is like water knowledge.

Rebbe Nachman says there are two levels: G-d is first [*rishon*], like G-d is the first and the last, and G-d is One [*echad*].

We say, *"Shema Yisrael HaShem Elokeinu HaShem Echad* [Listen Israel, the Lord is our G-d, the Lord is One.]" This is so important. I want you to know, in the deepest depths, that earth is on the level of G-d is first, and water is on the level of G-d is One.

Under the water we know that G-d is One.

The Hebrew word *"mayim"* [water] has no plural - water and waters, there is only *mayim*. Water accommodates more water gladly.

What is so special about water? What is water all about? The Gemara says that, in a *mikva*, if only one hair is sticking out of the water, then the *mikva* doesn't work. You must be completely immersed in the water. Inside knowledge....

Before Adam ate from the Tree of Knowledge, he was *mamash* so very connected to Above. This doesn't come from outside knowledge, from a book. This is *mamash* inside knowledge.

What's the difference? 'One and one equals two,' this is outside knowledge. 'One and one is One,' this is inside knowledge. The Tree of Knowledge is outside knowledge.

I want you to know, when you're in the water, completely covered with water, you have inside knowledge.

G-d cursed the snake; the snake is on the earth. Growing things are in the earth; a seed planted in the earth needs water to grow. Water connects the seed to the inside of the earth. So inside us we also need the water of inside knowledge to nurture our growth.

Water tells the earth, "Open your inside. Open inside."

Pure means open to receive, and impure means not open to receive.

Sweet holy knowledge is coming to us from heaven, but we need to be open to it, to be pure to receive it, so we must go to the *mikva*.

A pure person is someone who is so very open.

The more I connect, the more I remember. In Hebrew, the word *"choshech"* [darkness], is almost the same word as *"shocheach"* [forgetting].

You know what the Tree of Knowledge is? Why does it bring death into the world? Because it is disconnected from the inside.

You know what death is? Death means the soul is not connected to the body.

You know what water is? When G-d created the world there was separateness. You know what "G-d is hiding from the world" means? G-d is One, and the world is two.

You know what happened to Adam and Eve after they ate from the Tree of Knowledge? They became two, but Paradise is one.

Torah does not specifically mention that water was created, because after creation it would be two, but water is still one.

On Shabbos you know that G-d is One; Shabbos is peace and blessing. Always go to the *mikva* before Shabbos.

Rebbe Nachman says that *mikva* comes from the word *tikva* which is hope. Water is anti-death because dying and giving up hope are like the same thing.

Rebbe Nachman says that *mikva* is the water, the river that comes out of Paradise. *Mikva* water is pure on the level of oneness.

Why, in order to be kosher, is water from the *mikva* to be untouched, [not via a secondary implement]? Because it must be untouched water, coming straight down from heaven. *Mikva* water is pure and untouched on the level of oneness.

Water comes to the inside of your life.

The greatest crime in the world is when you are disconnected from your inside. If you live your life outside without being connected to your inside, what good is it? Water comes to the inside of your life.

What is the water doing to the earth? What is the water doing to you when you go into the *mikva*? The earth has to believe in itself in order to grow. The snake comes to Eve and says, "You want to be like G-d? Eat from the Tree of Knowledge." You know what the snake does to you? Why is the snake biting you in the soul? Because the specialty of the snake is to reduce you all the way down to nothing. The snake says, "You are nothing, but if you eat from the Tree of Knowledge then you'll know what's right and what's wrong, then you'll be like G-d, imitating G-d." But my knowledge of good and evil doesn't come from outside, it doesn't need eating apples to know what's right and what's wrong, it comes from inside. The snake thus cuts you down taking away your self-confidence all the time.

Humanity very much needs someone to lift us up. G-d says to Adam, "Cut off the snake's head." Take the lowest person and lift him up.

You know friends, people who never tasted the tree of life, what can you tell them about good and bad?

Rebbe Nachman says, the water of the *mikva* is *mamash* the highest from heaven. A person has to know that all their problems and brokenness, all their falling apart, is because they are not completely surrounded by G-d's heavenly love. If they go to the *mikva*, they will feel surrounded by G-d's love.

Deep inside nobody wants to do wrong. Deep inside everyone wants to be so good, but sometimes my inside and my outside are disconnected. Water connects the outside of the earth to the inside of the earth, water connects my outside to my inside, water connects my inside to the deepest surrounding light. Under the water in the *mikva* I am *mamash* completely surrounded by the most heavenly illumination.

You know what water does to you? *Mikva* makes you *mamash* into one. Every drop of water is one. The Zohar *hakodesh* says one and one is one.

Rebbe Nachman says that when you go to the *mikva, mamash,* it takes away all the fighting and all the anger. This has such deep meaning. Because *mikva* makes you connect to the reality that, "G-d is One."

Rebbe Nachman says that anger comes from thinking that I'm the master of the world; but in the *mikva* I know that only G-d is the master.

Compassion is better than anger.

Angry words can be like a knife in the heart because we're disconnected from our inside place, disconnected from our oneness.

Rebbe Nachman says that there is earth knowledge and water knowledge. Remember what was said before, that when Mashiach is coming, the world will be filled with G-d knowledge like water covering the ocean. Water knowledge is so deep, so pure, so beautiful, so good, so inside.

Rebbe Nachman says, some people think: "When I have a cold I shouldn't go to the *mikva*." *Mikva* doesn't make you sick; on the contrary, it's the most healing thing in the world.

Rebbe Nachman says, when I'm in the *mikva*, holy knowledge enters me. When I'm in the *mikva* I have vessels to receive knowledge from the heavenly Source, because I'm in another world in the *mikva*, not in this world.

When I go to the *mikva* I close my eyes, like when kissing, and I connect to a higher world, with deeper knowledge.

When I'm in the *mikva*, completely surrounded by heavenly water, I see that G-d is absolutely surrounding me. G-d is taking care of my every step. G-d helps every one of us.

When you pray in the *mikva*, when you turn your heart to G-d, when you pray, at that moment G-d is taking care of you.

Rebbe Nachman says, what did Eve do when she ate from the Tree of Knowledge? She disconnected herself from heaven and earth and she connected herself to outside knowledge, the knowledge of good and evil. *Mikva* is connection to inside knowledge.

Friends, open your hearts to this, anyone who wants to purify himself can go to the *mikva*.

Why did the snake go to Eve and not to Adam? Because Eve is a woman, and to bring children, life, into this world is so holy, it's G-d-like. Husband, wife, and children are connected to holiness and oneness by *mikva*.

Pureness is coming from heaven; holiness is coming from heaven. Pureness is a vessel for receiving the highest and deepest heavenly inside knowledge. Snake-talk is outside knowledge, but inside is the will of my soul, inside knowing. *Mikva* is giving strength to the inside of my inside of my inside, and connecting me to the highest place in heaven.

Water knowledge is inside knowledge.

Water is inside, *mikva* is inside, Shabbos is inside. Under water I disconnect from outside knowledge and connect to inside knowledge.

*Mikva* gives hope to people. The world needs to be purified, it needs hope.

Jerusalem is the *mikva* for Israel.

Rebbe Nachman says that to go to the *mikva* is to know that G-d is One; not that G-d is first, but that G-d is One, absolutely. You have to go to the *mikva* to be connected to inside, to oneness… deepest… highest… inside.

ℰᘏᘩ

# The Only Counteraction for Anger is if you're Filled with Joy

The very first thing when you decide to become a servant of G-d is that from that very instant on, you have to be filled with joy. Because G-d cannot stand sadness.

Sometimes I hate myself for it, but it's true; I can't stand *shleppers* / sad people, hanging on me when they're asking for help. If they could only say the same thing with joy, then, "No problem, of course I will help."

## Wholesale sin

There is, so to speak, 'retail sin' and 'wholesale sin.' An example of a retail sin is, let's assume I came here and I was so very hungry, and there was a piece of ham lying here and nobody was looking. Let's assume I took it and ran up to my room, and ate a little ham... Let's assume it was a terrible sin. But it was still a little retail sin.

But when I'm sad, that's not a retail sin, it's a wholesale sin. It is affecting my whole being.

If I eat a little piece of ham and come downstairs, and nobody noticed I stole the ham, nothing happens to the people around me. But if I come downstairs and I am sad, every person who looks at me gets the creeps. I change the vibrations of the world. It's not merely a wholesale sin, it's a world sin! And who am I to commit a sin against humanity, against the whole world?

The moment you go into the service of G-d, the moment you decide to become a perfect human being, at that moment it has to be clear to you that the greatest sin in the world is to be sad.

And Rebbe Nachman says, hold on with your last bit of strength to be happy.

You have to feel like you're drowning in the ocean, and you have just one piece of wood to hold onto, and the name of that piece of wood is joy. You have to fight for it with your very life. Because if you're not filled with joy, you're absolutely drowning.

## What should I do?

O.K. so you say, "Look, I'm sorry, I'm sad; what should I do?" The answer, or rather one of the answers, is like this:

Usually, sad people are sad because they believe that everything is bad, everything is black. "Everyone hates me, I hate everyone, everybody is rotten, everybody is ugly." So, Rebbe Nachman says, "Can you possibly find one person in the world who is not so ugly / terrible? You must have once met someone you loved. You think you're terrible? Let's assume it's true. But maybe, one day in your life...."

You see, if a person is sad, you can't argue with him because he's too stupid to argue with; you can't tell him he's not ugly; he'll tell you, "I know I'm ugly, I'm not stupid." So you say, "It's true, I'm convinced. But, was there one moment when your soul was shining? Was there one moment when you were beautiful? Was there one moment when your soul was shining? If you have got one such moment in your life, it's unbelievable. A lot of people live for 70 years without one good moment. You had one good moment, so jump out of your skin with joy, that G-d gave you one happy moment. And maybe G-d is ready to give you another happy moment."

### You're sick because you're so sad

Rebbe Nachman said something, which has been proven today. You're not doing G-d a favor when you're happy, you're doing yourself a favor, because, sadly enough, this is the sad truth - sickness only comes upon you when you're sad. If you're completely filled with joy, then sickness has no admission. Not a physical, nor mental, nor any sickness in the world; sickness cannot reach you. And even if, G-d forbid, it reaches you, it is so much on the outskirts of your being, that it takes practically no time at all to heal it.

But, if you're sad, then when sickness, G-d forbid, falls upon you, it takes over your whole being.

He also says that you are not sad because you're so sick, you're sick because you're so sad. If you were happy, you would not be sick. You're getting sicker because you are so sad.

### So what you have to do is...

Can you stop being clever for one hour? You're sad because, logically, cleverly, you have the right to be sad. You're right. So be a fool for one hour. Be G-d's fool for one hour. Have you ever seen fools? They're always happy. And this is not stupid, they have something holy. In Kabalistic terms, it's called *shtus dekedusha*, holy foolishness.

You think that when you are sad, you really have a little perspective on life? You are sad because you think that your life is not in order. Do you really know what's going on with you? Rebbe Nachman says; I promise that when you are sad, you can't even think straight. But if you are filled with joy, then you can really put aside one hour and really think clearly, "What am I doing with my life?"

G-d refuses to send messages to a sad person. G-d is ready to let you know what to do, but if you walk around with a long face, G-d is not interested in talking to you. But if you are filled with joy, G-d lets you know what to do.

The most important thing in the world is to pour out your heart before G-d. Talk to G-d.

When you're sad, there's such a wall between you and G-d, you can't pour out your heart before Him. But if you're filled with joy....

When someone is sad, you cannot relate to that person, they're so into their sadness they make two million walls around themselves. And you want to tell them, "It's OK, I'm with you, I love you, I care for you." But it doesn't reach them. But if they are filled with joy...

I want to tell you something unbelievable, without sounding sad. There were some people in concentration camps in Auschwitz, *Chassidishe mentsh*, [Hassidic men], who walked around filled with joy. And, can you believe, someone told me that there were two *Chassidishe Yidden* [Hassidic Jews], who would literally dance all through Friday night?

### How do I know I'm not fooling myself?

One of Rebbe Nachman's strongest teachings is that you can fool your head, you can fool your hands, but you cannot fool your feet. So if I say, "Do you notice how happy I am? I'm singing with joy." How do I know I'm not fooling myself? The answer is very simple. If someone says, "Do you want to dance?" and I say, "Really, I'm too tired," then I'm lying; I'm not happy.

Sometimes you go to a wedding and you just can't get up to dance, because there's absolutely no love in the air. Your feet pick up on it. Other times you go to a wedding and you absolutely can't stop dancing. In your head, you don't know the difference. But your feet always know. So Rebbe Nachman says, if you want to test your joy, watch your feet.

In Hebrew, the three major Holidays are simply called the *shalosh regalim* [the three feet (supports)], because when you are happy, it's the feet that know it. The fourth foot will be when the Mashiach [Messiah] is coming; right now the wagon is still riding on three wheels.

### I still can't get it together

Now suppose I say, "I know all this, but I still can't get it together." Rebbe Nachman says, you must know, whenever you do a good deed, at that moment they're not only opening the gates in Heaven for you to do a good deed, but at that very instant they are also opening gates for you to be happy. Because how can you do something for G-d without joy? So since G-d wants you to do it, He also opens gates for you to be happy.

So if you're sad and heartbroken, and someone calls you up and says, "Can you do me a favor?" and you answer, "Right now I'm too sad to do you a favor," it's crazy; right now G-d was opening gates of joy for you, and at that moment G-d would have opened up all the gates of joy for you.

So Rebbe Nachman says, if you can't get it together, find one person and do them a favor, and at that moment all the gates of Heaven are open.

Forget about doing someone a favor; do you know, when you are happy, how much life you give to the people around you? Do you know how much death you give to people when you are sad? Rebbe Nachman says, do you have a right to kill the people next to you?

So he says, do you know what you are doing when you're filled with joy? You're absolutely emanating life!

And he says that the greatest thing in the world is to give life to somebody else.

What's the most G-d like thing in the world? It's giving life to people, giving life to the world. So the moment you're filled with joy, you are absolutely on a G-d level, on the highest level.

**Erase pain from people's faces**

Most people have so much pain inside, not only they have nobody to tell it to, they don't even have words for it. Because most people are filled with pain. Rebbe Nachman says, they have so much pain, and they don't have words for it, but it is written on their faces. When you walk around with joy, and you make that person smile, you erase a little bit of that pain which has no words.

And when you erase that pain which has no words, eventually they open up and they tell you their problem. That's OK. The moment it hurts, it's already like, in the upper spheres. Because it was so deep, they couldn't get it out. But when you are filled with joy - you have given them a little life, then they can bear it.

**Guarding your children**

Then Rebbe Nachman says, the greatest way of guarding your children, so that they should always be alive, they should always be happy, they should always be well, is if parents are always happy. What they really need is for their parents to be filled with joy. And the joy of the parents is like a little wall around the babies.

**I don't need anything else**

One more thing. What is really called joy? How much joy do you need in order to say, "I am happy?" When I meet a girl I love the most, I don't have to say, "OK, what shall we do?" as if meeting was not enough, there has to be a little added attraction, a little movie, an little dancing. I am completely filled, I'm completely elated, that's it. Maybe we'll go to the movie also, but who cares?

So Rebbe Nachman says that joy is that this moment fills me so much that I don't need anything else in the world, I don't need anything else.

And he says, you know what it means to do a *mitzvah*, to do a good deed, to do someone a favor? That doing somebody a favor fills your heart so much that you could live on this joy.

Sometimes someone asks you to do a favor, and it's so heavy for you to do it. Because it was not done with joy. But imagine if you do it with so much joy that just this one deed could keep you going forever. You know how much life there is in that favor? How much holiness?

Then he says that you need a lot of *chutzpah*, you need a lot of audacity, to make it in this lifetime. And you don't have this audacity unless you are filled with joy.

ॐ

# Anger

One of the things we learned is that if you are standing on a roof, and you are standing near the middle of the roof, then there is no danger of your falling off, so theoretically it doesn't matter if there is a fence on the roof or not. But if you are standing right on the edge and you are in danger of falling, then you really need a fence to keep yourself from falling. So in the same way, if a person doesn't get angry, he doesn't need a fence, but most of us are getting angry all the time, so we need some kind of fence to protect us.

Rebbe Nachman says that a strong fence against getting angry is to make a vow. If you make a vow, you really have to keep it, because the Torah says not to say G-d's name in vain. So if you make a vow it is a very strong thing. It gives you strength to keep it.

But he also says; don't kid yourself. Don't make a vow that you're not going to get angry the rest of your life, because you'll break it, and it has no meaning. Even if you make a vow for just ten minutes - "I won't get angry," that is very good. If you can go for ten minutes without getting angry, then you have kept your vow, and it gives you more strength for the next time.

The Hebrew word for vow, *shvua*, comes from the word *savea*, which means satisfied, or full. A vow is really like food for the soul, it fills you with the strength to keep it. The Ziditchover Rebbe heard that Rebbe Nachman said he was making vows, so he said, "Even to make a vow for five minutes, you still have to be on the level."

If you are really immersed in anger, and you can't even make a five-minute vow, the only thing you can do is be like an ox plowing the field, and really work on it. Lift yourself up to the level where you can make a vow, then make a vow for five minutes.

Rebbe Nachman says, how do you have to talk to yourself when you make a vow? You have to call yourself; "Shlomo, the son of Pesia, don't speak evil." You have to talk to yourself, call yourself by your name.

ജരു

# Angry at Myself

One of the very deep teachings of Rebbe Nachman is, though I am sure you know it. Everybody knows it and feels it, but maybe we are not so careful with it.

What happens to me if I make a mistake? And I don't mean, "By mistake, instead of buying apples, I bought peaches." Sometimes I really make strong mistakes. Do you know what happens to me then? Deep, deep, deep inside, I begin to hate somebody.

And it's not that I make a mistake, and then I hate Moishele, or I hate Chanele. The way my hatred starts is that somewhere deep, deep, deep inside, I become so angry at myself. I am so angry….

### You need a big soul to love people

Let's say, in my life I have to meet thirty people. So G-d gives me a soul, my soul is so big, that I have enough in my soul to love thirty people for real. This is besides loving the whole world in general. A lot of people love the whole world, and yet they can't stand their own wives. I am not talking about that, but for real.

I have seen it a lot of times. Imagine somebody has two children, and then they say, "Let's have another child." And the husband, or the wife, just doesn't want to. It is not that they are bad. Deep, deep inside they know, "My *neshama*, my soul, is big enough for two children, but my soul isn't big enough for three."

I know a couple, and she absolutely wants to have ten children. Not that he is bad, but he says, "I can have three, I can have four. I can't have ten." This doesn't come from your consciousness. It comes from this deepest, deepest unconsciousness.

I am not a mechanic. If someone says to me, listen, "Can you fix a car?" I don't know how to fix a car. I don't know the first thing about it.
"Can you lift up ten thousand tons?" I can't.

Let's say I am supposed to love and be close to thirty people. So my soul is, let's say, thirty thousand feet wide. The first time I make a mistake, something happens to me inside; I am a little bit angry at myself. I am angry, and bitter. A little bit of hatred creeps in, and suddenly, my soul is too small now. I cannot love thirty people anymore. And only G-d in heaven knows how this operates, this depends upon closeness of the soul. But suddenly I hate somebody. I am angry at somebody. I am angry at myself.

I want you to know something. It is crazy, but I am sure it is clear to you. All the people who are yelling at other people, do you know what their problem is? Not that they are angry at other people; they do something wrong so much, their heart is full with anger... they can't... they can't.

## The test of Joseph

Our holy Rabbis teach us that Joseph had such a big test with the wife of Potifar, (without getting involved in the depths) and then he was in prison for twelve years. First of all, she threw him into prison because he didn't want to do anything. Then, for twelve years he was in prison, and she came three times a day. And you know that from prison in Egypt, you don't get out alive. You don't get out.... So she says to him, "One time – and I let you out of prison. A half a time, and I will let you out." He says, "No."

And then, he wasn't even angry at his brothers. And here I want you to open your hearts. How deep this is... If Joseph would have done something wrong with the wife of Potifar, he would have been so angry at himself, that he would never have had the strength to forgive his brothers. Because in order not to be angry at your brothers, your soul has to be complete.

You see, if my soul is absolutely complete, if I am whole inside with myself, between me and myself, then I am not angry. So if someone says to me, "Hey, listen, I did you wrong," I say, "Forget it."

You know, Joseph never said to his brothers, "I forgive you for selling me as a slave." He said, "Forget it. If you wouldn't have sold me as a slave, the whole world would have died from hunger. It is a miracle. Thank you so much for selling me as a slave." And this was not stupid Sunday morning Hebrew school teaching. It was for real. "*Ve'ata, al te'atzvu*. [Don't be downhearted.]"

## Inside fighting

Rebbe Nachman begins to say. Sometimes my mistake was caused by my body. Then my soul is angry at my body.

Imagine I do something just for my pleasure. In the meantime everything goes wrong, and my soul is angry at my body, "How could you do this?"

Sometimes my sin doesn't come from my body, it comes from my head. It was not physical pleasure, it was something else. Then my body is angry at my soul, "Why don't you have your act together?"

And the moment there is fighting inside of me. The moment I have inside fighting, there is one person that I hate each time I make a mistake. I may not ever know who this person is, but it always is someone who is close to me. The moment you make a mistake, you are angry at somebody. And, obviously, you are mostly angry at yourself.

## My soul is crying inside

One more thing. This is deep, deep, deep. Imagine I would hear a voice crying for help. Imagine I am sitting here, and deep, deep inside myself I would hear a voice of someone drowning in the ocean, crying for help, but there is nothing I can do. You know, imagine I would have ears that could hear what is going on in Venice, Italy, and someone is drowning there. I can hear them yelling for their lives. The only thing is, I am sitting here, and there is nothing I can do. What would my reaction be? I would be nervous. I would just blow my mind.

The truth is, whenever I make a mistake, my soul is crying so much inside. My soul is crying inside. And, even if I don't fix it... Let's say I am the president of General Motors, I am sitting here talking about a new car, and inside my soul is crying, and I don't do anything. So I don't know how to handle it; and the first time my secretary makes a mistake and instead of writing, "My dear friend," she writes, "My dearest friend," I want to kill her. Because I am beside myself. I am besides myself...

Rebbe Nachman says, I want you to know that all the people who start those big fights in the world, those big wars, it is because they do so much wrong, and they are so much besides themselves. How do you fight with yourself? They don't know how to do it. So they direct all this fighting to the outside. Towards others.

## A spiritually dead person

Now he says that there is an unbelievable Zohar that says, (we should all live long), my soul lives forever, and G-d forbid, at a certain point, my body dies, but the soul lives forever. But then, the Zohar HaKadosh says, there are some people whose soul died a long time ago, but heir body is still alive. Unbelievable. You know, sometimes you meet people, and they look like a carcass.

There is an unbelievable story about Eliahu HaNavi, Elijah the prophet, who came into a city, and he, with the wise man of the city, took a walk. They passed by the carcass of a dead cow, and the wise man of the city said, "Uchhh, it smells so bad." Elijah the prophet says to him, "I don't think it is smelling so bad. A cute little cow died, I am sorry that the cow died." Then, one of those people who is dead while he is alive, the real carcass, he is walking down the street, and the wise man of the city, said, "Oh, good morning, Mr. Max Cohen, who donated ten thousand dollars for the new temple." *Gevalt*, it's a living carcass!

First of all, a person has to know what a spiritually dead person is: when he can't even hear his own soul crying. You know what that means? The crying inside was so strong, that he couldn't bear it, he couldn't bear it. You know, physical suicide, is that I cut my veins, *chas veshalom* [G-d forbid]. Spiritual suicide is that I cut myself off from my soul. I don't want to hear it.

## Get up and dance like crazy

Rebbe Nachman says, imagine I hear my own soul crying. What am I supposed to do? Rebbe Nachman says, the first thing is to get up and dance like crazy. "Thank G-d I am still alive. Unbelievable. I thought I was gone forever." Imagine somebody commits suicide and he thinks he is dead. Then he wakes up, "Hey, it didn't work." *Gevalt*, he says, '*mazal tov,*' he is still alive. Oh, good, there is hope.

## I don't want to live like a cow

I want you to know one more thing. A lot of people, one side of them just wants to have a good time. Eat, drink, have a little money, have a good time, have a lot of power.

And on the other side, there is their soul; "I don't want to live like a cow." And what most people do is, they push it into a little closet, and lock it up; "I don't want to hear it."

What is my first step? My first step is that I take my soul out of my closet.

## *Hisbodedut*

Everybody is talking about meditation. According to Rebbe Nachman, the deepest meditation… (I am not knocking other meditations, G-d forbid. I am just telling you one side.) Rebbe Nachman says that you cannot be a servant of G-d unless you do *hisbodedut*. Just to sit somewhere and just *mamash* listen to your own soul cry. Because the truth is, the soul is so connected to G-d, and your own soul always knows best. Your own soul always knows best.

Remember, we were learning that the soul has clear prophesy.

Today, everyone makes money on 'prophesy,' I just saw an ad somewhere in New York, "Sister Toba, from New York. Clear Prophesy." You don't have to go to her and pay five dollars for clear prophesy. You see, the great prophets had prophesy for the world. You are not a prophet for the world; there are just a few who have prophesy for the world. But You are a prophet for yourself. And a prophet doesn't mean, "I know the future and the past." This is just a little side-kick of prophesy. The real prophesy is that your soul is telling you how to fix your life. How to fix your life.

## My own soul tells me what to do

A person came to the *heilege* grandson of the seer of Lublin, and he said, "Rebbe, I am broke. I am in such bad shape. I want you to know, I have nothing."

So the Rebbe says to him, "It is not true; every person has something. What do you have?"

In the book of Lamentations, there is a passage that says, *"Im yesh machov kemachovi /* is there pain like my pain?" *"Machov"* in Hebrew means pain.

The person answers, "Rebbe, do you want to know what I have? I have *machov*" - meaning pain.

But it also just so happened that there was a village right next to the Rebbe's city, where he was, with the name Machov.

"Oh," says the Rebbe, "Thank G-d, you have something. What are you *kvetching* [complaining about]? You are ok. Go to the city of Machov, and G-d will help you."

You know what I say; What do you do when you walk into a restaurant, and you order coffee, and you cannot pay? You have got to order another one, because you can't walk out, because you have no money to pay.

Ok, so he is sitting there in this restaurant in Machov, drinking one cup of coffee after the other. He cannot run out. Most probably it is the one hundred and seventy fifth cup of coffee, and they think he is not normal. He is waiting. The Rebbe said, "Go to Machov." Waiting.
Suddenly the door opens, and a very high officer from the Polish army walks in, and he says, "Moishele?"

He answers, "Yeah."

The Polish officer says, "Don't you remember me? Ivan, your neighbor?" Unbelievable. So this was a little Polish boy, Ivan, who was the neighbor of his father. His father, at one point, was a rich person, and the next door neighbors were poor people. His father paid for the education for this little boy Ivan. And, because of his father, Ivan hit it big in the Polish army.

He says, "Ivan, you are such a high officer?"

Ivan says, "Moishe, what happened to you? You were so rich!"

He says, *"Oy,* I went bankrupt."

Ivan says, "Moishele, you know something? I know you are good with numbers, and I need a good accountant in the army. Do you want to work for me?"

"How could I not?" he answers.

So, right there...

He goes back to the Rebbe to thank him, "Thank you so much for sending me to Machov. And my old bodyguard Ivan came..." Then he says, "Rebbe, what a miracle!"

The Rebbe said, "You don't understand, it was not a miracle. It was not even that I told you what to do. The truth is, whenever we don't know what to do, our own soul tells us what to do. Your own soul tells you what to do. The only thing is, you never took the time to listen to yourself. So I got it out of you. I said, 'What do you have?' And you said, 'Machov.' Ah, good."

## So what do you do?

Ok, so Rebbe Nachman says, what do I do, what do I do if I am completely torn apart?
Or, G-d forbid, I already reached the level that my own soul cries and I shut the door so that I shouldn't hear it.
Or, thank G-d, I am still hearing it, but I just don't want to hear it, it drives me crazy. It drives me crazy.
Or, maybe, G-d forbid I am *mamash* dead, dead inside.
You know, as long as I feel bad about it... as long as I know I did wrong, you are still ok. You are still ok. And I don't mean feeling guilty. Guilty means I walk around like... dejected.

So what do you do? The truth is, when your soul is crying that you did wrong, the soul also always cries into you what you have to do.

## G-d wants me to be a whole person

We always think, "G-d wants me to do this, and He wants me to do that." G-d wants me to be whole. G-d wants me to be a whole person. It is not a question of whether I did right or wrong; the moment I start doing wrong and make mistakes, I am just half myself. I am just half of myself.

*Gevalt,* if you could only tell this to the world: I want you to know, when parents come home, and they yell at their children, and they are looking for an excuse to yell at their children. The sad truth is, they did something wrong, and they are dead, and they are just yelling.

If a husband and wife yell at each other, it was not the woman it was not the man; it is not the other one: One of them, or both of them, did something wrong. *Chhhh.*

This is so deep. You see, the world always thinks, "I have to repent for what I did wrong." This is a very cute kind of repentance. Sure, we did something wrong, we will fix it.
We are talking about something so much deeper. How do I make my soul whole again?

People who hate, you know what their problem is? They did so much wrong already, and their soul has become so small, that they really can't love anymore. They are running out of soul. Right? They are running out of soul. They just don't have the capacity anymore.

## Real holy people

And who are all those real, real holy people in the world? Their souls are so whole.

Maybe, when they were born, G-d gave them the capacity of loving twenty people. And they worked their way up to forty, fifty, one hundred. And maybe, eventually, eventually, *mamash*, they have the capacity of really turning to every human being in the world.

I want you to know, the holy Bal Shem, the special thing about him - besides the holiness - was that towards every human being, he was not just giving him honor, he had this awesome, awesome, closeness. This awesome closeness.

I want you to know, I had the privilege of walking down the street with the Bobover Rebbe, one of the first Friday nights when he arrived from Europe. He moved into the neighborhood of Eighty-Fifth Street, on the West Side. And I don't have to tell you, the West Side, especially when he moved in, was all filled with drunkards, prostitutes, and dope pushers. Really heavy stuff. You know the way they look. I mean, I have nothing to do with them. It's another world.

That Friday night, someone had a baby, and the Rebbe wanted to visit them, and it was one o'clock at night. He went from Eighty-Seventh Street, to One Hundred and Tenth Street. Do you know what happened? We just walked along the street, and suddenly, all the drunkards, all the dope pushers, they waved at us, and we waved back at them. It was like after the Messiah had come.

Do you know how shy, without sounding coarse, how shy prostitutes are? They think very little of themselves. They don't think of themselves as the highest in the world. And they see a Rabbi with a *streimel* walking down the street, they should crawl back into their hole, right? There were two little prostitutes standing on the corner, and they waved at the Rebbe, and the Rebbe smiled. They suddenly looked so big, they looked holy. For one moment their soul was whole.

When you love somebody very much, it is not enough that you love them; the most important thing is to make their soul whole again. To make their soul whole.

When the soul is whole, there is no problem, you can deal with anything.

## White

Imagine, G-d forbid, that yesterday I did something terrible. My soul is now half the size. What happens to me this morning when I wake up?

Friends, I want you to pay attention to this, it's awesome: There is a passage in the Bible [Torah] that says, '*Vayashkem Lavan baboker.*' Laban was the father-in-law of Jacob. Lavan was called 'white.' It has millions of meanings, but in Kabalistic teachings, it is the story, but it is also beyond the story. So Lavan is white. *Vayashkem Lavan baboker.* The white stuff, so to speak, wakes you up in the morning.

You know what white is? Untouched. So the Zohar says that, every morning, something completely white and pure comes down from Heaven, and if I only know how to take it, my soul is whole again. If you could only hold on to that first second when you wake up.

My soul just came down from heaven, and I have a choice, I can put it right back in the box broken in half, the way I was yesterday. Or I can hold on to the way my soul is coming down.

## Two ex-professors

I will bring a very strong example.
A few years ago, it was in all the newspapers, all the psychologists were talking about it. There was a dispute between two very outstanding psychologists. One of them said: all the people in the bowery in New York, the drunkards, the downhearted, the broken, if you would only help them, they would be good. The other psychologist said: they like it there.

So, those two psychologists went down to the bowery, and they pick up two people. One is an ex-professor at Hunter College, and the other one is an ex-concert pianist. Unbelievable.

They pick them up, and they say, "Listen brothers, you have a suite at the most expensive hotel for two nights. And tonight, at twelve o'clock, we will take you out for dinner. All of your old friends from Hunter, and all your old musician friends will be there."

They take them to the plush hotel, and they are given a new suit, a new shirt, and new shoes. Absolutely new. And they hadn't had a decent meal for years.

The saddest thing in the world is that, the next morning, they were gone. They left those new suits on the chair, and they took their old disgusting, smelling, pants and shirt, and they left a note, "We don't like it."

Do you know what that means? They were already so broken… they were already so broken, that they couldn't take normal life.

You know what the Zohar says? What is the greatest sickness in the world? The greatest sickness in the world is if someone puts something sweet in my mouth, and I say, "*Gevalt* is that sour." Someone puts something sour in my mouth, and I say, "Ohh, it is so sweet." Absolutely perverted, it's the end! Not that I am not whole - I'm gone!

You see what it is, every morning G-d takes me out from the bowery. He says, "Hey brother, I give you a new pair of pants, new shoes…" White stuff is coming down from heaven. What are you doing with it?

Rebbe Nachman says, all the holy Rabbis, they made it in their life because they held on to that one moment. They held on to that first moment in the morning.

How did our father Abraham operate? If you remember, the morning prayer was initiated by our father Abraham. And I'm sure you understand, when I say, "Abraham initiated the morning prayer," it does not only mean that we take out a prayer book at a certain point and we pray in the morning. Waking up in the morning; this is Abraham. Because, what do you do when you live in a pagan world? What do you do when everything is broken? Hold on to that drop which is coming down from heaven. White.
You know what that means? Imagine if you could bring the world to the place that one morning every human being in the world would decide: "From now on I am something else." There would be peace in no time.

**The holy Tsanser**

The holy Tsanser, one of our holy masters, when he woke up…. He slept only an hour and a half in twenty-four hours. But you know, the waking up sometimes took six hours. You know what he did when he woke up? He would wash his hands, and sit up in his bed, and he would say, "Master of the world, today I want to serve You." He would *mamash*, yell, "MASTER OF THE WORLD, TODAY I WANT TO SERVE YOU."

Then he said, "*Oy*, you don't mean it yet. *Oy vey*, you are faking all around." He would yell at himself, "Are you for real?"
"Yeah, I'm for real! *Gevalt*, today I want…."

I'm sure that it did not take six hours every day, but there were days, obviously, that, he felt he needed it.

But sometimes I don't have time to wait for the morning, right? I want you to know something; physically there is a morning, and there is a night. But the morning doesn't have to be the clock morning.

Imagine I am *mamash* in darkness, into everything wrong. So Rebbe Nachman says, what is my morning? My morning is that I decide suddenly to look at myself and realize, "*Gevalt* am I holy. *Gevalt* am I good." Sure I made a few mistakes… You know, imagine Miss America needs a manicure, does she stop being Miss America? So I need a little manicure, maybe a pedicure too, maybe I need a shower. It is all outside stuff.

## The first step

The first step is that I have to, I really have to, sit down and listen to the crying of my own soul. Because, in my own soul, I have this holy prophesy.

## The second step

The second thing is, where do I begin? I begin in the morning. And it doesn't mean it has to be in the clock morning. In the morning it is easier, because it is morning and this holy white untouched energy is coming down from heaven.

Imagine you walk through a city early in the morning, just as the sun is coming out. There is something so pure in the air. I am sure you are aware of it. Something like… completely untouched by the world. *Mamash* heavenly.

I want you to know, the worst, worst, worst, time to yell at your husband, your wife, your children, friends, is early in the morning. It is unforgivable. It is unforgivable. Because right in the morning, my soul receives this white stuff from Heaven, untouched.

I don't want to say anything bad, but I have been in the house of some so called holy people. 'So called.' I heard the way they wake up their kids, "GET UP!" and they would say, "I didn't do anything wrong. On the contrary, I did it out of 'love'." What is their problem? Do you know what they destroy? Do you know what they destroy for their kids? Maybe their whole life. In the morning you have to be so soft. Very, very soft.

## Guard your tongue

Rebbe Elimelech says. Obviously you have to guard your tongue. You don't wiggle your tongue like a dog wiggles his tail, right? You want to say everything you think? Watch your tongue. But the most, most important time to watch your tongue is in the morning. In the morning….

Imagine, I wake up in the morning, and I say to my wife, to my children, "Did I tell you what my neighbor did? Ha, ha, ha." Do you know what I am doing, G-d forbid? Destroying the world. G-d is giving you a new suit - like the drunkard on the bowery – G-d says, "Ok, I am giving you a new suit, I am taking you to a plush hotel."

## You can make your own morning

So then Rebbe Nachman says, you can make your own morning. *Mamash*, sit down, and you start thinking; "One time in my life I must have done something good." Suddenly you remember, "*Gevalt*, ten years ago, I did one good thing." And you start working on it. Then you realize, "This was unbelievable, I really did it! Unheard of. And if I did it, that means I am ok. If I did it, that means, inside of me there is something very holy, something untouched. Because the way I act, I could be a murderer. Right? G-d forbid. So how come I did this? Ah, maybe I am not so bad."

I am sending a message to my soul, "Hey, I know you are angry at me for what I did, but I want you to know, one time in my life I did something good." And then there is already, like, this meeting between my body and my soul. Imagine I walk up to my friend and I say, "You are not a good friend, you are disgusting." So my friend says, "Yeah, it's true, yesterday I was disgusting, but last week I saved your life." Ah, it is already a little better.

**Holding on to my roots**

One more thing, and this is very important. When I am angry at myself, do you know what happens to me? I lose my grip on my roots. I lose touch with my own soul. Only when my soul is whole, am I really holding on to my roots. When my soul is half, my soul is a quarter, yes, I am hanging on to my roots with one finger, I am just hanging on. You know, a lot of times I meet people, they are completely uprooted.

Only when my soul is whole, am I really holding on to my roots.

ℰ◌ℜ

# Hisbodedus

You have to do *hisbodedus* all the time. *Hisbodedus* is translated as 'meditation,' but that is not what it is. *Hisbodedus* means being alone with G-d. Being alone with G-d.

You know, according to the world, meditation means, "being alone with yourself." I am not knocking it, it is also very important, I am sure it is very good, but that is not what Rebbe Nachman is talking about. Rebbe Nachman is talking about being alone with G-d.

You know, when we pray we say, *"Ata Hu HaShem levadecha.* G-d, You are alone." Do you know what that means? G-d can only reveal Himself to somebody who knows the secret of being alone with G-d. This is the deepest.

When people get married, the *chuppah* is very beautiful, but it is all nothing. Right after the *chuppah*, the bride and groom have to be alone a little bit. Because the real connection is by being alone. And alone with G-d doesn't just mean I am sitting there and I say, "Ah, I know there is one G-d. I appreciate it. G-d, 'hi'." It has got to be deeper than that. *Mamash*, pouring out your heart before G-d.

Rebbe Nachman was *mamash* pouring out his heart to G-d every second.

Rebbe Nachman said that he could not live more than three or four hours without talking to    G-d.

And the way to do it is, *mamash*, tell G-d everything. You know, we pray a lot to G-d. How about *Mamash* just telling G-d everything.

## Judge ourselves

When do we have time to look at ourselves and *mamash* judge ourselves properly? This is the deepest, friends.

I don't know about you, I know about me. We don't have the faintest idea how to judge ourselves: Am I good? Am I bad? Am I *gevalt*? Am I a creep? What am I?

And do you know when I have a little bit of closeness to my own heart? When I am alone with G-d. Because, when I am alone with G-d, you know what is shining? The inside of the inside of me.

And again, remember, being alone with G-d is not a head *gesheft* [thing]; "I sit down, I have a little mantra...." Please forgive me, I am not knocking it, but that is all head stuff. Being alone with G-d is inside, inside, *neshama* [soul] stuff, it is the deepest depths of my being.

## Don't be afraid to be a *gevalt*

On the one hand, we are afraid to go wrong, but we are also so afraid to be a *gevalt* [exceptionally good]. You know, today, psychology is talking a little bit about being afraid of success, but Rebbe Nachman already said that two hundred years ago, but even deeper. *Gevalt*, are you afraid to be as holy as the Bal Shem Tov? Are you afraid to be the holy of holiest?

And I don't mean ignoring the world, because some people think 'holy' means 'aloof from the world.'

## Holy means it is so close

Let me tell you the outside of it. Do you know what holy means? Why is G-d called holy? Because He is always there. He is *mamash* right there. You know, a holy person is not somebody who is far away. Holy means: "it is so close."

And friends, I want you to know, there is a torah from Rebbe Nachman, and *mamash*, I don't think you can be a Jew without knowing it:

Why is it that when we say "*Shema Yisrael HaShem Elokenu HaShem Echad*, G-d is One," we close our eyes? Rebbe Nachman says, if something is far away from you, you keep your eyes open. The closer it gets, the more you squint your eyes. Rebbe Nachman says that G-d is so close, you have to close your eyes in order to see it.

It's so deep.

And I want you to know something. Why is it that we cannot see ourselves, unless we have a mirror? Because we are so close to ourselves.

But when do you really, so to speak, have a little mirror for your insides, a little holy mirror? When you are alone with G-d. *Mamash*, at that moment, your inside is shining. And when your inside is shining, you are not afraid to be the highest.

### Holy arrogance

What is the deepest secret of life? The deepest secret of life is to be absolutely humble, and to be absolutely arrogant. *Mamash* arrogant.

They always talk about 'surrender,' it is a real pagan word. Do you know what it means to 'surrender?' "I am a *shmate* [rag]. I am nothing." *Chhhh*. "I surrender to G-d. I surrender to *Yiddishkeit*." What do you mean, 'surrender?' Rebbe Nachman always talks about just the opposite: to *mamash* reach such a high point.

Let me ask you a question: would you say a baby has to surrender and stop wearing diapers? One day the baby says, "Mother, I surrender. I won't wear diapers anymore." *Baruch HaShem*, you reached the level that you don't need it anymore. G-d doesn't want us to surrender anything. G-d wants us to reach so high.

The deepest secret of life is how to be absolutely humble, and how to be absolutely arrogant. Because, unless you are arrogant…

Rebbe Nachman talks about it a million times, *azut dekedusha*, holy arrogance. Without holy arrogance you can't do anything.

Is there anything more arrogant than praying; I am sitting here by myself, and I say to G-d, "*Mamash*, I want to talk to You." Really, you mean to say, G-d has nothing else to do than to listen to you? Praying is the biggest *chutzpah* in the world.

Why didn't G-d make a covenant with Noah, only with Abraham? When G-d says to Noah, "I am destroying the world," Noah didn't have enough *chutzpah* to tell G-d, "Don't do it."
G-d says, "If you have no *chutzpah*, I cannot deal with you."

G-d says to Abraham, "I'll destroy Sodom," and Avraham speaks up to G-d, and he says, "No, I don't want You to do it. If there are 50 *tzadikim* [holy people] there, and I will be able to turn the city over from being bad to being good."

I want you to know something so deep. What is the most important thing that we have to teach our children? Humility? Sadly enough, they will learn that a little bit in the world, because there are always enough people who knock us off and put us down. You know what parents have to give over to their children? Holy arrogance. Because maybe if learned from somebody else, it will just be arrogance. Not holy arrogance.

## The balance

This balance of arrogance comes from a very deep place in your heart.

The question is not, 'are you are arrogant or are you humble.' The question is really, what is your relationship to G-d. How do you look at G-d? How do you look at yourself?

The deepest question in the world is, can you really forget yourself for five minutes? Don't surrender. Surrender means, you make yourself like you are nothing. You are a *gevalt*. But can you forget about it for five minutes? Can you live in a world, where there is *mamash* only G-d?

Rebbe Nachman says there are three levels:
First, there is only me.
Then, there is me and G-d.
Then, there is only G-d.

Unless you experience for a few minutes every day that there is only one G-d, you are not balanced.

## Prophesy

When you are sitting, and you are talking to G-d, it has to be clear to you; every word you utter is clear prophesy, because, at that moment, you are connected to such a deep place.

Sometimes we don't know what to do. But imagine, if we would know really how to be alone with G-d, and I would stand before G-d, and I would say, "Master of the World, I don't know what to do." And suddenly, coming out from within me, from the deepest place of my soul, I would hear myself uttering the words answering what I have to do. No question, it is clear prophesy. You have to realize that G-d is sending words into you.

இ)இ

# A Free Gift from G-d
*Likutei Moharan Tinyono 78*

Rebbe Nachman says, there are two sources of life that a person can draw life from:

One source is from 'getting it.' With every word of Torah I am learning, I am filling my soul with life. Every good deed I am doing, I am getting life. It means; I deserve it, so I am getting it. It is as if I go to a bank, and have an account there. I write down on a piece of paper; "Give me ten dollars. Give me one hundred dollars." If I have it in the bank, I will get it. I don't need special pull.

Then, there is another source of life in heaven: you have nothing in the bank, you have nothing... and even whatever you do have has no meaning. It doesn't 'get there.' Imagine if I have one hundred dollars in the bank, but I go to the bank, and what I need to withdraw is two billion dollars. They say, "How much do you have in the account?" I say, "One hundred." It doesn't reach. It's not this kind of thing. They are talking about billions, and you talk about a few rubbles? It doesn't reach.

And you have to realize one more deep thing: on a material level, regardless of the magnitude of the amount, a billion dollars is still made up of one hundred dollars, but just so, so, so many more. On a spiritual level, however, the life level of 'getting it' without deserving it is from a completely different source. It is not even included in it. A hundred dollars has some connection to a billion dollars. A billion dollars is more, but it is made out of many many hundred dollars. But the life level which I can draw from, not by deserving it... just G-d gives it to you....

## G-d *wants* to create the world

When G-d created the world, there was nobody there to deserve it. There was nobody there. You cannot say, "G-d created the world because we deserve it. We were so good and so sweet, so G-d said, 'Ok let's create a world for them'." There was nobody there. So the very, very source of creation is not from deserving it. Not deserving it... G-d <u>wants</u> to create the world.

## Since I created the world, I am giving you the holy Land

And now Rebbe Nachman says the deepest depths in the world; the Gemara [Talmud] says, "Why did G-d tell us the story of the creation? The Torah is actually a book of laws. It should begin with the first law, so why does the Torah begin with the story of the creation?" So the Gemara and Rashi says, "Because someday the world will say to us, 'What are you doing in the holy Land? Why did you steal the holy Land from the other people?' So, therefore, G-d told us, 'I created the world, and since I created the world, I am giving you the holy Land'."

If you think of it in a very deep, deep, deep way, this means millions of things in the deepest depths.

Meaning to say that from the same source where G-d created the world, from that tremendous deep source where nobody can reach... Because my actions can't reach the creation of the world, because I wasn't even there yet. And the world was not created because we deserve it, but just because G-d wants it. It is much deeper than anything I can do to get there. And from that very same source, He gave us the holy Land. On that level.

## The real Torah is only in Israel

But now, why did G-d give us the holy Land? G-d gave us the holy land because the truth is that the real Torah is only in Israel. Because there are so many laws which cannot even be fulfilled in *chuts laarets* [outside of Israel], like all the laws of *truma* and *maser* [tithes], all the laws that have to do with the holy Land. And in fact there is an opinion, according to the Ramban, that even all those laws, for example, putting on *tefillin*, which I have to put on anywhere, but it is not the same. Putting on *tefillin* in Israel is on a different level.

That means that the real Torah was given in Israel.

## He wants us to deserve it

Now listen to this, this tremendous contrast, the deepest depths of the world:
On the one hand, G-d gave us Israel on the level that it has nothing to do with deserving it or not deserving it. But He gave it to us because He wants us to deserve it. He gave it to us because He wants us to do something, and to deserve it.

## It is not just a matter of deserving

You have to know that also in dealing with G-d, there is the level of buying from G-d, and there is the level of receiving a gift. Because, you have to realize, if there is such a thing as 'giving a gift' and 'buying' in this world, that means that such a thing also goes on in heaven. Because if there wouldn't be such a thing in heaven, it wouldn't exist here in this world either. Because the physical world is only like a little mirror of the spiritual world.

That means that also in G-d's dealing with the world, there are two levels:
One level is on the level of buying.
And one level is the level of getting a gift.

Buying means; I am learning, so I deserve it. I am doing a good deed, I deserve it. I am getting something as "payment" for what I did.

And then there is another level; giving you a gift. Giving you a gift... And this is every second.

**The sources of those two levels**

Which are the sources of those two levels, of 'buying' and of 'receiving a gift?' It's very simple: it is 'Mount Sinai,' and 'the creation of the world.'

On Mount Sinai, when G-d spoke to us and He gave us the Torah, He told us what to do, and what not to do. This is on the level of buying. It says so in the Torah, "If you don't deserve it, you won't get this. If you deserve it, I will give you this." Everything is on the level of deserving. You know, it is like G-d is dealing with us, judging us.

And the creation of the world… the level of creation of the world is that G-d <u>wants</u> to give to us: "I want to give it to you. Not because you are good, not because you are sweet, nor because you deserve it. But just because I want to."

**G-d's word is Torah**

And now Rebbe Nachman says one sweet little thing: you have to realize one thing, that every word G-d utters, is Torah.

What is Torah? What is the Torah? Is Torah only when G-d says you shouldn't eat milk and meat together? This is Torah? When G-d says, "Let there be light," this is also Torah! G-d says, "Let there be animals." This is also Torah. G-d says, "Let there be trees." This is also Torah. Everything. G-d's word is Torah.

But the truth is, that when G-d says, "Don't eat milk and meat together." this Torah is an open Torah. Everybody knows G-d says so, and so I am doing it. G-d's word is open to me. Revealed.

But when G-d says, "Let there be animals," "Let there be trees," this is the hidden Torah. It is the hidden Torah. Why is this hidden? Because it comes from a deeper source. Because this comes from the source of a gift.

**How deep does it reach into my soul**

If I sell something, how deep does it reach into my soul? It doesn't reach that deep. I can do business with my biggest enemy, right? It's nothing personal. Gifts, however, I only give to someone I love very much. And the greater the gift is, the deeper it reaches.

So the truth is, the strangest thing in the world, is that the Torah of creation is on a deeper level than the Torah from Mount Sinai. Because the 'Torah of the gift' is greater than the 'Torah of the buying.'

Mount Sinai is the 'marketplace,' where you buy, and the creation of the world is where you receive gifts.

Even on the level of giving gifts, there are also two levels. Sometimes I am giving you a gift which you need. But then that gift, which is also a very deep gift, but it is not so very deep. But imagine if I am giving you a gift, and it is actually nothing, you don't see anything. Imagine I would come up to someone, and I would say, "I am giving you a gift." And she doesn't see anything. And nobody saw anything. What a gift! It is so deep, it is so holy. It is from such a deep source that you can't see anything.

## It is just a gift

Our religion is really a 'non deserving' religion. We do not come to G-d and tell Him, "We deserve." For example, the way we want to pray on Rosh HaShanah, and the way the older generations *davened* [prayed] on Rosh HaShanah.... Some people today say, "There are a few sins I did, but in the meantime I did this good, and I did that good." They are not ready *mamash* to just receive without deserving.

You see, if you are on the level that you know that you are not deserving, then you are the most deserving. Because this is the way it is; G-d's wealth is for those who don't deserve it. And the moment you really know that you are not deserving, this is when you deserve it.

**Question:** You know you deserve it when you know you don't deserve it?

**Rebbe Shlomo answers:** You mean, you know already before? This is what Rebbe Nachman says: Don't think about it. Don't intellectualize it, because the moment you think about it, you are already diluting it, and it is not pure anymore. You have to know one thing: "I don't deserve it." You have to receive a gift. It is just a gift.

When you have a taste of the world, and you think you deserve it, then you cannot taste the world, because the world is a gift. It is a very deep thing.

The whole world is a gift from G-d. Nobody can say they deserve it.

## The world is only a gift.

The world is only destroyed by this whole attitude of deserving and not deserving. It is destroyed by people saying, "I am more deserving." What is going on between all the religions? "I am more deserving, I am better." All this is the destruction of the world. The world is only a gift!

But if you lift it back up to the level of knowing completely that, "I am not deserving." then you can put the world straight again. Then the world can be 'given' to us again.

When the Mashiach is coming, the world will really be here.

## Israel

The holiness of Israel… the holiness of the Land of Israel, is that it can only be received by our prayers.

Rebbe Nachman says something very deep. Where does our claim to Israel come from? The Gemara and Rashi says; Why did G-d tell us the story of the creation? The Torah is actually a book of laws, why did G-d tell us the story of the creation? Because someday, the world will say, "What are you doing in Israel?" And we answer them; "G-d created the world, He gave it to us." Meaning to say that our claim on Israel is on the level of creation: Just the goodness of G-d. Not because of deserving.

## You can receive life from that goodness

Mount Sinai is already on the level of deserving, because the whole basis of teaching is telling you what to do and what not to do. I am on a 'deserving or non-deserving' level. But the holy Land is given to us on the level of just, 'G-d wants to give it to us.'

And therefore when Moshe Rabbenu wanted to come to the holy Land, how did he argue with G-d? He didn't say, "I deserve it." He was begging G-d. He prayed several hundred prayers. And it says, "*Meotzar matnas chinam* [from the treasury of free gifts]." He was begging G-d, "Just from Your goodness… I know I don't deserve it, but I just want You to give it to me."

## Don't give up!

What did Rebbe Nachman start yelling at this point? He started yelling, "Don't give up!"
Because if your life depends on deserving and not deserving, then you can give up, because you know you are not deserving. But, on the contrary, if you are really not deserving, then you are the best customer for this holy G-d goodness of G-d's wealth, which is only for non-deserving. So therefore, on the contrary, you now should be filled with joy that now you can receive life from the goodness of G-d.

And, therefore, Rebbe Nachman says; what is the holiness of Israel, of the holy Land? The holiness of the Land of Israel is the holy thing that you don't give up. This is the secret of the holy Land. Because the holy Land is not giving up. I never give up, because G-d wants to give it to me. It has nothing to do with deserving or not deserving.

## Taste the holiness of the world

If someone wants to taste the holiness of the world… because, what is the goodness of G-d? The 'goodness of G-d' is also Torah. This is very very deep: it is also Torah. Because whatever G-d says, is Torah, "G-d created the world," is also Torah. When G-d says, "Let there be light," this is also Torah! G-d says, "Let there be animals." This is also Torah. But there is a revealed Torah, which was revealed to us on Mount Sinai, and there is a non revealed Torah, which is so very deep. This is the creation. This is the non-revealed Torah, which is even deeper. It is completely a gift.

So if someone wants to understand the secrets of the world, he has to receive that from G-d's goodness. Can you imagine, if you are learning the secrets of the world... because, what really is Torah? The Torah is: to learn the secrets of the world! That means you are learning on a deserving level, the secrets of the non-deserving.

## We really have vessels for this great light of non deserving

The highest level a person can be, the highest life level a person can be, is *mamash* to know that I am not deserving. That is the highest level a person can reach. This was the level of Moshe Rabbenu [Moses]. He reached the level of completely non-deserving.

And this is the level of the *tzadik*, of the holy person - that he knows he is not deserving. He *mamash* received it because he is really Torah, because he is learning all the time. Everything he is doing is good, yet he is on the level that he receives 'Mount Sinai' life on the level of 'creation.' This is the deepest depths there is.

## Prayer

What is the level of prayer? When I study, I receive life from Mount Sinai. When I pray... what am I praying for? I am praying for what I do not deserve. I am just praying because this is on the level of creation. You see, when I pray, I am not praying for things which can happen, and which are already in the world, I am praying for new things. Like, G-d should change the whole world. Why not? Because when I pray, I am praying on that level of before creation. So why not? Why not?

## If you learn and you know you don't deserve it

The moment you are learning, you already have this whole thing and you have this 'full stomach.' Like the Kotzker Rebbe says; some *Yiddelach*, with every page, their belly gets bigger, because they put the pages in their belly instead of in their heads. You know, there are some people who just look like pregnant women because their belly is full with pages. What kind of learning is that? If you would learn with your head, and with your soul....

Why was Moses the giver of the Torah? Because he received life on Mount Sinai on the level of not deserving. In other words, he was really the one, because the most deserving is non-deserving. Non-deserving is deserving. The creation is also just a secret... The non-revealed Torah is the secret of the revealed. You know, it is just all together.

### If you are not deserving

If you are just not deserving, so you receive life like a pistol in the back; "Keep on living, keep on living, keep on living." You see, G-d can give you life, and so you live, but G-d wants us to receive life on a Mount Sinai level, on a free choice level. That is the highest level there is; not only do I have free choice of my actions, I even have free choice of my life level, of what level I receive life. Because I am begging to receive this life of the non-deserving by free choice. This is *mamash* Torah. This is the deepest depths of life. It means I am really receiving it consciously, I am living this kind of life. Not just that I am just receiving, I am living it. You can have life but you are not living that life. And then you can have life and you are *mamash* living it.

### The holiness of a synagogue

Why are people together while they *daven* [pray], and why aren't they as much together when they are learning? Because when they are learning, they are on a deserving level. When you are praying, you are on the level of not deserving.

When we are *davening*, we are on the level of creation, on a completely not deserving level. Everybody is non-deserving, so they are all together. The moment I am studying, I am already saying; "I know more, you know less," or, "You know more, I know less."

(It is very strong. The truth is, this is one of the deepest Torah teachings of Rebbe Nachman, this is one of the deepest depths. We have to learn it a lot of times. It is just good to know this holy Torah. It is from Likutei Tinyono *ayin ches*. If you want to make a copies of it, it will be the strongest thing so some kids can walk around and learn it all the time.)

ഔ

# Only G-d can Help

On the one hand, it is so important to *daven* [pray] together. On the other hand, Rebbe Nachman says that when you *daven*, it has to be like there is nobody else in the world, just you and G-d. That's it.

Rebbe Tzadok HaCohen and all the Rebbes said; sometimes you pray, and you are angry that G-d didn't answer. But it is very simple, if I pray, and while I am *davening* I am already making plans "What will I do if G-d doesn't answer? So then I will have to do something else," then G-d says, "Listen, I don't want to interfere with your plans. Just go right ahead." You know, imagine I go to a doctor, and I would say, "Listen, if you are not so good, I also have an uncle, he's another doctor." Someone, a big doctor told me, "You know, Jewish patients are the worst, because everybody has an uncle who is a doctor, and right away they tell you that his uncle said something else. It's *geferlach*."

But you see what it is, when I *daven*, when I am asking G-d, it has to be clear to me that nobody else can help me. *Mamash*, absolutely nobody.

## Doing things in a natural way

And you see what it is, as much as G-d wants us to do everything in the natural way… Let's say, for instance, I need five thousand dollars, and I am going to sit here and learn Likutei Etzos and I hope that G-d will send me five thousand dollars right here on this table. It doesn't go this way. Because we are living in a world in which G-d puts certain borders. You want five thousand dollars, you have to work, you have to do something. And it says, "*uberachecha HaShem bkol asher tase* [G-d will bless you that whatever you do should be good]."

You see, the deepest secret is; I have to know that G-d wants me to work. If I have a herring store, I have to know that G-d wants me to have a herring store. But I still have to know that only G-d is feeding me, and the herring store is just a front.

So the question is, if G-d wants to feed me, what does He need a herring store for?

So? So you have a question. [You can't completely understand it, but so what? You don't need to completely understand it.]

Because this is the way G-d is operating in this world; that you have to do something, but it really is G-d's blessing.

But the most important thing is, when you *daven, mamash*, it has to be clear to you, *mamash* clear, in the deepest, deepest depths, that only G-d can help you.

## Connecting to G-d

When you learn Torah you exactly know G-d's will, and you know G-d's teachings. But when are you connecting yourself to G-d? Connecting to G-d is only when you *daven*.

And you know, it is very clear in the Gemara, that if you don't *daven*, you one hundred percent don't understand the Torah either. You don't understand the Torah… Ah, when you *daven*, you are already connected… ah, then when you learn, it is shining so deep into you.

Imagine, someone tells me a piece of Torah, it might be sweet. But if he tells me, "Do you know who said this piece of Torah? Someone who is your best friend." Ahh, I pay different attention to it. If you learn Torah, but without *davening*, and you really are not connected to G-d, so the Torah doesn't get in so deep. When you are connected to G-d, then the Torah gets in so deep.

**The power to pray**

This is something very deep. Why is it when we *daven*, suddenly all kinds of stupid thoughts, unimportant thoughts enter your mind. Not only stupid thoughts, but there is also something else, a certain arrogance. Suddenly you feel important when you *daven*. You think, "This one hurt my feelings, this one didn't respect me. This one did me wrong." Have you ever noticed it? Sometimes in the middle of *davening*, you start thinking arrogantly of everything stupid, "Twenty years ago, I remember, this person insulted me, *gevalt*. And one hundred and fifty years ago, *mamash*, I remember clearly, I remember it, on my way to the *bris*, someone insulted me."

What is going on here? Rebbe Nachman says, the truth is, that we have unbelievable power. Do you know what is the biggest power we have? We have the power to pray. It is awesome. You know, like the Gemara says, "Our weapon is praying." Meaning to say... you know the Gemara knew everything. If someone tells you, "You know, atomic power is *gevalt*, right?" But one *Yiddele* [Jew] saying Tehillim [Psalms] has more power. *Mamash* more power.

So when we begin to *daven*, suddenly we feel, *"Gevalt*, I have so much power." But if you don't know how to handle it, then the first thing comes to your head; "Ah, I am so important, how come this person didn't respect me?" But it is all nonsense, you have to get out of it.

So Rebbe Nachman says, this is because you really are *gevalt* very important, but it is in exile. It is garmented in a stupid way; the package is wrong.

ഇറ

# Wedding

Rebbe Nachman says that people come to a wedding, and then they walk out. One says, "It was a beautiful wedding. I liked the food." Another says, "I liked the music." Another says, "I met a lot of good friends there." They weren't really at the wedding.

Then someone walks out and says, *"Baruch HaShem*, thank G-d, those two got together!" He was there at the wedding.

**Children are a little piece of G-d's joy**

We lost our children because we didn't teach them the secret of joy.

Rebbe Nachman says, why is the joy at a wedding so strong? Because this is like the preparation to bring children into the world, and the greatest, greatest joy in the world is when a little baby arrives here.

You know what that means? That means, basically, that when a human being enters this world, not only does he bring with himself a soul, he also brings joy with him into the world. Because, the truth is, what is our soul? Just a little bit of G-d's joy. So when a baby is born, it is just a little piece of G-d's joy coming into the world. And in order to teach the world to prepare themselves for this holy joy, so people get married and for seven days the whole world is dancing, in order to prepare them to receive this holy joy which will come down from heaven.

If parents would know this secret of joy, they would watch over their children, I am sure there would be peace in the world. Because if parents would know that little children are a little piece of G-d's joy, they wouldn't like them to just go and be killed for nothing.

The world has maybe learned yet how to cry, but the world has not learned yet how to rejoice.

ഇ○ര

## Hearing your Soulmate

Do you know what it means to love somebody? To love somebody means that even if they don't say anything, you can hear it too. I want to bless *chosson* [groom] that, whatever your *kallah* [bride] wants to tell you, you should be privileged to hear it, and let it sink deep, deep into your heart. And *kallah*, whatever your *chosson* wants to tell you is only one billionth of what he really wants to tell you....

### The Silent Yell

It's unbelievable. Rebbe Nachman lived 200 years ago, and he is still around. So someone asked Rebbe Nachman, "How loud do you have to yell when you pray?" And he said, "You have to yell so loud, that no one can hear you." May every *chosson* and *kallah* hear each other yell so loud, that only you can hear each other. And I want to bless you that you should always hear your children when they yell so loud that nobody can hear them except their parents. And may you be the ones to hear them. And isn't G-d yelling so loudly all the time? You know why we say *Shuva Yisroel*? You know what a Jew is? Someone who can hear G-d yelling so loud that nobody can hear it.

ഇ○ര

## What is the Point!

This is an Ishbitser Torah teaching:
A circle needs a center. You cannot have a circle without a center. Four corners don't need a center.

There are people who live in the world of a circle, always connected to the center. They are always connected to the center.

And you know, friends, even if you do wrong sometimes… as long as you are connected to the center…

And you know, the center itself has a center. Do you know what the center is? The center of it, the most important thing in it, the essence of it is the point!

You know, I have seen people talking to you for ten years about *Yidishkiet* [Judaism], and when you walk away, you still don't know what they want, and they don't know either.

If you stop them and say, "Tell me, what is it to be a Jew?"

They say, "Send money to Israel. On Yom Kippur, drive to the synagogue, try not to be too late. And what else?… and join the breakfast club. Ahh what else… Make sure your children are going to a Jewish camp. It does not matter if it is kosher or not, as long as it has a Jewish flag over the dining room. What else…? Remind me of something else. By the life of me, I can't think of anything else."

I will ask you, "What is the center of Shabbos?"

They say, "You shouldn't work and you should enjoy yourself, and have fun."

'Beautiful,' right? They don't get to the point.

You know, friends, it is obvious that ninety-nine percent of the world doesn't know what the point of living is.

There is this awesome prayer of Rebbe Nosson for peace, and this is based on Rebbe Nachman's Torah teachings. Rebbe Nachman asks: What do people talk to each other about? The more pointless it is, the more people talk about it. Can you walk up to somebody and *mamash* say, "What is the point? Tell me. I know you for ten years, what is the point of our relationship."

What is the point? You keep Shabbos for one hundred years, but what is the point!


**Mashiach**

This comes from the holy Bal Shem Tov. Mashiach has a lot of meanings. Mashiach means 'the anointed,' and Mashiach comes from the world *lasuach*, to talk. Rebbe Nachman says, people don't talk to each other. They talk about anything in the world. Can you walk up to another person and say, "Listen brother, what are you really doing here? What are you really doing here? What is the point of your life?"

## What are you doing here?

Here is a little story which is just so heartwarming.

Rebbe Nachman became a Rebbe when he was fourteen years old. He got married when he was fourteen years old. Can you imagine, at the time, all the holy Chassidim of the Bal Shem Tov were still alive, but for Rebbe Nachman that was not enough. He wanted more than that.

So during his wedding reception, he walked around asking people, "What are you doing here?"

"What do you mean? I am here, I am a friend of the groom…." "I am a friend of the bride." Everyone said something else.

"What are you doing here?"

"I am related to the bride's mother."

"Good."

Finally he found one boy his age, fourteen years old, standing by the door. Rebbe Nachman said, "What are you doing here?"

And the boy answered Rebbe Nachman, "This is why I can't sleep at night. I don't know what I am doing here."

"Ahhh," Rebbe Nachman said, "There is one guest at my wedding… one guest."

Then he says to him, "Do me a favor, it is not for you and not for me here. Let's get out of here."

So he said to Rebbe Nachman, "I want you to know, that there are thirty young people in this city who don't sleep at night because they don't know what they are doing here."

Rebbe Nachman said, "Let's get together fast."

So then they walked out to the forest, and that night Rebbe Nachman became a Rebbe.

## *Tzitzis*

So the Ishbitser says, do you know when you need *tzitzis*? When you are in the world of four corners. Four corners - no more point. No more point…

When the spies came back from scouting the Land of Israel, and they told us, "Israel is not good, and also Moshe is no good, G-d is… the whole thing is bad." You know what they did to us? The whole thing has no more point. "There is no more point. What is the point of everything? Moshe Rabbenu took us out of Egypt to bring us to the holy Land!"

You know how many things we work on all our lives, and then in the end we are not doing it. Where is the point? So G-d, in His utmost mercy, gave us *tzitzis*.

And you know what the thing of *tzitzis* is? That on every corner, you make a little hole, a little point. For the moment there is a point.

And above all, when you come to a corner, G-d forbid, on the four corners of your pointless life, you are at the end, you are at the end... but *tzitzis* comes from the Hebrew word "seeing." You know what we do when we put on *tzitzis*? We put them over our eyes, and suddenly we see the point again. *Urisem oisoi* [and you will see it], G-d promises you, even if you are in the most distant corner, suddenly you put the *tzitzis* over your eyes, and *gevalt*....

You know, it is crazy, we have so many *mitzvas*, we have so many good deeds, but we don't kiss them.

Friday night, the *challah* is very holy, yet the only one who kissed the *challah* Friday night was Rebbe Levy Yitzchak of Berdichev. He couldn't stop kissing the *challah*. *Gevalt*. Friday night, *lechem mishna* [the two loaves], it blows his mind. Rebbe Levy Yitzchak of Berdichev kissed the *esrog*, kissed the *lulav*, kissed the *megilla*, we don't know how much he kissed them.

Ok, but that was because he was the deepest. But even people like you and me, we kiss the *tzitzis*.
Who do you love the most? Someone who connects you back to their center, who gives you back your point again.

Do you know why it is so easy to kiss children? Because children never lost their point. Until we un-point them, until we un-center them. Grownups, sometimes you would love to kiss them, but, *oy vey*, it is really hard, they have no point.

The point, you cannot see it; it is deeper than prophesy. It is just, that G-d opens your eyes. But you know the way G-d opens your eyes? When you close your eyes. Do you know, when we say *shema Yisrael*, why I close my eyes? Because G-d opens my eyes inside and I see there is really one G-d. There really is one G-d.

The *mezuzah*: Do you know how many people live in a house, but there is no point? People get married, they live in a house, but what's the point? What's the point!? *Mezuzah, gevalt*, G-d is the center of the world. G-d is the point of everything.

## Shabbos

Shabbos: Rebbe Nachman says, the world thinks that the week is seven days. It is not true. There are three days - Wednesday, Thursday, Friday - and the other three days - Sunday, Monday, Tuesday. Shabbos is the center. Shabbos is the point of everything. The Gemara says, the whole Torah is connected to *tzitzis*, the whole Torah is connected to Shabbos.

Why do we say good Shabbos to each other and it is so deep? Do you know what I'm saying to you when I say, "Good Shabbos." I'm saying, "G-d opened my eyes, and I see you." You know, there is a Wednesday and Thursday kind of seeing; "Your name is Max. You work for the UJA. You came to collect some money. I see you." This is not what the kind of seeing that I mean. I mean *Shabbosdike* seeing... connected to the point seeing.... You know how beautiful it is when people say, "Good

Shabbos" to each other. They are blessing each other that each should be connected to the point, that G-d should open each one's eyes.

You know, friends, until G-d opens your eyes, you can have pictures of everyone in the whole world, but you never have seen anybody.

The Gemara says, when you run, it is bad for your eyes, and when you make *Kiddush* it fixes your eyes. *Kiddush* is fixing your eyes. You know what the whole world is doing with wine? They get drunk, and they really lose their vision, right? What is a drunkard? He is off center, he can't walk or talk straight. You know what Friday night wine does to us? It brings us right back to the center. It opens our eyes in the deepest way.

ꟷ

## Rebbe Yisroel Dov Odesser zt"l

*At a Meeting with Rebbe Shlomo Carlebach zt"l and Rebbe Yisroel Dov Odesser zt"l. Rebbe Shlomo Carlebach singing:*

There is a *tzadik*, who is the beauty and the grandeur and the charming grace of the entire universe. And when this beauty and this grandeur are revealed, meaning, when this *tzadik* who is the true beauty of the whole world becomes famous and exalted in the world, then the eyes of the world open.

So this is the story: *HaRav HaGaon HaMekubal* [the genius Rabbi Kabalist] Yisrael Dov Odesser, *shlita*, was born in Tiberias in 1888 to very poor parents from Karlin Chassidus. From childhood already he demonstrated a soul yearning to *HaShem Yisborach* [G-d]. There was no doubt he was an extraordinary spirit.

This is his story: On the fast of the seventeenth day of *Tamuz*, Yisroel Dov Odesser erred and partook of food. As a result of this, he entered into a severe depression. After five continuous days of unremitting prayer, he took out a copy of Likutei Halochos of Rebbe Nosson. He noticed a small piece of paper just before closing the *sefer* [book]. After studying its contents, he became jubilant. This is what it said…

This is what the letter said; "It was very hard for me to come down to you, my precious *talmid* [student], to tell you that I enjoyed very much your *avodah* [work] laboring in the service of *HaShem*, and it was referring to you that I said, 'My flame will burn until the coming of Mashiach.' Be strong and courageous in your *avodah*. Na Nach Nachma Nachman from Uman. And with this I shall reveal to you a secret: *male vegadish mekav lekav*, an esoteric and ineffable name of a *malach HaShem* [angel of G-d]. And with the strength of your *avodah* you will be able to understand it. The sign is that they will say, 'You are not fasting.'"

The key to the redemption, the salvation of the entire world, is… So Rebbe Yisroel Dov Odesser, *shlita,* is making the name of the *tzadik* famous; printing his books in all languages throughout the entire world.

## Connect yourself to the *tzadikim*

He is a *Yid* [Jew], an *oved HaShem* [servant of G-d], an *alter Yid* [a Jewish elder], *mamash* [really] *shleptzach* with *mesiras nefesh* [he traveled with real self sacrifice all the way] to America, to be *mefarsem* and *mekarev Yidden* to *Yiddeshkeit* [to spread the word and bring Jews back to Judaism]. I have seen some old *Yidden,* who *mamash* don't know *leip nishet, bein yomom valayla* [some other old people often can't tell the difference between day and night]. But here is a *Yid,* an *alter Yid,* a *heilege Yid* [but he is a holy elderly Jew who is very clear-headed], and we are privileged to be in his presence, and let's hope and pray that he will be strong until Mashiach is coming, and we should all be there.

I can only say for myself, a lot of times, when the airplane is *shukkeling* [shaking] up in the air, and we get all shook up, I start saying, Na Nach Nachma Nachman MeUman, and *baruch HaShem* [thank G-d], it gives me *koach* [strength], and we are arriving *baruch HaShem* [thank G-d, safely].

Basically all my *chevre* [friends and followers], they know two things: when something goes wrong, they are saying, Na Nach Nachma Nachman MeUman, and, *Eloka de* Rebbe Levy Yitzchak ben Sarah Sasha *aneini* [G-d, please answer my prayer, in the merit of Rabbi Levy Yitzchak, the son of Sarah Sasha]. We mention *tzadikim* [we mention the names of holy people].

And you know, we are living in a world, where most of our young people are connected to every holy man of every other religion of the world.

You know, I will tell you something on a very simple level. I was some time in Washington in a Hebrew school. And the teacher tells me that she told the kids to write about ten people who affected their lives the most. They were fifteen to seventeen year old kids from a special class. And she was 'very proud,' fifty two students wrote about ten people who affected their lives the most. But you know, there was not one Jewish name!

And I have a strong feeling that this was *mamash misgale* [revealed] now to tell all the Jewish young people, "*mamash,* connect yourself to the *tzadikim,* to your own *tzadikim* [to the righteous Jews, to your own holy people]."

You know, whatever somebody does, there is always somebody who says something against it. Right? Because the holiness of this world is that you always have choice. Imagine if Yisroel Dov comes to America, and everybody says, "That's what it is." So what is so special about it? There always has to be someone who says something against it. Right? Which is ok with me. But I just want to say one thing, that I think it is unbelievable if we could really be *mefarsem* this among our young people all over the world, that whenever they need something, they should think of Rebbe Nachman, saying, "Na Nach Nachma Nachman MeUman," and connect themselves to *tzadikim.*

# Oral Law

When Moshe Rabbenu went up to Mt. Sinai, during the day G-d dictated the Chumash to him, during the night G-d explained the Mishna and Gemara to him [the Oral Law]. We don't know what Chumash [Five Books of Moses] really is. If someone says, "I know Gemara," he's probably lying, but maybe he isn't. But if someone comes to you and says, "I know Chumash," he's definitely lying [fooling himself]. Because Chumash is way out [beyond everybody]. So many times Moshe Rabbenu asked G-d, "Why don't you let me write it down?" - and he was begging G-d, "Why don't you let me change some of the wording, it would come out so much clearer." But G-d said, "No."

## Covenant

There's a verse that says that G-d made a covenant with us: the Gemara says that the covenant is the Oral Law.

What is a covenant? When you have a covenant with someone, you say something to each other. But what's the covenant between Israel and G-d? It's the Oral Law.

The Gemara puts it like this - and if it was real then, how much more real is it now! G-d says to Moses, There will be a time when the whole world will also know the Bible. So they will say, "We're just like the Jews," but the one who knows the Oral Torah, the one who knows what it really means - the world knows that they are the real Jews, the people who were at Mt. Sinai. And the ones who know the Bible via translation, they aren't real.

Maybe some of you know that the first time the Bible was translated, it was translated from the original Hebrew into Greek. And so, even today, we fast on the tenth day of Tevet, - one of the reasons is because it was on that day that the Bible was first translated. It's the saddest thing in the world. Because before then, any non-Jew who wanted to know the Bible came to Israel, and we taught him the Bible. In this way, we were teaching it, and so we knew that he knew exactly what was being said. But the moment the Bible was translated, any little person could buy himself a copy of the Bible, and think he knows what G-d is saying. So on that day we are still fasting, because it's a degradation of Mt. Sinai.

And so now the Bible has been in translation for about 2200 years, and the fact is people don't know the Bible yet!

Without hurting anybody's feelings, take a priest who writes commentaries on the Bible. He might be a sweet little man, but he cannot write commentaries on the Bible. It just does not work. And take a little *Yiddele* who writes commentaries on the Bible, and it does work... Because we have a covenant with G-d.

So, the actual words themselves can be translated, and for that you don't necessarily need a Jew, maybe. You don't need a Jew to know that the word '*Bereshit*' means "In the Beginning." But the real meaning of G-d's words was just given to us Jewish People, and that's not written down. It's just handed down from one generation to the other.

So whoever wants to come and learn what *HaShem* is really saying, can come and we'll teach him. But he has to come to us; we have to be the channel because it has to be given over from mouth to mouth.

Without going into a long story, I was once invited to give a concert in a monastery. So I began talking to them about the Psalms. They asked me, "Teach us one Psalm." So I took one and taught it to them, and I really know very little. But, regardless, they were *mamash* saying, "I never knew the Psalm was so good." And they all really know the Psalms by heart; they're good people, but they didn't know what the Psalms are saying. Because the Psalms were given to the Jewish people. I can <u>teach</u> it to them. But I cannot <u>give</u> it to them; I cannot give it over to them.

**Giving over**

There's such a thing as learning, and there's such a thing as giving over. You don't only teach children *Yiddishkeit*, you give it over to them. Sometimes, someone might have a great Rabbi, who can teach him the entire Torah, yet he doesn't give him over anything. And maybe Moshe the water carrier doesn't know much to teach his son, but *mamash* he gave *Yiddishkeit* over to him!

So G-d says to Moses, if I would write down the whole Torah, then the Jews could become strangers, G-d forbid, to their own Bible, to their own Mt. Sinai. But because it's not all written down, therefore, it's just given over to them. So the one nation who knows the Oral Law is the one nation that was at Mt. Sinai and received both the Written and the Oral Law, and the ones who don't know the Oral Law were not there.

**It was written down**

Later on, Rabbenu HaKodesh, the holy Rebbe, the only one who was called 'holy', realized that people began to forget the Oral Law. So, since there's a *passuk* [passage] that says that when the time comes to do something necessary for G-d, sometimes you may even have to do wrong in order to keep the thing up. So the Torah leaders of the generation decided to write the Oral Law down, because they realized that otherwise it would be completely forgotten.

**Only a *Yid* can understand it**

But the craziest thing is that even after they wrote it down, it's still not written down. Because, can you imagine, there's a book called the Gemara, yet there's not one non-Jew in the world who knows Gemara. They have professors, and they are studying it, yet they don't understand it.

And I'll tell you something deeper; if you don't keep Shabbos, if you're not a *frum* [religious] Jew, you also don't really understand it. Someone told me that he met a professor who was sitting on Yom Kippur, eating breakfast and smoking a cigar, and learning Gemara. *Gornisht*. It doesn't go into his head. If you're not on the level that you have the covenant between you and G-d, it doesn't get into your head.

Understanding the Gemara is not only to understand the words; it's a whole way of thinking. It's a G-d-like thinking, the deepest depths that there is. And this has to be handed down from Mt. Sinai. This is the oral tradition: I learned with Reb Shlomo Heiman, and Reb Shlomo Heiman learned from Reb Bera, and Reb Bera learned from Reb Chaim, and Reb Chaim learned from Reb Yosef Ber... all the way back to Mt. Sinai.

Because, what's the holiness of Rabbenu Hakodesh. He was able to write the Oral Law down in a way that if you don't have a Rebbe, someone to connect you to Mt. Sinai, you still won't be able to understand it.

If you don't know the entire Talmud, you cannot even learn one page, because there's this deep kind of interrelation between the whole Talmud. And with all the commentaries as well. The Oral Law is still only in the air, in other words, it's still just given over from one person to the other.

There are certain things that, if I write them down, they stop being a secret. But with other deep things, I can write them down, from today until tomorrow, and yet it still remains a secret.

People who love each other very much have all kinds of secrets between them. They can write a letter, and the whole world can read it, but nobody knows what they're talking about because they're so close to each other.
Rabbenu HaKodesh was so holy that he knew exactly how to write it down.

And, again, if you don't know Torah *shebal peh*, you don't know Torah *shebechtav*. G-d wrote down the Torah in such a way that, even if you translate it into all seventy languages, you still cannot understand it. And Rabbeinu HaKodesh wrote down the Oral Law and still did not destroy, even for one minute, the holiness of its being a secret.

## Whatever I know of G-d

Rebbe Nachman says, what is the Written Torah and the Oral Torah? He says, whatever I know of G-d, whatever I know of *Yiddishkeit,* can't be written down.

The Bal Shem Tov can write down all the things he said, but what do I really know about the way the Bal Shem Tov believed that there is one G-d? That's Torah *shebal peh*. And yet I know that he was there on that level, and today I'm a little bit of a *Yid* because he was there.

What do I really know about the way Avraham our father knew G-d? There are absolutely no words for it.

Then Rebbe Nachman says that learning is Torah *shebechtav*, and praying is Torah *shebal peh*. Because how can I explain to you what I'm praying? The greatest secret between me and G-d is what I am praying. Even the words - we have a *siddur* [prayer book], and for two thousand years all the *Yiddelach* are praying the same words - and yet it's not the same words. And not only is it not the same words for two people, but when I *daven Shmonah Esrai* in the morning, the *Shmonah Esrai* from *Shacharit* is already a different *Shmonah Esrai* from *Mincha*. Because what do I know what I feel in the morning and what I feel at night? This can't be written down; it's the Torah *shebal peh*.

ഇൗൽ

# Eating

This is one of the top Torah teachings of Rebbe Nachman. You know, most of us always think of life in terms of, "What am I doing with my life? How much money do I make? What's my future? What's my past?" This is cute and sweet, but it's the outside of it. Inside - life itself is so deep.

Rebbe Nachman says, at the moment when you put food into your mouth, if you want to, you can receive life on the highest level. You can take a bite of an apple and receive eternal life, or you can just receive the apple. It's up to you.

The story goes that: Most Breslov Chassidim were poor. Reb Nosson, the greatest pupil of Rebbe Nachman, was once invited by Rebbe Nachman's grandson, who was very wealthy. He didn't feel right going there, but since he was invited he went, though, the whole day he was crying inside, "*Gevalt*, my Rebbe was so holy, and here this grandson is into money." Reb Nosson relates, "I came to the house…" and due to the affluence, he regretted that he went, since he wasn't accustomed to this kind of riches. And then the food was brought in, and he says, "*Oy vey*. With these of golden plates and golden spoons, who knows? Forget it!" But then, he continues, "Rebbe Nachman's grandson walked in, and he made the blessing, *hamotzi* [blessing over the bread]." And he says, "The way he put the food in his mouth, I swear to you, I haven't seen it since Rebbe Nachman." *Mamash*, the grandson was eating with the utmost readiness to receive life on the highest level.

ഇൗൽ

## Tell it Straight

This is one of the deepest, deepest depths of Rebbe Nachman. How close do you have to be to a person to tell them something straight? Basically, a stranger can ask me, "How much is one and one?" I'll tell him "two." I don't have to love him, and he doesn't have to love me. I'll just tell him "two." But there is certain language which is only used when you love somebody very much. It's the deepest depths, right? On the one hand, maybe it's not as clear. But on the other hand, it's so much deeper.

                ℬⓌ

## The world is getting better

You know, Rebbe Nachman says that the world always thinks there are nations. But the whole thing is an illusion. There are no nations; there are only people. And where do you start making peace? You can't make peace between nations. You can only make peace between people. So let it start right here, with us, my friends.

I have to share something with you an unbelievable, true story. I don't know how it will turn you on - it turned me on. Exactly two weeks ago I had the great privilege, to perform in Hanover, Germany, for ten thousand young people. Can you imagine? The Protestant Church had a big convention, and for the first time in their history, I, a 'Jewboy,' was invited to sing. And so I performed for ten thousand. Now, listen to this!

There was a huge stage set up in the middle of the city, and before I was to begin, the Bishop spoke. I don't want to say anything bad, but there were thousands of people, and nobody paid any attention; everybody was drinking beer. I thought to myself, "I'm supposed to appear next, *oy gevalt!*" I thought, "I'm quitting, I'm just going to disappear."

And, really, let's face it, what can I tell them [what are the right words that I could possibly tell them]? But I knew one thing, you're not permitted to quit, ever. So I got on the stage. And there were thousands of kids sitting and drinking beer; and it didn't look like they really cared too much about anything. Anyway, I yelled from the depths of my heart, and said, "My most precious brothers and sisters, I'm bringing you a message of love and peace from the Holy City of Jerusalem!" And I don't know what happened, it was a miracle from G-d: Thousands of kids got up and streamed to the stage. And we started singing and dancing. It was just unbelievable! And I said, "You know something? Fifty years ago, our forefathers did not dance together, but we do! What a world! There is one G-d! The world is getting better!"*

*(Sichot HaRaN 239)

                ℬⓌ

# Mixing the Ingredients

Rebbe Nachman says, imagine I make a pie. I have all the ingredients, and I just have to stir it. Actually we stir it all the time, because we're living all the time. OK, but imagine I want an ingredient called love. But if this love is in the pie, it has to be soft. If it isn't ground up, if it is thick like a stone, it won't mingle, it will stick out. It's not mixed, it just doesn't mingle with the other parts. Do you know what is happening then? It's just obnoxious. It's good, it's sweet, it's a strong ingredient, but it just isn't mixed in, it's just so coarse. It doesn't go.

Some people keep Shabbos, but sometimes your nose tells you, "I can't stand their Shabbos." Why? Their Shabbos isn't really, really, really integrated into their whole being and their whole life. It's sticking out like a stone, coarse, so coarse it just doesn't mingle.

It isn't that we need a 'great fixer,' but a 'great mixer.' You have got to know how to do it. Coarse just doesn't go.


## Hitbodedut

How do you un-coarse all those ingredients? The only way, Rebbe Nachman says, and he's very strong about this, is that you have to be alone and talk to G-d. You've got to be alone, and you've got to get yourself a little control.

And the whole thing is, Rebbe Nachman always taught, that while we pray, *mamash* we're completely annihilated. Because if you pray, and then, after you prayed, you're as coarse as you were before, nothing happens to you. Nothing happens… Something has to happen.


## Taste real goodness

What do we know about 'real good?' Let's say, for instance, we say, "This is not so bad, this is better, and this is good." What? Did we ever taste 'real good?' I don't know if maybe you ever tasted real evil, but did you ever taste 'real good?' There is something that is good. Did you ever taste it? Even if you have it, you wouldn't taste it, because we're immune to it. You know, if I have chewing gum in my mouth, someone can put the most delicious thing in my mouth at the same time, and I would be unaffected by it because of my chewing gum being there. Some people chew spiritual gum all the time. They chew the same thing all the time, two words, three words, three ideas, or one idea, chewing it all the time. And in the meantime, someone puts the most beautiful thing into their mouth and they don't taste it.

**The soul really wants to be good all the time**

So Rebbe Nachman says, when can you taste the real goodness? There is no way… there is no way…. The only part that can taste real goodness is your soul. But if your soul is sleeping, if your soul is not real, it's not even worth talking. How can you taste it? How can you bring out your soul? This is one of the strong things of Rebbe Nachman. Rebbe Nachman says, if you ask, "What is the soul?" Know that the soul is longing. Longing, that is the soul. That's the strongest thing of the soul. Not wanting. Not 'I want.' Longing means yearning. Yearning! Rebbe Nachman says, I can be alone and *mamash* be completely yearning, and then I can *mamash* taste real good.

ഇറ

# A Taste of How Holy your Soul is

Someone came to Rebbe Nachman and he was talking about our father Abraham. So Rebbe Nachman says to him, "Obviously, you don't have the faintest idea who our father Abraham was. How could you know? But whatever you think our father Abraham was; you are about one million times deeper than that. You are millions of times deeper."

You know friends, whatever we think any holy person we know in the world is, we ourselves are much deeper.

When does G-d give us a taste of how holy your soul is, how holy your *neshama* [soul] is? When G-d gives you a taste of that light which is really burning inside of you, of that great fire….

You know friends, let me tell you something, if I know that I am very talented with numbers, so I know, "Maybe I should study mathematics, and be a scientist." If I know that I am talented in music, so I know, "Maybe I should study music." You know what our problem is? All of us, we don't even know our talents in serving G-d, we don't know our talents in making the world more beautiful. Because we never taste it.

So I want you just to hear this. This is a torah from Rebbe Nachman, I am giving you in one sentence:

*Harotze litom tam ohr haganuz,* If you want to have a taste of the hidden light inside of you, *yarbe behisbodedus,* There has to be moments, moments, moments, where you extract yourself from the whole world. *Mamash,* and you are just so close to G-d. And as I told you before, the moments you can be close to G-d have nothing to do with what you did before and what you will do after. You know sweetest friends, I want you to know something, when you love somebody very much, you can make a deal with them; "I don't care what happens between us, one minute a day I want to be close to you." You know friends, why we Jewish people made it after the destruction of the holy temple? Because: three times a day I am close to G-d. Three times a day, when I pray, all the gates of Heaven are open. Three times a day I am not in exile. Three times a day the holy Temple is rebuilt.

When you get a taste of your own *neshama*, your own soul, whenever you do somebody else a favor with all your heart. *Gevalt* is that holy, *gevalt* is that good. Someone asks you for a favor, and you *mamash* do it without reservation, with all your heart. At that moment, you get a little glimpse, you get a little taste of what you really have inside.

You know friends, I want you to know, when someone asks us for a favor, we always think we are doing them a favor. It is not true. G-d wants to give you a taste of who you are.

Imagine I am up all night crying before G-d, "Please let me know who I am." Right. The next morning I am very tired. Someone calls me up and says, "Can you do me a favor?" I say, "Listen, not now, I was up all night crying to G-d… Please call me next week." *Gevalt*, G-d wanted to give you a taste of who you are. Right?

It is not awesome to taste good *cholent*. But it is awesome, awesome, awesome, awesome, to have a little bit of a glimpse of my own *neshama*.

## What is it to pray

The *heilege* Rebbe Nachman, the Holy Bal Shem Tov's grandson, once when the Chassidim asked him, "Rebbe, what is it really to pray? How do you pray?" So he says, "I want you to watch my little grandson Yisrolekle, who is three years old, he knows how to pray. He is my true follower."

You have to realize something; the holy Rebbe Nachman, sadly enough, passed away when he was thirty nine. He got married a few days after his *bar mitzvah*, and so, when he was twenty five, how old was his daughter then? Twelve, right. So she got married, right? So when he was thirty nine, he had grandchildren already.

So the Chassidim began watching this Yisrolekle. And you know, little kids of three, when they want to tie their shoelaces, sometimes they don't have so much control yet, so he tore the shoelace. And you know, I don't know about you, but most sophisticated people; if they tore your shoelace, they would put a new one in, or go out and buy one. But not Yisrolekle, he is Breslover *chossid*, right, a follower of his grandfather. When he tore his shoelace, he put the shoe down, walked to a corner, and he began crying from the deepest depths of his heart, "Rebono Shel Olam, Master of the World, I tore my shoelace, please get me another one."
*Gevalt*, right.

I want you to know, you can get shoelaces by buying it, but that shoelace has no taste. Imagine if you get a shoelace from the One, from the Only One, *gevalt* is that good, *gevalt* is that good, so good.

❧⊷⊶☙

# Yerushalayim

Everything in the world has a certain holiness. When I walk on the street and I give a poor man a dollar, it is holy, when I wake up in the morning and put on *tefillin*, it is holy. Whatever I do is holy, but it is only one certain side of holiness. But then there is something which has like the headquarters for holiness. Whatever is holy in the world is included there. This is the holy Land, this is what Eretz Yisrael [the Land of Israel] is all about. Eretz Yisrael is the *klalius kol hakedushas* [the Land of Israel is the inclusiveness of all the holiness]. People always say to me, "Why are you talking so much about Yerushalayim [Jerusalem]? Bombay is also holy, Amsterdam is holy." Every city has a certain holiness, because if it would be completely void of holiness, it would not exist. There might be bad things also, but there has to be something holy, otherwise they wouldn't be. Yeah, I am not knocking it, it is a little bit holy, but Eretz Yisrael is something else. Eretz Yisrael has the holiness of all the holiness. Meaning to say, imagine if you would take all of the holiness, whatever there is; all of the *mitzvas*, all the good deeds, all the cities, all the houses, and you would put it all in one pot. This is what Eretz Yisrael is all about.

## The Beis Hamikdash is the center of the world

The world always thinks that since Eretz Yisrael is holy, so Yerushalayim is more holy because it is the capital, and the Beis Hamikdash [Holy Temple] is even more holy than Yerushalayim. It is the other way around. It is very clear in the Rambam and the great commentaries that the holiness begins with the Beis Hamikdash, this is the center of the world. The center of the world is the Holy Temple, and this is like *kodesh kodoshim* [holy of holies], and Yerushalayim is holy because it is close to the Beis Hamikdash, and Eretz Yisrael is holy because it is the land in which Yerushalayim is. So everything begins *mamish* in Yerushalayim, in the Holy Temple.

## *Menios* [obstacles]

You know, friends, if I decide to be a comedian, do you think anybody would say anything bad about it? It would be very easy. If I decide to do anything in the world that is stupid, there is nobody against me. Nobody says something against it. The moment I want to do something holy, there are obstacles, *menios*. Rebbe Nachman teaches one of the deepest torahs: The more important something is, and the more holy something is - the more obstacles there are in the way. Meaning to say, if you want to do something, and there are absolutely no obstacles, don't waste your time, because obviously it is very very unimportant.

There is this famous classic story, the *heilege* Reb Shalom Shachna (the father of the *heilege* Rizhiner) without getting involved in the depths…. In Rizhin, *mamish*, they had a different way…. The *heilege* Reb Shalom Shachna grew up in the house of Reb Nachum Chernobyler, because *nebech* his father passed away when he was three years old. When he was *bar mitzvah*, he already had a lot of Chassidim, all his age. And what do you understand about Rebbes, Rizhin is very majestic, everything has to be clean. But the streets of Chernobyl were full of mud, so one Shabbos he said, "You know, it is so bad for me,

Shabbos morning I have to go to the *shul* [synagogue], and then my shoes and my pants get dirty from the mud. I want you to build me a *shul* right next to my house." But they were all thirteen year old kids, they have no money. Most of them were married already, they had little *shverele* [in laws]. So word got around that they want to build their own *shul*. Like Young Israel youth *minyan*, you know, *lehavdil* [not to compare]. So they decided, "Why not?" So everybody gave them money. Do you know what they did? They *mamish* sold their *tefillin*, their *tallis*, and everybody had just one pair for the whole *chevra* [group of friends], and the whole city was helping them.

By Pesach time, they had just about finished the *shul*, and suddenly Reb Shalom Shachna says, "I don't need the *shul* now because there is no more mud. Why do I need the *shul*? I can go to the big *shul*." But they understood enough about the Rebbe to know that this was probably not the real reason.

They stopped building it and left it hanging in the air.

On Rosh Hashanah by *davening*, suddenly someone said, "Remember I gave you some money to build the *shul*. What happened to that money?" So the *Yid* answered, "Why, do you want to tell me that my son stole the money?" So he says, "No, I don't want to say that he stole, but maybe he did." Before you look around, the whole *shul* was *mamish* a fist fight, one says, "He stole it." one says, "He didn't steal it." and the whole *shul* was turning over.

The next thing that happened was that Reb Shalom Shachna said, "OK, it is time to finish the *shul*." And don't ask, everybody was yelling and fighting like crazy.

On Simchas Torah, when the atmosphere was a bit more open, one of the kids said to Reb Shalom, "Rebbe, we don't doubt your reason, I am sure you know what you are doing, but we can't understand you. Before Pesach when everybody was helping us, and it was so good, you told us to stop, and now when everybody is fighting over it, you told us to continue to build it."

He answered, "That's what it is. Because I heard from my holy father, the *heilege* Malach, the 'holy angel' who heard from the Bal Shem Tov, who heard from Eliyahu Hanavi, that anything you do that there is no opposition, don't do it. It is a waste of time."


**Moving to Israel**

Have you ever seen, when anybody wants to move from New York to Chicago, how hard is it? So he moves to Chicago, it is not hard. Ahh, but when you want to move to Eretz Yisrael, hey, this is already heavy.

Have you ever seen, even just the checking in is so hard, you are just checking in to the airport, you just want to go there, and they drive you crazy. You know, I have flown every airline in the world. You check in, and nobody bothers you. You go in, you mind your own business, you sit down, and that's it. El Al airline *mamish*... everything comes so hard; Either you are too early, or you are too late, or someone sits in your seat. *Gevalt*.

Do you know what a Trans World Airline stewardess told me? "We don't know what it is. We are flying all over the world and everything is peaceful, but when we fly from New York to Tel Aviv, there is something in the air, everybody is... it drives us crazy." One stewardess said, "I am not an anti-Semite, but I can't take it." I told her, it has nothing to do with being an anti-Semite, I understand, I see it with my own eyes, it is because there is something... it is so hard to get to the Holy Land. It is so hard to get to the Holy Land.

## Higher than paradise

I want you to know something awesome. Rav Kook says, everyone knows that on Shabbos you have to be in a higher place than during the week. Imagine if we would not have been driven out from paradise. If Adam and Eve would not have eaten from the tree of knowledge, and they would not have been driven out from Gan Eden [paradise], where would they be Shabbos? You see, now that we were driven out from paradise, so the highest we can hope for is to be back in paradise on Shabbos, but if we would not have been driven out from paradise, where would we be on Shabbos? And only Rav Kook can say such holy torah. He says, if they would not have been driven out from paradise, they would have been in Eretz Yisrael. But not Eretz Yisrael we know now, the real Eretz Yisrael after Mashiach. *Gevalt. Yerushalayim Ir Hakodesh* [Jerusalem the Holy City].

Why was the snake so eager that they should eat from the Tree of Knowledge? According to Rebbe Nachman, it is not just the *averah* [sin], that G-d told them, "Don't eat from the Tree of Knowledge." and they ate it. Do you know what was at stake? Going to Eretz Yisrael. *Gevalt*. It was Friday afternoon, right. The snake knew; "In a few minutes, *gevalt*, they are going to Eretz Yisrael. No, I won't let them."

Everybody knows, Lavan [Laban the Aramite] is not the *Nachash Kadmoni* [primordial snake], Lavan is not really the snake. Lavan is just the *Yetzer Hara* [evil inclination] who wants to drive us crazy. But Esav... Esav [Esau] knew that Yaakov [Jacob] was sitting by Lavan for twenty years, why didn't he come to kill him? Esav doesn't mind if Yaakov is sitting in Padan Aram (outside of Israel), "So let him sit there." He doesn't mind if a Jew sits in Dallas Texas, even with fifteen *Shtreimelach* [traditional fur hat] and one hundred *tzitzis* [Jewish garment with fringes] hanging around. Ahh, Yaakov wants to go back to Eretz Yisrael – Esav doesn't let you. Everybody knows, Esav is Amalek. When did Haman come? For seventy years we were sitting in Babel, and nobody wanted to kill all the Jews. When it was the end of the seventy years, and it is time to go back to Eretz Yisrael - hey hey hey, then Haman comes, Esav comes, Amalek comes the *Nachash Kadmoni* comes, "I won't let you go to Eretz Yisrael."

**The Spies**

Can you imagine how much the *menios* [obstacles] are, that even though the Meraglim had clear *ruach hakodesh* and they were *mamish* the holiest people beforehand, but then they come back and they can't help it, they say something bad about Eretz Yisrael. It was the same mistake, it was still the fixing of the *Nachash*, it was the fixing that *mamish* does not let you go into Eretz Yisrael. The most heartbreaking thing in the world, we see it all the time. I want to tell you something awesome. Basically the spies were Rebbes, they were all Rebbes, and you know, according to the Torah, *acharei rabim lehatos* [the majority decides]. Imagine there are twelve people in the Sanhedrin [Rabbinic high court], ten say he is guilty, G-d forbid, and two say that he is not. What is the *halacha* [law]? The *halacha* is like the ten. Right? Ok, here were twelve spies; ten spies say Eretz Yisrael is bad…. This is an awesome torah. Do you know that Moshe Rabenu gave Yehoshua a special *bracha* [blessing] that he should not listen to the Meraglim. Do you know something? It was *mamish* against the Torah, because the Torah says, *acharei rabim lehatos*, if the ten Meraglim come back and they say, "Let's not go to Eretz Yisrael." and two say, "We should go." who are they not to listen. So you know what it is, I have a very strong feeling that the deepest, deepest fixing is that Israel was *mamish* built by non-religious people. Let's face it, right, because sadly enough, the religious people have so much trouble even with the Rebbes. It is so true. And I want you to know, there are some so-called *Rebbelach* in Eretz Yisrael, I mean some are good, but some still smell from the Meraglim sometimes.

**You don't know who I am**

I want you to know something awesome which is the deepest depths. Let's say I am madly in love with this girl, her name is Maxine (it is a good name) and we are driving around in New York, and she says, "Guess where I live." Ok, let's assume if I love her very much, and I am class, so I drive down to Scarsdale, I see *mamish* super class houses, I say, "Maxine, I have a feeling you live here in this neighborhood." She says, "*Gevalt*, you got it. This is where my parents live." But imagine if I am driving down with Maxine, and I come down to the bowery, to a broken house, it smells bad, full of cockroaches, and I say, "Maxine, are you maybe living here?" So she says, "Are you crazy?!" I say, "Ok forgive me." Will she ever marry me? No. Do you know why? I say, "Why don't you forgive me, it says in the Torah that you have to forgive." She says, "Yes, I forgive you, but if you can think that I am living there, then you don't know who I am. You don't know where I belong." You know, G-d never forgave us for the Meraglim. So the Alexander Rebbe asks, why did G-d forgive us for all the other sins and not for this sin? G-d says, "Yeah, I forgive you, but if you think that I will give my children a bad land… that is what you think, that I am sending my children to a dirty filthy place? Who do you think I am? What do you think *Yidden* [Jews] are? Where do think *Yidden* belong?" It is awesome, such a good torah. I want you to know that whatever you think of Israel, that is what you think of *Yidden*.

## Not part of this world

So here Rebbe Nachman says, that in this world it is so hidden, it is so full of obstacles, that you *mamish* can't get through. You see what Rebbe Nachman says; That means that Eretz Yisrael is not really part of this world. You know, imagine I am an expert on Holland, I am an expert on Italy, I am an expert on Germany. I know geology, I know agriculture... yeah, you can hang yourself, but you do not know anything about Eretz Yisrael. Because Eretz Yisrael, Israel is not part of the world.

Do you know why Calev had the strength to see Eretz Yisrael in a different light? Because he went to the grave of Avraham Yitzchak and Yaakov. Avraham Yitzchak and Yaakov are also not part of this world. Why was Eretz Yisrael given to Avraham Yitzchak and Yaakov? It is not just a gift, G-d says to him, *El haarets asher areka* [Go to the land which I will show you]. It is *mamish* heavenly. Imagine if someone would show me something heavenly, you know, the level I am on, I would not even see it. I wouldn't see anything.

## Different eyes

I have to interrupt myself because I want to tell you something unbelievable. It is a true story, it happened a few years ago. Here on the West Side street there is a non-religious person, *nebech* it should never happen, he *mamish* had cancer. The doctors said that it is too late to operate, and *nebech*, he is dying from cancer, *chas veshalom* [G-d forbid]. His next door neighbor is a Gerrer chasid. So the Gerrer chasid says to him, "Listen, you have nothing to lose, go to Eretz Yisrael, go to the Gerrer Rebbe, maybe...."

Everybody knows, the Gerrer Rebbe is already around 92 years old, *mamish* very sick, I don't mean *chas veshalom* sick inside, but his outside.

So he comes to the Gerrer Rebbe, and the Gerrer Rebbe says to him, "Did you bring your X-ray?" He says, "Yeah."

I mean, the Gerrer Rebbe is not a doctor, right. So the Gerrer Rebbe, you can just picture it, the *heilege* Gerrer Rebbe, an *alter Yid* [Jewish elder], his hands are shivering a little bit. The Gerrer Rebbe looks at the X-ray, and he says, *ich zei gornisht* [I don't see anything]. He opens the *beis medrash* [study hall] door, and he says to one of his *gabaim*, Yankel, *ziest epes* [do you see anything]? He looks, *ich zei gornisht. Ich zei gornisht...*

It is a true story, the next day he goes to Hadassah hospital for an X-ray, and they say, "What do you want? There is nothing there."

Do you know what I mean to tell you, those Rebbes have different eyes. Different eyes.

So Calev *mamish*, went back to Avraham Yitzchak and Yaakov. What gave him the strength, why did he have different eyes? He had different eyes because he connected himself to Avraham Yitzchak and Yaakov.

**Clean the air**

So Rebbe Nachman says, even Calev, suddenly he realized that he *mamish* does not have the strength.

Remember the torah from all the Rebbes. I walk on the street and I feel very good. Suddenly I come to forty-second street and third avenue, and suddenly there is so much anger in my heart. Suddenly I think, "Oh, I always thought that this person is my friend, ach, nah, he is not my friend. And this one is disgusting, and this one is terrible." I walk five blocks and I come to let's say, thirty fifth street and third avenue, and is say, "Ahh, the world is so beautiful." What is happening? Am I crazy? I might be crazy anyway, but do you know what it is, when I walk on forty-second street and third avenue, just a few minutes before I went, someone was very angry and insulted. And the whole anger is still on that street corner. So when I walk there, the whole anger comes upon me. I walk down to thirty fifth street, and there *mamish* two minutes before someone said something so sweet, the air is good. I want you to know, why did Moshe Rabenu send the spies, why did we send the spies? Moshe Rabenu didn't know that Eretz Yisrael is beautiful? Everybody knows that Moshe Rabenu sent them there to clean the air. *Mamish*, to clean the air. They were supposed to go there and clean the air, because the most perverted people were living there.

I once had the privilege of walking with the Bobover Rebbe on Friday night from 87th street to 110th street. And suddenly the street looked so beautiful; every drunkard looked like a Rebbe, and every prostitute looked like a Rebbetzin. Because the Bobover Rebbe is so holy, *mamish*, it cleaned out the whole air.

So Moshe Rabenu send the twelve biggest *Tzadikim* [holy people], and they thought that when they come to Eretz Yisrael they will pave the way. But they weren't strong enough, because the air was so bad that even they did not have the strength. Even they didn't have the strength….

**Don't rely on your own holiness**

And why did Calev have the strength? Calev had the strength because he *mamish* went to pray…. Yehoshua made it because Moshe Rabenu blessed him. Why did Calev make it, and why didn't the ten Meraglim make it? The Meraglim were relying on their own holiness.

Let's assume that all of Israel would tell me; "Shlomo, we want you to go to Syria and talk to *Yemach Shemo* [may his name be blotted out] the president, and you will pave the way for peace between us and Syria." And the whole time I am thinking, "Let's face it, they could have not chosen anybody else. Let's face it, I am a *gevalt*." I am going to Syria, and the whole time I am looking in the mirror, and I think,

"*Gevalt, baruch Hashem*, finally all of Israel knows who I am." I can charge more for concerts when I come back. Imagine I come back, and advertise; "Exclusive! I was in Syria." You know what; I would be the most awesome failure in the world. Do you know when I will be successful? When it will be clear to me that it is not my doing. It is not, "I am holy, or unholy." That is all stupidity. I don't even count. I am going there with the *koach* [strength] of Avraham Yitzchak and Yaakov. *Gevalt*, G-d gave the land to Avraham Yitzchak and Yaakov, *mamish* because of their *zechus* [merit]. *Bezchutam* [in their merit] I am going there. The Meraglim, sadly enough, they were very holy, but they still had a little bit of an idea that it is their *kedusha* [holiness]. Calev knew exactly; "It is not my *kedusha*." He went to the grave of Avraham Yitzchak and Yaakov, Sarah Rivka and Leah. He was *mamish* saying, "Rebono Shel Olam, please, I am begging you, I am begging you, let me see the holy land. Let me have the *kedushas haAvos* [the holiness of the forefathers]."

## Two holinesses

And I want you to open your hearts. Every person has two holinesses. Every person has the holiness of his own Torah and *mitzvas* [good deeds], every time you do a *mitzvah* you are more holy, every time you do an *aveira* [sin] you are less holy. But then, you have the *kedusha* of Avraham Yitzchak and Yaakov. The only thing is, that the *kedusha* of Avraham Yitzchak and Yaakov is shining into you by your good deeds. But then sometimes it is shining beyond my good deeds. Nothing to do with it. Beyond my good deeds.

So you see how deep this is. If Eretz Yisrael would have been built by religious people, that means; "Their own holiness." That is right back to the Meraglim (who relied on their own holiness). So Eretz Yisrael was built by people who *mamish* don't have any of their own holiness. They *mamish* are holy because of Avraham Yitzchak and Yaakov. Their holiness is because they are *Yidden*. Simple as it is.

You know, Rav Kook says a hundred times, sometimes you meet a big *tzadik* who is very holy, but the holiness which is shining out of him is not overpowering. Sometimes you meet a person who is not such a *tzadik*, but at a certain point in their life, just, the holiness of being a *Yid* shines like crazy.

I will tell you something awesome, all of the big *Tzadikim*, Rebbe Elimelech, and all the Rebbes who were brought over to Israel after the war to be reburied; they looked like they were alive, because they were so holy. You know something, in 1947 or 1948 whenever it was, three Israelis were killed in Cairo, they were absolutely non-religious. And now, about 40 or 50 years later, they were brought over to Israel to be reburied in Israel. How do you think they looked like? They absolutely looked like they were alive. Even their garments looked like they came out from the laundry. What is their holiness? Their holiness is that they died for the holy Land. What is shining into them is the holiness of Avraham Yitzchak and Yaakov.

## The essence of all the *kedushas*

And here I want you to open your hearts in the deepest way. If I put on *tefillin*, it is very holy, but *tefillin* does not connect me to the *kedusha* of Eretz Yisrael. Because Eretz Yisrael is the essence of all the *kedushas* of the world. Eretz Yisrael is the headquarters of all the *kedushas* of the world. So what connects me to Eretz Yisrael is *mamish* only the *kedusha* of Avraham Yitzchak and Yaakov.

You see what it means when we say that G-d gave the land to Avraham Yitzchak and Yaakov, it does not mean just that when Abraham was alive, G-d says to Avraham, "Avraham, I am very thankful to you that you are my missionary. You are talking about Me to the world, so I am giving you a gift." The *kedusha* of Avraham Yitzchak and Yaakov is the essence of all *kedusha*.

### The holiness of the Land

I want you to know something deeper. It is not that G-d gave the Land to Avraham Avinu. The Land is holy because G-d gave it to Avraham Avinu.

Remember the most awesome torah in the world from the Peshischer, which is just mind blowing. The Peshischer says, G-d says to Avraham, "I will give you the Land which I will show you." So the Peshischer says; Avraham Avinu has clear prophesy, Avraham Avinu can sit there in New York and G-d can say, "See over there, that is the Land." Why does he have to go there? So the Peshischer says the deepest torah in the world. Eretz Yisrael without one Jew living there, doesn't look like anything. Do you know how deep this is. Until Avraham Avinu gets there, the Land is not really holy. Ahh, one *Yid* is in Eretz Yisrael, Ahh, then it is *kedosha*.

### It is a gift

The Meraglim thought that Eretz Yisrael is given to us because of Torah and *mitzvas*, because of our own *kedusha*. So they said, "*Ki chazak hu mimenu* [we *Yidden* do not have enough strength]. They are not stupid, *chazak mimenu* does not mean 'too strong for G-d' *chazak mimenu* means, 'too strong for us,' 'We don't have enough strength.' They had clear prophesy, they *mamish* had, like, a computer in their head. They counted in heaven how much Torah and *mitzvas* we have and they saw that we didn't have enough Torah and *mitzvas* yet to conquer the holy land.
So what is the problem?
G-d does not give the Land to us for our own Torah and *mitzvas*. G-d gives it to us because of the *kedusha* of Avraham Yitzchak and Yaakov. Ahh it is so deep.

Do you know what the Zohar Hakadosh says? Eretz Yisrael is not given to us because of the Torah and *mitzvas*, because we deserve it. It is a gift.

### You have to want it

And do you know why G-d gives it to us? Because of tears. *Gevalt*. Eretz *Yisrael* is *niknes beyisurim* / Eretz Yisrael is given to us for our tears. It means that you have to want it so much. If I am putting on *tefillin* in the morning, and I do the *mitzvah*, maybe I am not crazy about *tefillin*, but I am just putting it on. So the *mitzvah* is given to me. But Eretz Yisrael is only given to us if you cry for it with all your heart. It doesn't mean that you have to sit there and cry. But *mamish* you have to *mamish* want it. And you know something, if I don't want something, then every little thing can stop me from doing it. Can you imagine how much G-d wants us to want Eretz Yisrael that it is so hard. It is so hard.

## What gives a person strength

Ok now, this is *mamish* the deepest depths. What gives a person strength to stand by all the trials? I want to be a little bit of a holy *Yid*, but then the first test I have, I am falling through, because obviously I did not want it the most. Because if I am crazy about this, then I am not going to let anything stop me. Imagine I am on my way to make ten million dollars, and you offer me one hundred dollars, I am not falling for it. If I want to be *mamish* a *gevalt Yid*, then all the tests in the world won't count.

Let me ask you something. What is the strongest thing a person wants? There is an unbelievable drive, in all of mankind, to want to be free. There is not such a thing as a person who does not want to be free. Everyone wants to be free. I will do anything to be free. And here I want you to open you hearts. Yosef Hatzadik.... The wife of Potifar comes and she says to him, "You do it one time and you will be free." And I want you to know, the wife of Potifar was not even married to Potifar. She was a slave. And she was even ready to convert, she said, "I will go to the *mikva*." Because in those days, you don't need a Beis Din [Rabbinic court] to convert. Like the daughter of Pharaoh, she went to the *mikva*, and is *mekabel ol malchus shamayim* [accepts the yoke of the kingdom of heaven], and she is a *Yid*. Reb Tzadok Hacohen says, there was absolutely.... But do you know what Yosef Hatzadik wanted more that freedom? He wants to be a *heilege Yid* [holy Jew]. He wants to be a *heilege Yid*.

And Rebbe Nachman says, why did he have the strength to want so much to be a *heilege Yid*? Because nobody is connected to Eretz Yisrael more than Yosef Hatzadik. Yosef Hatzadik *mamish* wanted to go back to Eretz Yisrael, but he wanted to go back as a *heilege Yid*. He didn't want to go back as a crippled Jew. All alone, he held out. Everybody knows, Rachel is the master of bringing us back to Eretz Yisrael. What is Rachel shining into us? What is Mashiach Ben Yosef all about? Mashiach Ben Yosef is shining into us that we should want the most, most, most to go back to Eretz Yisrael as a *heilege Yid*. I don't want to go back as a *shlepper*, as a spiritual *shlepper*.

Rebbe Nachman says the deepest torah in the world. Moshe Rabenu comes to the *Yidden*, and he brings them a message, "You are getting free." What else do you need? Have you seen in all the movies: I come to a little plantation, and I tell all the brothers, "I am giving you freedom." They jump out of their skin. Rebbe Nachman says, what did Moshe Rabenu say to the *Yidden*? "I am taking you to Eretz Yisrael." Hey.... Do you know what a *Yid* is? For a *Yid*, the deepest depths in the world is not to be free. Because the essence of all holiness of a *Yid* is Eretz Yisrael. So Moshe Rabenu comes to the slaves, and what is he telling them? *Mamish*, "*Vehotzesi, vehitsalti, vegoalti, velakachti*." He says, "*Yidden*, we are going to Eretz Yisrael." It is an awesome torah, not to be believed.

## Receiving life

Rebbe Nachman says, imagine, G-d forbid, someone is on life support, he is breathing oxygen. How much is this person alive? He is alive, right? Even if a person is *chas veshalom* on life support, he is also a little bit alive, but *nebech*, do you want to live like this? No, *chas veshalom*. Then you take a person who is *mamish* healthy and strong like a lion. He is alive. Do you know, the life energy which is coming down in *Chutz Laaretz* [outside of Israel], and the life energy which is coming down in Eretz Yisrael, is like a person who is living and breathing, and the other one is on oxygen. We are not on the level to feel it. Even in Eretz Yisrael we are not strong enough to feel it. Rebbe Nachman says that the life energy which is coming down in Eretz Yisrael is something else. Something else...

Why is it that Eretz Yisrael is even more important than freedom? Listen to this; is there anything deeper than, 'I want to be alive?' I think that when I am breathing and I am hanging around that I am alive. No. A *Yid* knows that there is something available which is really meant for me: *mamish, mamish, mamish* to be alive. *Mamish* to be alive.

## Receiving face to face

The Gemara says, if you are in *Chutz Laarets* it is like you are a little bit of a pagan. If you are in Eretz Yisrael you are *mamish* connected to G-d. I want you to know something, we always think 'pagan' means that I bow down to a tree. No. The Zohar Hakadosh says, when I love somebody very much, I give them what I want to give them face to face. How do I give something to a person that I don't like? I throw it from my back. In the Torah, idols are called, *Elokim Acherim*, the way it is translated by most is 'other gods.' Right? Do you know, the way the Zohar Hakadosh translates it is *Elokim Achorayim*. That means G-d gives you life, but He throws it from his back. Unbelievable. That means, in *Chutz Laaretz*, you are an *eved elokim acherim*, you are serving G-d, but the way G-d gives you everything is that He just throws it from his back.

## The air of Eretz Yisrael

And again, let it be clear to you, the truth is, Rebbe Nachman says, Tzadikim, even in *Chutz Laaretz*, wherever they are, is *Avira d'Eretz Yisrael* [the air of the Land of Israel]. You know, some Tzadikim, wherever they are is Eretz Yisrael. All the Rebbes said, when you come to the grave of the holy Bal Shem, it is *mamish* the air of Eretz Yisrael. Some of us have had the privilege of being by Rebbe Nachmans grave. You cannot say that by Rebbe Nachmans grave *chas veshalom* G-d throws from his back.

What is Yisrael? Do you know what Eretz Yisrael means? *Yashar Kel* / receiving strait from  G-d. The land where we are receiving face to face from G-d.

Why was Yosef Hatzadik privileged to feed the whole world? Yosef Hatzadik was always connected to the deepest life. Yosef Hatzadik is giving out life, Yosef Hatzadik is giving out food, Yosef Hatzadik is connected to the highest level of life.

The truth is, he says, in *Chutz Laaretz*, the life level is very very *shvach* [weak]. Yet, he says, a *Yid* has to know, that whenever I say *Shema Yisrael Hashem Elokenu Hashem Echad* [Hear O' Israel, the L-rd is our G-d, the L-rd is One], at that moment I receive life on the level of Eretz Yisrael.

Why is it that when we didn't go into Eretz Yisrael, then G-d gave us the *mitzvah* of *tzitzis*? Because when you wear *Tzitzis*, you also receive a little bit of life on the level of Eretz Yisrael.

Why is it that when I put on *Tzitzis*, it says, *Ureisim Oso* / I can see G-d. Because when I wear *Tzitzis*, at that moment I am receiving life from G-d face to face.

Rebbe Nachman says, every *Beis Medrash* [synagogue] where you learn Torah, and you *daven* [pray] is a little bit Eretz Yisrael. It is *mamish* true, sometimes you are completely out of energy, and you walk into a *Beis Medrash*, and you receive a little more life.

## Yerushalayim

And this is all Eretz Yisrael, but Yerushalayim, ahh, Yerushalayim is deeper than all this. Because so far we were only talking about Rachel. (Yosef Hatzadik is the son of Rachel and has the aspect of Rachel.) Rachel *mevakah al baneha*, Rachel brings us back to Eretz Yisrael. Ahh, but Leah, the *heilege mama* Leah, is *Yerushalayim Ir Hakodesh*. What is Mashiach all about? Building the Beis Hamikdash [Holy Temple]. The Beis Hamikdash is; *Ayin lo rasa elokim zulatecha* [No eye has seen it but G-d] Whatever I think life is, whatever I would like to receive life from, It's not it. It's not it....

## Pray for Eretz Yisrael

Rebbe Nachman says, let it be clear to you that every prayer that you pray for Eretz Yisrael is *mamish* hastening the redemption. Because only in Heaven they know exactly.... Remember I told you before that the spies thought that you get Eretz Yisrael by Torah and *Mitzvas*? Eretz Yisrael is; *Ki beisi beis tefila yikare lekol haamim* [My house is a house of prayer for all nations], it is *mamish* praying and *davening*. Each time a *Yid* prays for Eretz Yisrael, not only is his prayer heard, *mamish*, he is hastening the redemption, *mamish*, he is hastening the redemption of all of Israel.

Then he says, let it be clear to you, you can only go to Eretz Yisrael if you connect yourself like Calev did. Connect yourself to Avraham Yitzchak and Yaakov, you have to connect yourself to all the Tzadikim.

## It is like the house is burning

Rebbe Nachman says, imagine a father is angry at his child, and suddenly the house is on fire, will he remember that he was angry at his child? Because, when the house is burning, he says, *"Gevalt,* it is my child, *gevalt."* I want you to know, when it comes to *Chutz Laaretz,* why when we are in *Chutz Laaretz,* humanly speaking, G-d is a little bit angry at us, we are not that close. When it comes to Eretz Yisrael, it is like the house is burning. When it has to do with Eretz Yisrael, suddenly everything is forgotten. Everything is forgotten....

When a *Yid* says, "Rebono Shel Olam, take me to Eretz Yisrael." *Gevalt,* right. On a simple level, if I am angry at my child, and let's say my child is in Alaska, and I talk to him on the phone, and I am a little bit angry. Suddenly my child says, "I want to come to visit you." *Gevalt* is it deep. You see, the lowest *Yiddele....* And therefore it had to be the non-religious Jews to pave the way for us, to pave the way for us that even if we are not so good, even if we are not so good, a *Yid* says, "Rebono Shel Olam, I want to go back to Your house." The door is open.

## Garments

The Vorke Rebbe says, why did Yaakov walk in to receive the blessing in the garments of Esau? He says, if Yaakov would have received the blessing in his own garments, we would not have gotten anything because we don't have it, we don't have these kinds of garments, we don't have the garments of Torah and *mitzvas.* So he walked in with the garments of Esau. That means that even a *Yid* who on the outside he looks like Esau, smells like Esau, lives like Esau, *gevalt,* Yaakov Avinu brought down the blessings even for him.

So you see what it is, the Meraglim realized that our garments are not good enough yet for Eretz Yisrael. And here I want you to know something awesome. Every person in the world, even a Rebbe, looks at you, at your garments. There is one person in the world, or, two people who *mamish* don't see your garments. It is your father and you mother. You see, the Meraglim walked in like Rebbes, and they looked at the garments of the *Yidden,* on the level of garments we were not on the level yet to conquer Eretz Yisrael, maybe we will never be. But Yehoshua and Calev, they walked in connecting themselves to Avraham Yitzchak and Yaakov. Do you know what we need the most, the moment we talk so much about *Yidden,* about how a *Yid* looks like, if he is *frum* [religious] or not, then we are again talking to G-d about garments, we are *mamish* stopping the redemption. What we have to do in our generation is forget about the garments.

I don't want to say anything bad, but just a few days before the war (with Iraq in 1992), I don't want to say anything bad, but one person got up and he says, "Do you know why there is so much danger? Because a lot of people eat ham, and some are not *frum* [religious]." It's disgusting. And all of the real Rebbes in Eretz Yisrael said, "What a *chutzpah!* Now? Now is the time to say bad things about *Yidden*? Now is the time to say; *mamish* every *Yid* is the holy of holiest!" And the fact is that all the miracles happened to every *Yid.* Imagine if the missiles are falling and only a *Yid* who keeps Shabbos, his house doesn't explode, and *chas veshalom*, a *Yid* who doesn't keep Shabbos… And I want you to know, the missiles always fell on Friday night, were most people in those housed did not keep Shabbos, and a miracle happened that nothing happened and no one was hurt. Do you know why? Because G-d was showing us: in Eretz Yisrael, G-d looks differently at a *Yid*.

And I will tell you something else, if we ever want all of Israel to keep Shabbos, "*Haaretz asher areka* [The Land that I will show you]." If you look at a *Yid* like he is so holy, then he looks back at you and says, "Yeah, I really am holy, I should keep Shabbos." But if you look at him and say, "You are dirty, you are filthy…" – Listen, if I would tell a little girl, "You know, your dress if full of stains." So is she going to watch out for another stain? She says, "It is dirty anyway, what should I do?" Ahh, you put her in a new dress, and you say, "Ahh, you know, you look so beautiful, please watch out for a stain." She will be very careful.

The *heilege* Rizhiner, had a custom that whenever one of his children got married, that he would tell the *yichus* [dynasty] of his family, and the other side was supposed to tell their family tree also, so here the Sadigura's daughter is marrying the grandson of Reb Hershele Rimanover. And everybody knows that Reb Hershele Rimanover's father was not a Rebbe, he was a Tailor. The Rizhiner begins to say, *gevalt*, my father was Reb Shalom Shachna, and my *zeide* was the *Heilege* Malach, and my *elte zeide* was the *Heilege* Mezritcher Magid. Then he says, Reb Hershele, now it is your turn. He said, "I want you to know, my father was a tailor, and he told me, "When you have a new suit, try not to tear it, and if you have an old suit, try to fix it." "Ahhh, *gevalt*," the Rizhiner said, "*gevalt* what a *yichus*!"

The Gemara says, *Yerushalayim lo nischalka leshvatim* / all of Israel was divided by the tribes, but Yerushalayim belongs to all the *Yidden*. Yerushalayim belongs to all the *Yidden*….

Do you know, the holy wall was conquered, I think, by six soldiers. Two were religious, and four where not. Four were not… *gevalt*. I want you to know, not that I am so sensitive, I was somewhere, and a person walked in without a Yarmulke, and I just had this feeling… I asked someone, "Who is he?" He said, "He is one of the six soldiers who conquered the holy wall." You know the *kedusha* of that soldier? Awesome, right. Eretz Yisrael is something else.

## Shmita

The earth also has garments and insides. The garments of the land is: How much is growing, how much money you can make on it, if it is fruitful, if it is productive. That is the outside of the land. Do you know what *shmita* [seventh year when the land is not worked] is? The inside of the land. I don't care if it is growing, I don't care… the Land! Eretz Yisrael….

## A special place

This is a torah from Reb Leibele Eiger, which is mind blowing. We don't find Eretz Yisrael, only by Avraham Avinu. Why wasn't there Eretz Yisrael before Avraham Avinu? He says the deepest depths. You know, I like all of New York, then I meet someone I love very much, I need a special place to meet. Until Avraham Avinu, G-d did not need a special place in the world where to meet this person. This is awesome. From Avraham Avinu on, the *Heilege Zeise* Avraham Avinu, G-d needs a special place. G-d says to Avraham Avinu, "I will meet you in Eretz Yisrael." Do you know what the Beis Hamikdash is all about? G-d says to every *Yid*, "Do you know how precious you are to me? I want to meet you in a special place." But this is deeper than garments. If you will tell me, "Oh, the Wall is broken, achh." You don't know what is going on. You don't know what is going on. Because, imagine I meet this girl, and I love her very much. Then I say, meet me on 42nd street and 8th avenue. It looks to you like a stupid place. That is only because you don't know what is going on. When I meet this girl, suddenly it looks to me like the Beis Hamikdash. Something else.

## Yom Yerushalayim

The craziest thing is that always the Shabbos of Yom Yerushalayim is always *Behar, Bechukosai*. And you see what it is, if you didn't keep *shmita*, that means that you are interested in the garments of the Land. G-d says, "You are a garment person? I will look at your garments, you don't deserve to be in Eretz Yisrael." And if you are a *shmita* person: your connection to Eretz Yisrael is beyond garments, your connection to every *Yid* is beyond garments…. You know, children are born without garments, do you know why? *Nebech*, they are begging their parents; don't judge my garments. Do you know when children are angry at their parents? When their parents look at their garments: Are you beautiful, are you clever, do you have good marks, will you marry a rich girl? All those garments. So one more thing. Rebbe Nachman says that brother Satan has only a hold on the outside of Eretz Yisrael, not on the inside, not on the inside of Eretz Yisrael.

## How long it takes to fix

Do you know, if Chava would have not eaten from the tree of knowledge, we would have walked into Eretz Yisrael. And you know something, sometimes you make a mistake, and you want to fix it, and you know how long it takes to fix…. You know, sometimes you go to the wrong street, and you want to make a U turn, and it doesn't go. You drive around for hours. I want you to know something, last week someone was driving me, and he missed the exit, so he says, "I am getting off at the next exit." First of all, the next exit was twenty two miles after. *Meshigene of toit* [crazy]. And I was supposed to be there at a certain time, and I am already late. Twenty two miles… and then when he came to that exit, and he wants to go back, he couldn't find it, he went wrong again. You know, it was clear to me: It is not so simple, when you make a mistake, you don't fix it in one second. You don't fix it in one second…. What takes the longest for us to fix? To go to Eretz Yisrael. Because, there are two sides; not eating from the Tree of Knowledge, and *mamish* going for Shabbos to Eretz Yisrael, or *chas veshalom*, we eat the Tree of

Knowledge. We haven't gotten there yet. Yeah, we go, but we still haven't tasted the inside of Eretz Yisrael yet. Do you know what the Tree of Knowledge is? Everything is outside stuff. Everything is outside stuff....

We should have the privilege of being inside *Yidden*, inside, inside. Do you know what the Bal Shem Tov brought down to the world? The *Heilege* Bal Shem Tov brought down to the world that you look at a *Yid* at his inside, not the outside. You look at everything inside, inside.

And I want you to know, the outside of the Torah is always the same; you have to keep Shabbos, we have to put on *tefillin*. The outside is the same. But the inside gets deeper and deeper and deeper.

You know, it is unbelievable, Rebono Shel Olam gave us the Torah on Mount Sinai. How many books, how many commentaries, what have we done to the Torah... I mean, if you walk into a bookstore in Eretz Yisrael, and from one year to the other, how many books come out! You know, there is a *passuk* [passage] that says, *Asos sforim ad ein ketz* / to come out with books endlessly. Not to be believed. *Mamish*, we should live to see this.

## Inside

Every Shabbos, the *parsha* [Torah portion of the week] is the same *parsha* as last year. But it is getting deeper and deeper and deeper.

You know what is so special? The Bible is translated into every language in the world. Without saying anything bad, do you know how many religions preach the Bible every Sunday? Have you ever seen one little minister or priest come out with one decent book of commentaries on the Bible? Why not, they have good heads, they invent missiles. Can't they say something about the Torah? No. Because the Torah was given to us. The outside of the outside, the words, is for the world. Torah *shebalpeh* [the oral tradition], the inside of the inside, is just for us.

And we should be privileged to be connected to the inside of each other, the inside of Eretz Yisrael.

If someone comes back to you and says, "Israel is full of non-religious Jews." You are right, but you are the outside. The outside of the outside. On the inside. The inside of the inside, on the inside of the inside we are getting closer every second.

Each time a *Yid* says when he *benches* [says grace after meals], *Uvenei Yerushalayim Ir Hakodesh* [rebuild Jerusalem the holy city], you are bringing Mashiach closer, because the Rebono Shel Olam needs so many prayers, so many tears to bring Mashiach.

## *Parnossah*

And I want to tell you one more thing, a lot of people ask, what is a *segula* for *parnossah* [livelihood]? I want you to know that the *heilege* Ishbitzer says, "I promise you that if you *bench besimcha* [say grace after meals with joy], you will have *parnossah*. If you say grace after meals with joy, you will always have what you need." Listen to this unbelievable thing; if Rothschild gives me a million dollars, and I say just, "thanks." Is he going to give me another million dollars? Not over your dead body. Imagine he gives me a million dollars, and I can't stop thanking him, and I *mamish* bring all of the *chevre*, and we are dancing like crazy. So he says, "I like it. I am ready to give you another few times." So if the Rebono Shel Olam gives you a little piece of bread, and then I knock off a *bentching* like crazy, what a *bentching*! G-d says, "Hey, if this is the way you thank me for a piece of bread, I will give you more."

But I want you to know, that each time in benching I say, *"Uveney Yerushalayim."* It is for real. *Mamish* for real.

છારુ

# Prayer

Someone says to Rebbe Nachman, "How loud do you have to yell when you pray?" He said, "You have to yell so loud that nobody can hear." This is the specialty of us Jewish People. But sometimes I bless all the Jewish people that we should yell so loud that sometimes the world should hear us.

છારુ

# Days are Coming

*(Transcribed by Moshe Dovid Hacohen)*

Shalom again my sweetest friends. I'm sure you know this passage, it's a passage in the prophets. We're living in a hungry world, a very hungry world. You know, if you're hungry for bread you become ugly, because you're so hungry that you can't bear it, but if you're hungry for G-d, the more hungry you become, the more beautiful you are. People hungry for bread hate one another, they suspect each other of taking away their bread. But people hungry for G-d realize that it's the greatest privilege to make somebody else hungry as well. When you're hungry for bread you're empty, but when you're hungry for G-d you are so full, you're so full. Basically there are only two types of people in the world: there are the empty people who are hungry for bread, and the full people who are hungry for G-d.

I'm sure that you all read the prophets, but I'm not sure if it's known to you that the prophets were not like little *shleppers* standing on street corners of Jerusalem, *nebech*, with nothing to eat. G-d's prophets, real prophets, especially before the destruction of the Second Temple, were the richest people in the world. They were perfect people - physically, mentally, spiritually, and divinely. Do you know, each prophet had a little school for prophecy with hundreds and thousands of young people and they all had instruments.

One can't receive G-d's prophecy simply by standing and looking at a red light. Rather the prophets would stand and begin singing and playing musical instruments, and then suddenly the gates of Heaven were opened and they prophesized. Hearing prophecy is not like listening to a news broadcast, because most of the time anyone listening began prophesizing as well. A true prophet is not someone who says: "I had a prophecy but who are you to be worthy of one?" Rather the prophets lifted you and me up to the highest level.

So I just want to share this with you. The prophet says, "There will be a time when there will be a hunger in the world..." So why did the prophet say this two thousand years ago? When it comes time we'll know about it. I want you to open your hearts sweetest friends. The prophet is telling us that there will come a time when there will be such a hunger in the world. People will be so hungry that when someone will come and tell you "I'm hungry for bread," don't believe him - he's ashamed to tell you that he's really hungry for G-d. You know that when a neighbor knocks on your door and asks for some eggs to bake a cake, do you know what he really means? "*Gevalt* am I hungry... I'm so hungry for some holy words, so lonely, and so hungry for one friend. Could you just give me a hug?" When a person stops you on the street and asks for the time, you think that he doesn't have a watch? He may have two watches, but he's just telling you: "My life is just slipping by... I just don't know what to do with it anymore." Imagine that you're standing on 42nd street and somebody asks you where 48th street is. You think that he can't read? What he really means is "I don't know where to go."

You know, sometimes a child comes home from school and his mother says to him: "If you're hungry I'll give you some peanut butter." It's cute, right? Those mothers are the failure of our generation. Your child is not hungry for a peanut butter sandwich, he's hungry because he was sitting in school for five hours and nobody kissed him, nobody told him how sweet he is, how beautiful he is...

And you know what, it's strange. The people that are a little bit hungry for G-d, a little hungry for something holy, tell you that they're hungry. However, the people who are desperately hungry are ashamed to tell you so, because they're *mamash* so desperate and they don't want you to know how desperate they are.

We are living in a world, where all of us, you and I, can do so much. You know friends that the difference between healing somebody spiritually, mentally or divinely and healing someone physically is very simple. Physical healing takes time. You know why? Because there are two levels: the level of creation and the level of beyond creation. G-d created the world in six days and our body was created as part of them. Therefore the process of healing takes time as well. Our soul however, was not created during those six days. It is beyond creation - it is part of G-d. To cure one's soul takes no time at all. However, it takes someone else's soul, someone else's Divine Spark, someone else's utmost holiness to do so. And today everyone is aware that most of the time when one's body is very sick and weary, it's because he just can't find the person who will fix his soul.

You know friends, I'm sure you know better than I do what the sign is of a good doctor. Imagine, G-d forbid, that you are lying in bed sick, and one doctor after another walks in. How do you know which one is a good doctor? It's simple. If the moment a doctor walks in you already feel better, even before he examines you, before he gives you medication, even without saying anything, then you know that he is a real doctor. He has fixed your soul; he did something to you without medication.

There is an unbelievable story about the Maggid of Mezrich, who lived around two hundred years ago and was one of our holiest Chassidic Masters. A wealthy man from Vilna, which was the capital of Lithuania at the time, came to him to ask his advice regarding business. The Maggid told him: "I just want you to know one thing. It's not the doctor who cures, rather it's G-d's messenger, an angel, who goes along with the doctor. A little doctor has a little angel, and a great doctor has a great angel." The man said to him: "You know Rabbi, I came to talk to you about my business not about healing." The Maggid repeated the same thing and told him to remember it. The businessman thought to himself, "He's obviously senile, I'm talking to him about business, and he's talking to me about angels!" The man went home and told everyone that the Maggid was not a holy Master and that he was crazy.

Two weeks later this man had a heart attack and was dying. His children rushed out to find the best doctor possible. At that time, the Czar of Russia was in Vilna and since this businessman was very wealthy, the children were able to arrange for the Czar's doctor to come to see their father. The great doctor walked in and he saw that the man had maybe a minute to live. He told the children to rush to the drugstore to buy some very strong medication. They rushed out and brought it, but since the medication was so strong he decided to examine him again before giving it to him. He checked him and said, "This medicine is too powerful. Go back and get me something less strong." They came back with it ten minutes later, but after reexamining the patient the doctor said that this medicine was too strong as well. He then sent them back to get something even less strong.

This went on five times and the patient, without even receiving any medication, was already sitting up. The doctor said to the sick man, "This is crazy. When I walked in you were dying. I haven't given you any medication and yet you're already sitting up!" The man replied, "I'll tell you something crazy. A holy man once told me that it's not the doctor who does the curing, it's G-d's messenger. G-d gives the doctor the power to heal. (What is an angel? It is a certain energy that G-d gives you.) And a little doctor has a little angel and a big doctor has a big angel." The doctor exclaimed, "I must meet this great Rabbi." You should know that this doctor later became one of the holiest Masters. But he didn't stop being a doctor; on the contrary, he even became a greater one, because he learned from this whole story that one has to cure the soul first.

How would the Holy Masters of the Chasidic tradition fix someone's soul? A person would give them a piece of paper with his and his mother's name on it, and they would fix his name. Only then would they have a look at the person himself.

Something is happening to the world. I'm sure that you realize it even more than I do. The world realizes that we have to cure each other's soul. But you know that there is something very special in Chasidic tradition, in Kabbalistic terms. You can cure the body but you don't cure the soul - you fix the soul. Curing takes some time. Fixing however, is something very deep. It doesn't require an action, if you know how to do it. For example, you can walk down the street smiling to yourself or singing a song and you can fix a sad person's soul as you walk by him without even realizing it.

If you don't mind friends, let me tell you the story of The Great Fixer. This is a story told by our Holy Master Rebbe Nachman of Breslov, the Holy Baal Shem Tov's grandson. It's a very deep story so open your hearts, because this is the most important thing that I want to share with you:

What is the greatest fixing of the world? What is it that the world needs most, even deeper than love? If I tell you "I love you," it's very cute, but it won't fix you. What we need is utmost joy and bliss. We *mamash* need joy, as simple as it is. And naturally, it goes without saying that people who hate don't know what joy is.

According to Kabbalistic tradition, sadness has a little of the dust of paganism on it. Because if you really believe in G-d, if you really believe that G-d is doing everything, then what is there to be sad about? Why are you *krechtzing* (whining)? You know that G-d is taking care of you, you realize that you're in good hands. Imagine that someone is in the hospital, G-d forbid, and he has the greatest doctor in the world, a doctor who can cure him in a second. If he keeps complaining about his illness, it's stupid. It means that he doesn't really believe that the doctor can cure him.

So the story is that the King of Sadness wanted to see if the world really was still in good shape, if everybody in the world was sad.

You know sweetest friends, what makes a sad person happy? If he meets somebody else who's also sad. What a joy! Have you ever seen the way two sad people meet? They really experience joy! One says: "I want you to know that so and so died, and this one died, and the other one says: "Let me just add a few more names." And they *mamash* cry with joy!

So the King of Sadness is walking around the world and he comes back to his capital overjoyed. His kingdom is so strong that the whole world is sad. He hasn't met one happy person. This means that his empire is really everlasting. However, before he enters the capital, the most horrible thing happens to him: By a broken-down house, on a broken-down porch, by a broken table, on a broken chair, he sees a man sitting and playing, maybe a guitar or a harp. He has some leftover food on a plate, he's singing and, worst of all, he's happy! The king knows that this is the end of the world, because one happy person can save the whole world. One happy person can destroy his entire kingdom. He realizes that he must get rid of him.

The king walks up to the broken house, disguised as a simpleton, and says to the man, "Hey friend, who are you?" The man replies, "You don't know who I am? I am the Great Fixer. I walk the streets of the world and yell at the top of my lungs, "I am the Great Fixer. Is anything broken? Bring me your broken hearts, your broken lives, your broken worlds - I'll fix them." People give me a few pennies for my work and with that money I buy myself a little feast."

And Rebbe Nachman says that when you tell the story you have to say, "And the feast'le was a feast'le" - "אין דיא סעודה איז גיווען א סעודה" - a feast'le is a feast'le.

You think sad people know how to eat? They push the food down their throats. You have to be a Great Fixer in order to receive G-d's light when you eat, and then "the feast'le is a feast'le."

The King, knowing what he has to do, runs back to his palace. The next day the Great Fixer walks as usual down the streets of the world and yells "I am the Great Fixer..." People open the windows and tell him "Didn't you hear? There's a new decree from the king that there is to be no more fixing in his kingdom."

It's a bad scene, what can you do! But the Great Fixer has to have a feast'le. There has to be one feast in the world.

The Great Fixer walks down the street and sees a rich man chopping wood. He says to him "You know, it doesn't befit a rich man to chop wood. Why don't you let me do it?" He chops wood all day, gets a few pennies, buys a little something to eat, and as Rebbe Nachman says, "The feast'le was a feast'le."

The Great Fixer is sitting at his house in utter bliss and singing a song when the king comes back to visit and says, "Hey brother, how are you doing today?" He answers, "Did you hear? The king is crazier than ever, he forbids fixing!" "So what did you do?" asks the king. "I chopped wood, and in fact, I have a job tomorrow as well chopping wood," answers the Great Fixer. The king goes back to the palace and the next day when the Great Fixer goes to his job'le to chop wood, the rich man says, "I'm sorry, there's a new decree that there is to be no more chopping wood in the country." It's a bad scene, but the Great Fixer thinks to himself, "I can always do something else."

He walks down the street, looks through a window, and sees a rich woman sweeping the floor. He says to her, "What's the matter?" She answers, "I just couldn't find a maid today." He tells her that he'll gladly sweep for her. He sweeps the floor, gets a few pennies, and as Rebbe Nachman says, "The feast'le was a feast'le."

Once again he is sitting in utter bliss singing his song when the king comes back and says, "Hey Brother, what's going on?" The Great Fixer replies, "The king is getting crazier, he said that there is to be no more chopping wood." "Well what did you do?" "I'm sweeping floors and in fact I'm going back tomorrow to sweep floors as well."

It goes without saying that the king decrees the next day that there is to be no more sweeping floors. Whatever job the Great Fixer finds, the king finds a way to stop it, as he wants to cut off the feast. Finally the Great Fixer can't find anything to do. But he has a tremendous idea.

He sees a sign that the king is looking for soldiers. However, soldiers are only paid every half a year. He walks up to the Induction Office and asks if he can become a soldier on the condition that he be paid two pennies every night. They tell him: "It's the first time we've heard of such a thing, but why not?" And so, the Great Fixer becomes a soldier and gets a big sword. As he doesn't know what to do with it, he walks up and down, smiles a little bit and pretends that he's busy and happy.

That night he goes to the office, gets his two pennies, and has a little feast. Once again the king is back. The king says, "Hey what's going on?" He says, "You know, I told you the king is crazy..." "So what did you do?" "I became a soldier and I've been promised two pennies each night for the next half a year." The king obviously goes and decrees that soldiers should only to be paid once every half a year.

This time it was really a bad scene, because they only told him at night that he wouldn't be paid for his day's work. And the Great Fixer must have a feast, as Rebbe Nachman says, "A feast'le has to be a feast'le." There must be at least one person in the world that's keeping the world up with his joy. But leave it up to the Great Fixer.

He goes to a pawnshop and pawns his sword, and now has enough money to support himself for half a year. A soldier, however, must have a sword, so he buys himself some silver paper [1]. And since he knows how to fix things, he takes the silver paper and makes it looks like a sword. The Great Fixer walks happily up and down and once again the feast'le is a feast'le.

I'm coming to the end now - open your hearts.

The king comes back and asks how he is. He told him that he pawned his sword and has enough money for half a year.

But you know my sweetest friends, that a soldier who pawns his sword receives the death penalty.

The king thinks to himself, "This time I don't have to worry, for tomorrow I'm going to kill you." He is overjoyed. The next morning he goes to the prison and he asks if there is anybody who is to be executed that day.

You know, in a sad world they always find someone to kill...

They reply that indeed there is someone. The king says, "I will personally supervise the execution and I will appoint the soldier who will kill this person."

All the soldiers line up and the king walks around dressed royally so that the Great Fixer won't recognize him. He sees the Great Fixer, walks over and says to him, "I, the king of the world, appoint you to kill this man with your sword." Leave it up to the Great Fixer. He answers, "My dear king, let me tell you something. I have never killed a person and I really have no intention of killing anybody, so you'll have to appoint somebody else." The king starts yelling, like a wild beast, at the Great Fixer.

You know friends, only sad people are afraid of anyone. If you're really filled with joy then you are no longer afraid.

The Fixer turns to the King, "Are you sure that this person is really guilty?" This is too much. The King screams back, "Who are you to question me? I commanded you to kill him." The Great Fixer realizes that he can't talk to the king, so he turns to the whole world and says, "Brothers and Sisters, let me tell you something. I want you to know that I'm the Great Fixer. I know magic. And I know one thing: When

---

[1] Another version is that he replaced the sword with wood, stuck it in its' sash and kept the sword's handle intact.

somebody is guilty then the soldier pulls out his sword and kills him. However, if the person is not guilty then the sword turns into silver paper!" The Great Fixer pulls out his sword and everyone sees that it's silver paper.

So the little convict goes home and the Great Fixer goes home and as Rebbe Nachman says: "The feast'le was *mamash* a feast'le!"

## Fixing

Sweetest friends I just want to share one more thing with you. Imagine if the absolutely most sick and incurable person in the world would be well for one day a year. What would happen? He would make it. Because you know what happens to people when they are incurably sick, when they can't walk or move? They think to themselves that they can't do it anymore. But if they would see that for one day a year they can do it, then they would realize that, yes, they may need fixing, but it is possible. If you want to cure and fix a person, the first thing to do is to make them whole again for one minute.

You know, if someone comes to you broken, what's the first aid, mentally and spiritually that you can do for him? The first aid is to show him that, sure, he may be sick and need curing, but for the moment he's not sick at all.

And here I want to share the deepest depths with you. You know what it means to stand and pray before G-d? For one minute, when you stand before G-d, you're not sick. And you know friends, what the difference is between meeting someone who loves you a lot and meeting someone who only loves you a little bit? When you meet someone who loves you a little you may not be as sad but you're still broken, you're still sick. When you meet someone who really loves you, you love him so much that you're not sick. You're so whole.

The same is true from a worldview. The world is always talking about peace. Imagine if we could establish peace in the whole world for one minute. We would *mamash* have peace the next day. But the world doesn't believe in it, they don't believe that there will ever be peace. Because they have been so sick, for so many thousands of years, that they can't imagine that someday people will really love each other.

I want to tell you the utmost deepest depths. It may sound simple. G-d says in the bible, "*V'ahavta l'reacha kamocha*" - which is sadly enough translated as: "Love your neighbor."

King James should live long wherever he is, but *nebech*, his Hebrew wasn't so good and a few more things weren't so good about him. It goes without saying that he completely mistranslates the bible. If I wouldn't know the bible in Hebrew and I would look at King James translation, I wouldn't understand it at all.

The verse doesn't say, "Love your neighbor." What does the word "neighbor" mean? Is it someone from the same street, from the same city, someone that has the same bank? Rather, the verse says *"Reacha"* which means - "the person standing next to you."

Open your hearts friends. G-d doesn't say that you must love the whole world forever. Rather that every person that you meet, for that one moment that you meet him, turn your whole heart to him. And you know friends, if we could only do that. You know how deep this is? G-d doesn't ask me to love you forever. Maybe I don't care for you so much. You may not be on the same wavelength as me. You may not be plugged into the same thing as I. Your soul and mine, as much as they are both a part of G-d, are not so connected. But for one second, when you are standing before me…

And I want you to know the deepest depths. You know, whatever you think of G-d is, sadly enough, whatever you think of yourself. If I am convinced that I am a creep, I can fool you, but the truth is that I am convinced that G-d is also a bit creepy. Because I know one thing - that I am G-d's image. But if my G-d is so exalted then I must be exalted too. If I have one little taste that G-d is the holy of holiest, the most perfect of all perfect, that means that I have it inside of me as well. You know friends, when we stood on Mount Sinai and G-d spoke to us, the miracle wasn't only that G-d spoke to us. At that moment we were all physically, mentally and spiritually completely perfect.

I don't know how much you know about the Jews of Poland before the Second World War. I bought a book that just came out in Israel, which tells the following eyewitness account:

One of the holiest and greatest Rabbis opened a new school in the city of Lublin. He accepted four hundred of the most gifted children from the age of five to seventeen. Sadly enough, there were only seven children left after the war. When he opened the school his Holy Master, the Tshotkover Rebbe, came to Lublin for the opening. Listen to this unbelievable thing. You know that opening a school to study G-d's law is really like Mount Sinai. So, the Tshotkover Rebbe arrived on Thursday and left Monday night. And during the four days that he was there nobody died in Lublin. Can you imagine, not one person died! There so much G-dliness and the spirit of perfection in the city that nobody died.

And you know sweetest friends, I don't have to tell you that dying is not only a physical state. We die a million times a day. If we could just lift ourselves up to those few moments, to be alive for one moment a day, to love a person for one moment a day. And I just want to bless you and me that we should be holy enough to give over this "one moment" to our children, the holiness of "one moment." You know the people who have those "one moments" will make it. They will always make it.

One of our holiest Masters, who lived around one hundred fifty years ago, was called the "Ohr HaMeir" - The Shining Light. He was one the greatest pupils of the great Seer of Lublin. One night he stopped at an inn, at a kretchmer, to sleep. As he looked like a very holy rabbi, the innkeeper told him that he had a very special room for him. He gave him this very beautiful room in which there was a big clock hanging on the wall. All night long the Ohr HaMeir couldn't sleep. He walked up and down, up and down. And you know, in little wooden houses like those kretchmers, when you walked right the whole house bent right and when you walked left the whole house bent left. So the poor innkeeper couldn't sleep either.

Finally at three o'clock he figured it was no use trying and that he may as well make some hot tea to bring to the holy rabbi. He knocked on the door, brought him some tea, and said: "Holy Rabbi, is something wrong with the bed, why can't you sleep?" The Ohr HaMeir replied: "No, G-d forbid, this is a beautiful room." "So why can't you sleep?" asked the innkeeper. The holy rabbi looked at him and said: "Let me ask you something. This big clock hanging on the wall, is it by any chance the clock of my Holy Master, the Seer of Lublin?" The innkeeper replied: "Yes, but don't think that I stole it. His son was here for two weeks and couldn't pay rent, so he pawned this clock. He'll come back in a few weeks to redeem it." "But I don't understand," he continued, "what does your sleeping have to do with the clock?" The Ohr HaMeir told him: "My dear friend, let me tell you something. There are two kinds of clocks in the world. A clock says 1, 2, 3, 4. All the clocks of the world say, "One hour less, one hour less, one hour less..." When you hear this, you think, "Who needs this, let's go to sleep and forget the whole thing." But then there is the clock of the Seer of Lublin which says, "One hour closer, one hour closer..." So how could one fall asleep?

I want to bless you and me and all of us, we *mamash* need different clocks, we need a real time change. Have you ever seen the way people go to sleep? They're so sad, because another day is gone. And I want to share something with you. G-d blessed me in his infinite mercy with two little children - one is three and one is six. Sadly enough, I'm not always home because I travel a little bit, but whenever I'm home the most important and holy function for me is putting them to sleep. You know, when children go to sleep they know exactly what level you're putting them to sleep on. Whether you're putting them to sleep on the level of "one day less, one day less..." or if you're telling them, "one day closer, tomorrow you'll be one day closer." Then they'll want to go to sleep so fast, so that they'll be able to do it again the next day and do it even deeper.

And you know, basically sweetest friends, you can reach so high and so deep with joy. You know, our Holy Master, Rebbe Nachman teaches us that whatever you see is in this world, is a result of it being in Heaven as well.

If someone calls you up on the telephone crying that he really needs a hundred dollars, you'll probably give it to him. Five minutes later he calls up again, sobbing: "I made a mistake, I need two hundred…" You're already a little bit annoyed, you think to yourself that you won't answer the phone anymore that day. Two hours later the same person calls up again, sobbing and crying: "You know I hate to impose upon you, but I made a mistake with my accountant and taxes, I really need five hundred dollars." So you're already unplugging the phone, changing the phone number…

But imagine that you call someone up with the greatest joy and say, "Listen Brother, I have something for you to do that can save my life, your life, the life of the world. Right now you could do the greatest thing in the world, you could do me a big favor." He says: "Why not, what can I do for you?" "Can you dish me up a hundred matzos, I need it." Two hours later I call up and say, "I'll tell you something, this is your day, not only can you give a hundred matzos, G-d in His infinite mercy is giving you the chance to give me two hundred matzos!"

So Rebbe Nachman says that we have this kind of feeling because G-d has it as well. If you stand before G-d and *krechts* [whine], "G-d, I don't know why you created me, but let me tell you something, it's a bad scene. Anyway, I'm created now, and it's not so good…" So G-d says: "Thank you very much, really, I'll give you anything you want, just don't bother me again." And when you bother Him again, He says, "Oy vey, not again…" But when you come before G-d with great joy, all the Gates of Heaven are open.

Friends, we need Gate Openers. And let me tell you this little story. One time a person had a child who was very ill. He came to our Holy Master, the Baal Shem Tov, and told him that his child was very sick. The Baal Shem Tov was so holy that he not only knew the good people, he knew all of the thieves too. He told this man to wait. The Baal Shem Tov then went and came back with a minyan of ten thieves. They recited the Psalms and the child got well in no time. The next day the Baal Shem Tov's holy pupils, the really holy people, asked him: "Rebbe, if you wanted to recite the Psalms, did you have to bring ten thieves? Couldn't you have taken take ten decent people?" The Baal Shem Tov replied: "Don't you understand? The Gates of Heaven were closed. I needed ten thieves to break them open!"

So friends, I want to bless you, me and all of us that we should all be holy thieves. Thank you so much. Shalom!

# Glossary:

Alef: first letter of the Hebrew alphabet

Asara ma'amaros: ten pronouncements / sayings with which the world was created

Avraham: Abraham, the first Patriarch of the Jewish People

Atzvut: dead kind of sadness

Avoda: work

Azut d'kdusha: holy arrogance

Bal Shem: The Bal Shem Tov, founder of the Hassidic movement

Beis Din: Rabbinic court

Beis Din Hagadol: High Rabbinic court of 71

Beis Hamikdash: the holy tabernacle, Holy Temple

Beis medrash: Synagogue study hall

Ben: son, the son of

Bench licht: light Shabbos candles

Bentsh gomel: say a special blessing thanking G-d for helping us

B'simcha: filled with joy

Bet: 2nd letter of the Hebrew alphabet

Challah: loaves of bread eaten on the Sabath

Chanuka: Jewish holiday of light

*Chas veshalom*: G-d forbid

Chassan: groom

Chassidishe mentsh: Chassidic man

Chassidishe *Yidden*: Chassidic Jews

Chassidus: Chassidism

Chevra: group of friends

Chhhh: an expression

Chodesh: Jewish month

Chossid: Chassid, of the Jewish spiritual movement

Chumash: Five Books of Moses

Chuts laarets: outside of Israel

Chuppah: Jewish marriage canopy

Chutzpah: audacity

Daven: pray

Davening: praying

Davener: someone who prays

David HaMelech: King David

Ellul: a Jewish month

Esrog: citron

Emuna: faith

*Frum*: Religious – careful to abide by the word of HaShem

Gabbi: shamash / beadle / secretary

Gaon: genius

Geferlach: a bad scene

Gehinnom: Hell

Gemara: Talmud / the oral law

*Gevalt*: strong (Yiddish expression originaly having a negative meaning: 'help!' Rebbe Shlomo Carlebach zt"l transformed the word to have a positive meaning: 'tremendous!')

Gornisht: it is nothing, worthless

Gut: good

Gut yom tov: have a good holiday

HaNeor balayla: One who is awake at night. (The title of Rebbe Nachmans teaching on Hisbodedus)

Haggadah: read at Passover, recounting the Jews' leaving Egypt

HaKodesh: holy

Haneor Balayla: if you are up at night

Hanevia: the prophetess

Hashmonaim: Maccabi

Hatzadik: the holy person

Heilege ziese: holy sweet

Heilege: holy

Halacha: Jewish law

Hevre: group of friends

Hisbodedus: being alone with G-d

Ich veis: I don't know (Yiddish expression)

Kaddish: prayer, said when ten men pray, honoring G-d

Kallah: bride

Kavod: honor

Kiddush: blessing over the wine on the sabbath and Holidays

Kishkes: stomach

Koach: strength

Krechts: cry

Krechtzing: groaning

Kvetching: complaining

Kriyat Shema: reading the prayer, Hear O Israel

Lasuach: to talk

L'vatala: to nothingness, to unimportant things

Lechem mishna: Double loaves of bread on the Sabbath

Lulov: palm branch waved together with a citron, willow, and myrtle on the holiday of Succoth

Maimonides: Rambam

Mamash: really

Maos Hittim: Money given to the poor to buy wheat for Yom Tov

Marirut: bitterness, which is living sadness

Megilla: Purim scroll

Mehadrin min hamehadrin: very high stardard of doing good deeds

Menorah: candelabrum lit on Hanukah, hanukiyah

Meraglim: The spies that were sent by Moses to the Land of Israel
Michuyav hamitziut: really existing
*Mikva*: ritual bath
Mincha: afternoon daily prayer
Mishna: Jewish oral law
*Mitzvah*: good deed
*Mitzvas*: when you do something good
Mashiach: Messiah
*Nebech*: unfortunate
Nefesh: soul (lower level of the soul)
Neshama: soul (higher level of the soul)
Niggun: a tune, a song
Neggina: singing a song
Noam Elyon: holy sweetness which flows down from Heaven
Olam hatohu: chaos world
Olam Hatikun: the world of correction
Oneg: bliss
Ohr Haganuz: the hidden light of creation
Oral Law: Gemara / Talmud
Oy: oh
Oy vey: oh, no!
P'gam: a blemish
Passuk: passage, verse from the Torah
Peyos: sidelocks
Rabbenu: Our teacher
Reb: Rebbe / Rabbi
Rebbe: Chassidic master
Rebono Shel Olam: G-d
Rosh Chodesh: New month
Rosh HaShanah: Jewish new year
Ruach: soul (mid level of the soul, between nefesh and neshama)
Sanhedrin: Rabinic high court
Schmendrik: fool
Sefer: holy book
Sefira: level, emanation of the light of G-d
Sforim: holy books
Shabbos: the Sabbath
Shabbosdike: Sabbath like
Shacharit: Morning prayer
Shalach Manos: food gifts given on Purim
Shames: beadle / secretary of the Rebbe
Shasim: books of Talmud
Shebalpeh: oral tradition

Shema: Hear

Shema Yisrael: Hear O' Israel

Shlemazel: lazy, simpleton

Shleppers: poor, sad people, tramp

Shlita: May he live long

Shmendrik: fool

Shmonah Esrai: Prayer

Shukkle: shake

Shul: synagogue

Siach hasadeh: The little grass in the field

Siddur: prayerbook

Siddurim: prayerbooks

Simcha: joy

Simchas Torah: Holiday of the Torah

Streimel: Traditional fur hat

Sukkah: temporary dwelling on Succoth

Sukkot: Jewish holiday of Succoth

Tallis: prayer shawl

Talmid: disciple, student

Tamuz: a Hebrew month

Tefillin: phylacteries

Talmud: Gemara, the Oral Law

Taka: actually

Torah: Bible, Pentateuch. Sometimes means; a teaching from the Torah

Torah shebal peh: Oral Torah

Torah shebechtav: written Torah

Teshuva: returning to G-d

Tzadik: holy person

Tzadikim: holy people

Tzitzis: four cornered garment with fringes

Yarmulke: skullcap

Yerushalayim: Jerusalem

Yerushalayim Ir Hakodesh: Jerusalem the Holy City

Yeshiva bochur: young Jewish student

Yesod heafar: the element of earth (of the four elements: air, water, fire, earth)

Yid: Jew

Yiddelach: Jews

Yiddele: Jew

Yidishkeit: Judaism

Yivul: fruit of the field

Yom Kippur: Day of forgiveness

Yom Tov: Jewish Holiday

Zie gezunt: goodbye, be healthy

Zohar HaKadosh: Holy book of Kabala

Z"tl: may the memory of a holy person be for a blessing

## Expressions:

A bad scene: a bad situation, hard to imagine

Blow my mind: mind boggling, amazing

I am not knocking it: I am not saying anything bad about it

In the craziest way: in the most amazing way, paradoxical

Intellectuals: they have everything in their head, and nothing in their heart

It doesn't go: it does not work, it doesn't make sense

Let's put it this way: Put in another way

Not to be believed: amazing

Right?: Do you understand?

So: very

Straight: orderly. (Or it sometimes means; overly conforming and uptight.)

Strong: intensely, powerful, *gevalt*

Taste: experience, receive, understand

Top: epitomy, best, greatest

Top man of: the person who epitomizes the concept of…

That is all head stuff: It is only intellectual without feeling and depth

Way out: amazing, very high concept

With it: composed and in control, together with

ഔറ

CPSIA information can be obtained at www.ICGtesting.com
Printed in the USA
BVOW05s1648260114

343067BV00007B/49/P